What's In a Relative?

Household and Family in Formentera

Kinship has often been seen as a marginal topic in the anthropology of industrial societies. In this ground-breaking study, based on ethnographic research in Formentera, in the Balaric Islands, the author demonstrates that European kinship can become central to anthropological explanation, once it is understood from a symbolic and cultural perspective. The book is an outstanding example of ethnographic analysis which is sensitive to the findings of demographic and historical research as well as to the perspectives of both the American and European anthropological traditions. This theoretically innovative work on a relatively neglected area in Europe is essential reading for all who are interested in what anthropology can teach us about European society and culture in general.

Joan Bestard-Camps is a Lecturer in Social Anthropology at the University of Barcelona.

Explorations in Anthropology
A University College London Series
Series Editors: Barbara Bender, John Gledhill and
Bruce Kapferer

What's In a Relative?

Household and Family in Formentera

Joan Bestard-Camps

Translated by
Robert Pitt

BERG
New York / Oxford
**Distributed exclusively in the US and Canada by
St Martin's Press, New York**

English edition first published in 1991 by
Berg Publishers Limited
Editorial Offices:
165 Taber Avenue, Providence R.I. 02906, USA
150 Cowley Road, Oxford OX4 1JJ, UK

First published as *Casa y familia: Parentesco y reproducción doméstica en Formentera*, Institut d'Estudis Baleàrics, Palma de Mallorca, 1986

Library of Congress Cataloging-in-Publication Data

Bestard-Camps, Joan.
    What's in a relative?: household and family in Formentera / Joan
Bestard-Camps.
       p. 216 cm. — (Explorations in anthropology)
    Translated from the Spanish.
    Includes bibliographical references.
    ISBN 0–85496–586–6
      1. Kinship—Spain—Formentera. 2. Family—Spain—
      Formentera.
    3. Formentera (Spain)—Social life and customs. I. Title.
    II. Series.
GN585.S7B47   1991
306.85'0946'756—dc20   90–394
                                            CIP

British Library Cataloguing in Publication Data

Bestard-Camps, Joan
    What's in a relative?: household and family in
    Formentera. — (Explorations in anthropology).
    1. Spain. Kinship
    I. Title II. Series III. Casa y familia. *English*
    306.830946

    ISBN 0–85496–586–6

Printed in Great Britain by Billing and Sons Ltd, Worcester

Contents

Tables, Figures and Genealogies

Tables

Figures

Tables, Figures and Genealogies

Genealogies

Abbreviations

B	Brother
BD	Brother's daughter
BS	Brother's son
BW	Brother's wife
D	Daughter
D Ch	Daughter's children
DD	Daughter's daughter
DS	Daughter's son
F	Father
FB	Father's brother
FF	Father's father
FM	Father's mother
FZ	Father's sister
H	Husband
HB	Husband's brother
HF	Husband's father
HM	Husband's mother
HZ	Husband's sister
M	Mother
MB	Mother's brother
MF	Mother's father
MM	Mother's mother
MZ	Mother's sister
S	Son
S Ch	Son's children
SD	Son's daughter
SS	Son's son
Sib	Sibling
SW	Son's wife
W	Wife
WB	Wife's brother

WF	Wife's father
WM	Wife's mother
WZ	Wife's sister
Z	Sister
Z Ch	Sister's children
ZD	Sister's daughter
ZH	Sister's husband
ZS	Sister's son

Acknowledgements

The author would like to thank Dr Jordi Gayá for his help with the translation. He also wishes to express thanks to the Institut d'Estudis Baleàrics for their financial assistance in the translation of this book.

Preface

Although the English-speaking reader may be familiar with anthropological monographs on Southern Europe, it is a rare treat to be able to read in English what native anthropologists write about their own societies. The lopsided structure of the international anthropological community means that Anglo-Saxon anthropologists, and to a lesser extent Northern Europeans too, have had, and still largely have, a practical monopoly of knowledge concerning Southern Europe, at least in the international arena. What was inevitable some years ago, when the native Southern Europeans had not yet developed an anthropological expertise, is not acceptable today when a pleiad of social anthropologists, many trained abroad, are engaged in systematic research in the different regions and communities of their own countries. Many excellent monographs from Southern Europe are unavailable to the wider anthropological public (who tend to read English, but not Spanish, Italian or Portuguese), and hence are quoted only by the specialists (or worse, used without acknowledgement).

It is thus with great pleasure that I welcome the translation of *Casa y familia* into English. A lecturer in the Department of Anthropology at the University of Barcelona, Dr Bestard-Camps belongs to the new breed of Catalan anthropologists who, by the 1970s, had enthusiastically decided to dedicate themselves to the development of anthropology in their own homeland along scholarly lines, forcefully shedding the decades of unimaginative, slovenly and parochial musings that had characterised the Francoist era. Like many who aspired to become anthropologists at that time, Bestard-Camps came under the influence of the spellbinding work of Lévi-Strauss, and particularly of his *The Elementary Structure of Kinship*. His own anthropological project owes a lot to the inspiration of this book. But it would be erroneous to assume that *What's in a Relative?* is a case of mimesis. This would be to ignore the fact that the author is also well steeped in the Anglo-Saxon anthropological literature, and has mind of his own.

Three main features characterise the book. First, its boldness: it is a text in the grand style of anthropology – a microcosm is taken as the starting-point, a pre-text for wider theoretical considerations. Second, its originality: focusing exclusively on kinship as the key to the understanding of cultural continuities and discontinuities, of social identity over time, it is a brave undertaking, particularly because it deals with a Euro-Mediterranean society. Finally, its scholarly character: the book shows a masterly command of the anthropological, historical and sociological theories and literature at three levels – local, European and Mediterranean, and general. Not many texts can equal the wealth of scholarly knowledge displayed in *What's in a Relative?*, as the seminal Introduction so well exemplifies. Furthermore, unlike most anthropological monographs, the theoretical discussions are not confined to the Introduction; in fact they permeate each and every one of the chapters and sections of the book.

Dr Bestard-Camps chose as his area of theoretical interest what Lévi-Strauss called the complex structures of kinship. But, how to study kinship in societies where it is not the structural centre of social life? The island selected to become his research laboratory (an expression that Bestard-Camps perhaps would not endorse) was Formentera, one of the smaller Balearic islands, off the coast of Spain. There, kinship is elusive from a social structural point of view, but it is important in the construction of the social experience of the natives. For the islanders, genealogies are a way of thinking about social continuity, and hence they open the path to the understanding of their history and of their identity. Local genealogies are a form of memory which helps the understanding of the lines of rupture and correspondence between social time and family time.

The author makes it clear that kinship concepts cannot be reduced to either a universe of norms or a system which can easily be manipulated through social strategies. Kinship notions are symbols which provide meaning to personal relationships and make possible certain types of social experience. The kinship discourse is not a closed system which dominates only a single aspect of the social structure; in fact it goes beyond the domestic domain into other cultural realms. There is a symbolic use of kinship in the areas of 'hierarchy, status and identity'.

The centrality of the house (*casa*) in the life of the islanders of Formentera is one of the key aspects of the book. The houses (*cases*) are patrimonial lines, that is, corporations, moral persons, with a name and property attached to them. It is through them that individuals are placed in the social game; they condense in one concept the residence of the domestic group and the descent line of a number of generations. The author emphasises that marriage alliances are the crux of the kinship system, and that the change from hierarchical to homogeneous marriages means a transition to a system in which the houses cease to be central and the interest of the individual prevails.

Except for the study of family and domestic units, most ethnographies on Mediterranean Europe have ignored the centrality of kinship, which is usually explained away by reference to the economy (marriage and inheritance strategies) or the political sphere (clientelism). The author seeks to avoid the two major pitfalls of kinship studies in complex societies: economic or political reductionism and the normative or organisational perspective. But if in Mediterranean Europe the kinship discourse no longer speaks the language of social organisation, it must follow that its symbolic aspects are central (unless one is prepared to accept that kinship is a remnant from times past). As I have said before, symbols refer to the way in which groups perceive themselves, their identity and their historical memory. In other words, the symbols of kinship are different forms of thinking about time and refer to the different ways of integrating personal, social and family time.

The Formenterans believe that kinship has to generate solidarity; that is why their matrimonial strategy is to marry neither too close nor too far (both in terms of geographical and kinship distance). A distant cousin seems to be the preferred type of marriage. The positive attitude towards distant cousin marriage is justified by saying that it is a way of bringing together what was in the process of being lost. Marriage with close cousins is rather uncommon, exceptional. A too close marriage would show family egoism and it would fail to create solidarity; in any case the rationale of the islanders is to say that there is no point in uniting what is already united. A too distant marriage, on the other hand, would also be unable to generate solidarity because of 'cultural' incompatibility. However, social reproduction imposes marriage cycles among patrimonial lines which are socially equal (that is, with the same status, class, location, etc.) but not identical (they do not belong to the same house or have the same 'blood'). Because of the small size of the island, this means much closer marriages than the ideal previously expressed.

The 'traditional' type of marriage came under pressure at the beginning of the twentieth century as a result of temporary migration to the Americas. The return of the enriched sailors produced a much greater homogeneity in the pattern of land distribution, and hence the hierarchical element among the houses became less important. It was possible, then, to practise a different type of marriage, unrelated to hierarchical principles. Consanguinal marriages ceased to be statistically important because there was no longer any need to protect patrimonial lines at a time when the island had become socio-economically levelled. This situation called for wider types of marriage.

I would like to conclude this brief preface with two points that transcend the strict limits of the book. First of all, *What's in a Relative?* is implicitly a text about culture in so far as it is a solid reflection on the role of kinship within a social whole. The author manages to avoid a simplistic conception of social change based on either a materialist or an idealist view of society. In this he is faithful to the Weberian dictum that no one-sided interpretation of history can be right. He makes it clear that the kinship idiom cannot be reduced to infrastructural factors such as ecology, demography or economy; but neither can it be constituted into an entelechy. Only a conception of society as an ongoing, changing social totality in which no primacy is given to any factor can account for the role of kinship. Second, there are a number of implications for research. The book brilliantly confirms, if it needed demonstration, that without historical depth, anthropological work (at least in Europe) is bound to be descriptive and superficial; indirectly, it shows how even secluded communities such as Formentera cannot be properly understood without reference to a wider world system. At the methodological level, Dr Bestard-Camps exemplifies how with theoretical sophistication one can test a number of hypotheses by reference to a single case-study.

What's in a Relative? is an excellent monograph in the best tradition of social anthropology and it deserves to occupy an honourable place among European ethnographies; with this

English translation it will be available to a much wider public. But the book goes beyond the purely ethnographic to tackle some crucial issues concerning the role of kinship in complex societies. And in this the author discharges himself with great sensitivity and skill to produce a work which is of the greatest interest and of a high scientific level.

Josep R. Llobera

I

Introduction

There is no privileged zone in culture from which the others necessarily derive, and society is neither the family expanded nor the polity
generalized.

Geertz and Geertz (1975: 157)

I.1. Kinship in Formentera

From the beginning of my fieldwork in Formentera my research
was intended to be an analysis of the role of kinship in a peasant
society. My methodology followed classical anthropological tradition: I collected genealogies, researched the land inheritance
system and analysed kinship practices in different social situations.[1] Formentera offers a number of advantages for this kind
of enquiry. It is a relatively small island (82.08 km^2), which had
2,965 inhabitants in 1970, of whom 82.87 per cent were dispersed (Vallés 1973) and the remainder concentrated in three
parishes: Sant Francesc Xavier, Sant Ferran and El Pilar.
Throughout its history there have been periods of population
increase and periods of depopulation, and at the end of the
seventeenth century the island was inhabited by people from
Ibiza, the Pitiusa Major (Vilá Valentí 1950). Since the nineteenth
century the men of Formentera have left the island temporarily
to go as sailors or labourers to South America and Cuba, staying
away for three or four years but without breaking their ties with

---

1. I gathered data concerning the population's ideas about kinship by means
of oral interviews, and also used documents such as the census lists kept in the
Formentera Council Archive and in the Historical Archive of Ibiza, the notarial
protocols in the Notary Archive of Ibiza and family documents kept in various
households of Formentera. I have also used the matrimonial dispensations kept
in the Episcopal Archive of Ibiza.

their native community. From 1960 onwards the island has felt the impact of tourism (Gil Muñoz 1971 and Nieto 1976). Although tourism has changed the traditional way of life in significant ways, there are, nevertheless, significant continuities with the past. The island has well-defined natural resources, a homogeneous cultural tradition, a well-defined family structure and a population that has not moved *en masse*: temporary emigration has been compatible with maintaining the agricultural work necessary for subsistence, and there is a high incidence of local endogamy. This is, therefore, a case where it is possible to study the continuity and discontinuity of kinship relations in detail.

At first, I felt that my focus on kinship should lead me to concentrate on the classic topics of an ethnography based upon 'social structure' – the kinship system, family types, domestic organisation, marriage and inheritance systems – and upon infrastructural aspects like ecology, economy and demography. However, if kinship is not the centre of this kind of social structure, this argument necessarily leads to the marginalisation of what was constituted as the object of analysis. Kinship either tends to be relegated to the domestic sphere, or becomes an epiphenomenon of the infrastructural aspects of society and loses its specificity.

From the standpoint of social structure, kinship practices in Formentera have very irregular and contradictory facets. They can be important with respect to reciprocal help in some kinds of family agricultural labour, but can equally be replaced by another kind of relationship like neighbourliness, friendship or the relationship between employer and employee. Although we can find a wide acknowledgement of remote kin, there are no corporate groups corresponding to organised kindreds. Beyond domestic obligations we can hardly talk about a social action determined by circumstances of kinship. In some contexts, we can find intense relationships between collaterals, but in others they are absent. As a normative system of inheritance, kinship seems to have the rigidity of patrilineality, but adaptive strategies in particular situations transform it into a flexible and scarcely determinant system of inheritance practices. We might talk about a political discourse expressed in terms of kinship language, but political recruitment can be attributed to modes of clientelism where kinship plays no major role. Not everyone agrees about his or her ascription to a kinship unit, and 'family' or 'household' can refer to different groups depending on the circumstances. It is possible to find families with a deep genealogical memory, while others reduce their family history to the present. In short, we have a classic example of cognatic kinship in which the lack of differentiation in recognising kin allows the introduction of non-kinship principles for determining social organisation.

Social relations in Formentera are not organised in the language of kinship; this idiom appears only in the private sphere, and it is marginal in relation to other principles of social structure such as property, locality and social class. From this perspective, kinship can hardly be considered an explanatory category in analysing social structure, except by presenting it as a survival, still operational, from a 'traditional' peasant society in rapid process of social change and integration into the market system. Such an interpretation could only be based on an idealisation of the peasant family in a past that has nothing to do with history. Juxtaposing a 'traditional' family characterised by a domestic mode of production, a strong patriarchal dimension and a stem domestic type with a 'modern' nuclear and private family seemed to me a simplification of social change that was not in accord with family experiences remembered by the old people of Formentera nor with notarial records, census lists and the spatial structures of the old houses, nor with what can be observed among present-day families.

In spite of the fact that the language of kinship may be thought marginal with respect to social structure and that the rules of behaviour defined by kinship rarely extend beyond the limits of the household, it became clear from my fieldwork that a kinship-based discourse still remained significant. When people explained their own personal histories, they talked about family, they constructed genealogies and they classified their relatives. The discourse of kinship seemed neither marginal for the construction of their social experience nor isolated from other social languages. Faced with these fragments of a kinship based discourse I felt that it was worthwhile 'to ask another question and see what the pay-off might be', as Schneider (1972: 59) had suggested in his attempt to bring about a change in the traditional hypotheses concerning kinship, which had previously been linked to problems of social organisation.

Oral discourse on kinship in Formentera allows us to consider genealogies as a way of thinking about social continuity. Talking about family involves a regular movement between past and present. The spatial perception of kinship is based on relations in the past and the use of the idiom of consanguinity is related to the definition of personal identity in time. It seems that genealogies not only give us facts about family groups, marriage customs and inheritance strategies, but also give us insights into a complete realm of perception and understanding of history and a way of making sense of several aspects of social life. The conceptions of kinship presented in the lists of names in genealogies, in reminiscences and in discourses about the family cannot be reduced to a system of norms or social strategies. They are symbols that give meaning to relations between people, and they delimit several sorts of social experience. The discourse of kinship should not, therefore, be considered as a closed system exclusively controlling one part of the social structure such as the family, or the rules of marriage and inheritance. Kinship symbols are not simply restricted to the realm of the household, they are correlated with other cultural languages, and they are relevant to more social contexts than just that of the family. In Formentera kinship language does not dominate the social structure. However, kinship may be recognised as having a symbolic use related to local models of hierarchy, status and identity. Ideas of consanguinity and affinity are associated with patterns of hierarchy between households, with relationships between families of similar status and with the local differentiation and global homogeneity of the island.

The allusions to the past in genealogical narratives, the significance of kinship as a way of thinking about social continuity, and the flux between past and present in family memory have led me to interpret kinship in the context of local history. I have regarded oral genealogies as a form of memory and I have related them to other written forms of memory (census lists, marriage registers, land documents, notarial protocols and folklorists' and travellers' descriptions) in order to attempt to establish the continuities and discontinuities between family time and social time. Through these different kinds of sources I have not only compared facts in order to compile information and to try to find analogies or contradictions between what people say and what people do or between normative systems and social practices, I have also tried to fuse the different sources together, while continuing to pursue a detailed analysis of the oral discourse of families: their reminiscences of particular experiences in Formentera. In this way I seek to restore a general meaning to a multiplicity of particular memories and at the same time to understand kinship in history, without starting either from a model of the traditional family built on an idealised past or from a static model based on the idea of the universality of the nuclear family. To overcome this dichotomy, I have considered family memories in relation to the history of the community, looking for different forms of continuity and change in family experience. I have analysed continuity through residential forms and normative systems, demonstrating that discontinuity manifests itself on the level of family control over its social environment. Although household composition showed continuity, different ways of inhabiting the domestic space seemed to me to reflect the dynamic between the collectivity and the domestic group.

Through the reconstruction of the genealogical lines of some families of the island, as preserved *selectively* by family memory and private documents (for example, baptismal records, matrimonial contracts, wills), distinct patrimonial lines have been identified within the network of kinship. I have called them *houses*, following European juridical and ethnological tradition. Houses are corporate groups with a name and rights of property. They are units of kinship: through them their members are recognised in the social network. They link the concepts of residence and descent. The house in Formentera is not only significant as a residence; it is also seen as a line of continuity between ancestors and successors. The best legal expression of this kind of family continuity is seen in the marriage contracts of heirs of the house.

I have analysed the house, the most relevant element in the kinship system, in terms of the two principles of social reproduction: descent and alliance. The house, considered as a descent line, does not form any kind of descent group, given that residence is an element of succession, that only one member of the sibling group is the successor and that the male line can be supplanted by the female one and the lineal succession by the lateral one. This kind of flexibility under the rigid principle of house continuity is also exemplified in the different modes available to houses for the orchestration of alliances. In their matrimonial strategies it is possible to find close alliances that change remote consanguineous kin into affines, and also alliances outside the limits of consanguinity, but within the realm of homogamy. The interaction of house alliances moves within the narrow circles of matrimonial compatibility and, at various times, combines close alliances with more remote ones.

In the analysis of social reproduction of houses in circumstances of social change on the island, I found the transformational pivot of the kinship system in matrimonial alliances. What has changed is the *field* of marriage: from close matrimonial strategies that created deep local differences, there has been a change to marriages founded upon the social homogeneity of the island. This principle of homogeneity challenges the hierarchy that can be found inside the house and the system of social differences in which houses participated. I have analysed the way in which changes in the meaning of matrimonial alliances have led to transformation of kinship units, showing how houses are no longer the centre of the system and how their language of social continuity has given way to individualist interest.

In this interpretation of kinship in Formentera I have not pretended that its family model is the expression of a type we can generalise to wider cultural areas (Catalonia or the Mediterranean, for example). However, I offer some data and interpretations that could be useful in comparative terms, and have myself made use of other monographs in this way. Neither have I written a comprehensive ethnography of all cultural aspects of Formentera, since I have collected only those data I thought relevant in order to analyse problems of kinship. This does not mean that I have regarded the island as a kind of natural laboratory to test some hypotheses. In any fieldwork, even on a small island, it is impossible to check all the variables of a cultural analysis. I have only raised some issues concerning kinship which arise from an anthropological perspective (without making any pretence that there exists a homogeneous tradition in the discipline in this field) and considered them in a concrete situation. Through the analysis of naming practices, different conceptions of identity, domestic forms and experiences and practices of succession and marriage, I have tried to present the principal axes along which kinship develops in a particular culture and which allow us to distinguish the specific attributes of kinship in its social relations. Enquiring about kin in specific situations, I have tried to answer the question 'what's in a relative?'

I.2. Paradoxes in the Study of Kinship

A superficial look at the history of anthropology may lead to the conclusion that the subject of kinship has been one of the major topics in the discipline. Some important texts[2] give the impression that the discipline has accumulated a body of positive knowledge of the subject, and the degree of abstraction with which the theme is treated could encourage the hope that anthropology has finally converted itself into a 'hard science', the 'pure or theoretical' science of which Radcliffe-Brown (1950) speaks in his famous 'Introduction' to the *African Systems of Kinship and Marriage*. This abstract and theoretical character of kinship studies, completely unintelligible to the uninitiated, could give it the status of a fundamental discipline within anthropology. Kinship is to anthropology what logic is to philosophy or the nude to art: it is 'the basic discipline', argues Fox (1967) in one of the most common university textbooks on kinship. Kinship has also generated some of the most sophisticated conceptual devices of any anthropological topic; one need simply recall the polemics on alliance theory or the dispute about the Crow–Omaha systems.[3]

However, when anthropologists began to study rural communities at home, although a chapter about family and kinship was an obligatory part of each ethnography, kinship seemed neither relevant nor important for the study of this kind of society. What is said in these chapters often seems trivial, an ordered repetition of what we still know or believe we know from our own family experience, and a sense of theoretical insecurity troubles any anthropologist trying to study the domestic groups or kinship relations in any European peasant society. As G. Augustins (1982: 39) remarks: 'faced with questions of social organisation in European peasant societies, the anthropologist finds himself without any protection: the grand theories of descent and alliance, worked out for societies with rules of affiliation to a group or for the choice of a spouse, have no use here'. Unlike those of 'primitive' societies, ethnographies

2. See Fox (1967), Buchler and Selby (1968) and Kessing (1975).
3. The polemics on alliance theory arose in the wake of Lévi-Strauss's seminal contribution (1968, first edn 1947) and was continued by Leach (1951), Homans and Schneider (1955) and Needham (1960). The analysis of Crow–Omaha systems used a formal language not common in other domains of anthropology: see, for example, Lounsbury (1964) and Héritier (1981).

of European peasant societies introduce kinship as a peripheral
subject, and other spheres of social life take the role which
kinship systems have played in studying 'primitive' societies. It
has seemed reasonable to speak about kinship only as an epiphenomenon of the economy (e.g. in inheritance or marriage
strategies) or as a tool of politics (e.g. in patron–client relationships). Moreover, it is often assumed that modernisation processes will result in the end of even a mediating role for kinship,
leaving economic and political relationships in their pure form.

Mediterranean anthropologists have neither developed any
relevant theory for the analysis of kinship nor have they generally even reached a consensus about adequate theoretical questions. The one exception has perhaps been the study of
household types and their inner family relations. The northwest Mediterranean coast, for example, has bilateral kinship,
personal kindreds and a lack of descent groups. Kinship, however, has been judged trivial, and without any interest, except
where it could be used as a vehicle for social relations, political
influence or clientelism.[4] The Mediterranean anthropologist,
unlike those working in other cultural areas, does not have a
solid group of theoretical questions with which to analyse kinship successfully. As Davis (1977: 198) has noted: 'kinship
studies in the Mediterranean have not reached the same depth
in their analysis as elsewhere. Kinship studies on Mediterranean bilateral systems have been carried out on the easy sup-
position that such a familiar kinship system does not require
further research. Authors have only asked about the use of
kinship, without previous study of the system itself.' If, on the
south Mediterranean coast, marriages with a parallel cousin
have caused 'a kind of scandal' for alliance theory (Bourdieu
1980: 271), on the north Mediterranean coast 'the relative autonomy of the nuclear family and the absence of clear marriage
rules have induced little interest in kinship studies' (Pitt-Rivers
1977: 114), and the minimal role of kinship in the formation of
corporate groups has also meant that descent theory has regarded this kinship system as a marginal subject of study.

An anthropologist with a standard knowledge of kinship,
faced with the state of kinship studies in Europe and the Mediterranean and trying to begin an analysis of kinship in a
southern European society, could form the same impression as

4. See the classic study of the Mediterranean area by Campbell (1964).

a sociologist of the family who writes of 'a methodologically naive and conceptually underdeveloped discipline centred on trivial problems and rife with value judgements, more useful for journalism and social work than for serious sociology' (Anderson 1971b: 8). Given the importance of the topic, the work of the sociologist of the family might seem to offer a way to a new scientific approach, constructing explanatory theories based on the rigorous verification of hypotheses. However, the anthropologist, notwithstanding the very sophisticated and developed theories of kinship which exist for other kinds of societies, will usually find that the study of kinship in our own society has been considered marginal and extraneous to the analysis of social organisation. Anthropological theories have asserted that kinship groups outside the nuclear family have no significance in industrial societies, in contrast to the role of kinship in those societies on which anthropologists have based their kinship theories. Parsons' (1943) thesis of the structural isolation of the nuclear family has been used to this effect, as a kind of intellectual fudge for avoiding kinship analysis in our society. Compared with the 'traditional' European or 'exotic' kinship systems studied by anthropologists, the nuclear family could be considered as 'isolated' and hence irrelevant for studies of social organisation, an entity divorced from the holistic and synthetic studies that anthropologists made of societies. The deep-rooted prejudice of industrial societies that kinship has no social relevance became the basis of an intellectual procedure for distinguishing different societies and the methods of analysis appropriate to them. Within this framework, the meaning of the isolated nuclear family, so alien to other cultures, was still not explained. Rivers' suggestion (1914: 703) that we should study descriptive systems once the 'lesson of classificatory systems' has been learned had no chance of being carried through, given that the explanatory strength imputed to classificatory systems kept descriptive systems within the private and domestic realm.

Kinship studies have preserved the view, which arose under evolutionism, that kinship governs 'primitive societies', while in modern societies kinship has been restricted to the domestic sphere and hence can be considered peripheral to an understanding of such societies. We could accept Radcliffe-Brown's dictum (1950: 11) that in order to understand any aspect of the social life of any African people it is necessary to have a complete knowledge of their kinship system, only if we assume that this statement could not be extended either to modern societies or to rural communities. Such an approach implies that western society bases its behaviour on utilitarian and economic motivations, while in 'primitive' societies social behaviour is determined by kinship. As I have already stressed, if kinship has been analysed at all in complex societies, it is only as an agent of political control or property inheritance. This is the reason why one of the key concepts in the study of kinship is 'strategy', that is, the instrumental use of certain kinship relations with motivations outside the obligations between relatives. Talking about inheritance or matrimonial strategies usually means that kinship has been subsumed under other basic structures like politics or economics. From this point of view kinship is considered as an expression of other phenomena, such as material conditions, economic structures or social norms. In this sense, it can be said that kinship is judged a peculiar idiom without its own rules and that its systemic character is determined by other social phenomena. But in opposition to 'the idiom of kinship' approach, I will argue that kinship can indeed be regarded as a symbolic system with its own rules.

Kinship research in peasant communities has been focused mainly on normative and organisational aspects. Key themes have been the structure and composition of households and the analysis of peasant families as units of production and consumption. Several aspects of kinship, like descent as a set of inheritance rules, marriage rules as norms which control alliances between families, and kinship networks as a set of social relations that allow different adaptive strategies, have been topics of research on the relationship between family and social structure in rural communities. Thus, the normative and organisational aspects of kinship have been given prominence, while its internal structure and meaning have been considered as trivial and theoretically irrelevant. As an element of social organisation, kinship appears peripheral in all spheres except in the domestic domain. 'Thus', comments Strathern (1982: 75), 'analyses concentrate on the family as a unit of consumption or agent of socialisation, of solidarity within small neighbourhood groups, of personal authority structures, and of the "adaptiveness" of the nuclear family to social mobility'. Attention has been focused chiefly on the organisational effects of kinship structure and the conditions for its manipulation. However, the forms of kin classification, the symbolic system of the idiom of kinship and the link between social and kinship categories have all been regarded as obvious.

If bonds between kinship and social networks are regarded as self-evident, the analysis of the relationship between kinship and social classes can lead to statements which are clearly contradictory, such as, on the one hand, that 'in the absence of property, societies do not tend to produce extended kinship networks' (Sabean 1976: 98) and, on the other, that while peasant elites are developing a 'bureaucratic' or an 'anti-kinship' model which denies 'extra-family' relations, other community groups maximise the kinship relationship (Leyton 1975: 4). These assertions presume a necessary relation between peasant property and the 'kinship model', on the one hand, and between modernisation and the 'anti-kinship' model, on the other. They can be considered, however, as variations in the social behaviour associated with the use that is made of the same kinship structure, and as different perceptions within social groups of the same kinship categories and of the public dimension of kinship relations which seem to open or close social possibilities according to context.[5] It is neither the economic conduct of social groups nor their greater or lesser structural integration that regulates the social use of kinship; it is the use of different codes of the idiom of kinship that allows variations in kinship relations. As Fortes (1978: 22) remarks: 'the sphere of kinship has its inherent structural properties and cultural content. Matrimonial, parental and sibling relations belong to and arise in this sphere, providing models for the organisation and conduct of human affairs which can be transferred by metaphor, metonymy and other social processes to other cultural and structural spheres.'

The dichotomy which places kinship at the centre of theoretical analysis of 'primitive societies', but relegates it to the margins of the private domain in modern ones, can be regarded as an ideological prejudice rather than positive anthropological science. There has not always been complete agreement about the nature and meaning of kinship, and neither has kinship always been regarded as trivial for the analysis of our culture. A less presentist reading of the history of kinship theories does not

---

5. Schneider (1968) has analysed the meaning of American kinship in terms of the contrast between what is fixed (of the order of nature, the 'substance') and what is changeable (of the order of law, the 'code').

necessarily relate it to any of the basic domains of anthropology. Instead of agreement about the subject-matter of kinship, there have been conflicting points of view, discontinuities in the development of kinship theories and observations and proposals without any subsequent application. It seems as though Lafitau's initial description and later omission of the Iroquois kinship system could be regarded as the paradigm for kinship theories rather than the exception.[6] It is enough to remember the polemic on the meaning of classificatory terminologies raised by Morgan (1871). McLennan's proposition (1886: 273) that classificatory terminologies are merely 'systems of mutual salutation' relating to courtesy and ceremonial codes could suggest that it would be more useful to abandon the study of kinship terminologies in favour of descent systems. The rediscovery of Morgan by Rivers (1907) elicited further interest in terminologies and their relationship to social organisation. However, at the same time Kroeber (1909) suggested that 'kinship terms reflect psychology, not sociology', and originated a split between studies of the mechanics of kinship systems and the logic of kinship terms.[7] Malinowski (1930), for his part, repudiated 'kinship algebra' as a suitable method to approach family life, based as it was on the assumption that notions of kinship first arise in the family and then 'extend' to wider social groups.

These debates allowed the specification of 'jural' and 'social' aspects of kinship. However, since Durkheim (1897: 316) defined the social character of kinship and established one of the basic assertions of kinship studies – 'kinship and consanguinity are different things' – it seemed as if kinship, ever more replete with social functions and with explanatory power within the social structure, had lost its specific significance and had become one of those 'odd-job' words that produce major analytic difficulties and are of no real use in analysis (Needham 1974: 42).

6. Histories of kinship theory have normally followed a linear plan outlining the presence of forerunners in the field, founders of a new subject and researchers of specific problems in the field (Tax 1937). It would be better to write a history in which kinship is not presented as being so homogeneous as some anthropological texts have supposed. For a history of attempts to make kinship the central focus of anthropological theory, see Langham (1981). For a critical history of definitions of kinship, see Schneider (1984: 97–112).

7. On the different approaches of Rivers and Kroeber to kinship analysis, see Schneider (1968).

'Kinship' in anthropological jargon is one of those rubrics under which special anthropological observations can be organised and it becomes an academic convention which lumps together many topics with different meanings. It does not refer to any distinct class of phenomena, and major theoretical difficulties can arise if we try to define its nature and specific function and are 'tempted to describe the use of important "odd-job" words as if they functioned like normal words' (Wittgenstein 1976: 75). That is exactly what happened when the polemic about the nature of kinship erupted.[8] In order to define the specific meaning of kinship, it was necessary to assume that it depicts a set of relations, primarily genealogical, though with an ultimate connection to its biological character. Otherwise kinship had to be considered (as many social anthropologist did consider it) as an 'idiom' of social relations without any specific content. The difficulties arose when anthropologists began to consider the 'substance' of kinship. It was difficult to distinguish kinship from other aspects of social relations if it was regarded merely as an 'idiom' expressing them, thus prompting Leach (1961: 305) to remark that 'kinship systems have no "substance" except in relation to land and property. What social anthropologists had designated as kinship structure was just a way of speaking about property rights. The kinship system as a self-sufficient and self-regulating frame of reference, and as a discrete category of jural rules, was, thereby, called into question.'

Consensus about the advantages of kinship as a rubric to organise analysis of social data has been destroyed, and kinship, as the analytic centre of papers and monographs, has given way to other topics such as economic relations, social control, dependency relations, etc., in which kinship relations have a subordinate role (Barnes 1980: 294). Kinship is no longer regarded as a privileged 'idiom' through which other social relations are expressed, but simply as a fragment of other social discourses. The same thing has happened to kinship as to other concepts originated in the early days of anthropology. What seemed a set of

8. We allude to the polemic about the meaning of kinship genealogies. Gellner (1954, 1960 and 1963, all reprinted in 1973) added a biological element to the meaning of genealogies, whereas Needham (1960) and Barnes (1961 and 1964) defended the exclusive social character of kinship. Beattie (1964 and 1965) suggested that kinship has no meaning on its own. Schneider (1964 and 1965) regarded the specificity of kinship language as a system of symbols and initiated the cultural accounts of kinship.

clear and distinct phenomena became an illusion (Schneider 1972: 50–1). In ethnographies of 'primitive' societies, 'kinship systems' have lost their charm, and if there ever was agreement about the meaning of kinship, it was only in the mythical time of the ancestors of the discipline. As Geertz and Geertz (1975: 153) remark, what once upon a time seemed so indubitable – 'that kinship forms a definable object of study to be found in a readily recognizable form everywhere, a contained universe of internally organized relationships only awaiting an anthropologist to explore it' – has now become one of the more implausible principles of anthropology.

In order to overcome the contradiction of regarding kinship as an 'idiom' without any specific substance in itself, but with a content in economics or politics, Schneider (1964) suggested analysing kinship in its 'pure form', as a system of symbols and meanings. To do that, its content had to be sought in the appropriate place, in American or European societies, where kinship was separate from other institutions and social relations, in contrast to 'primitive societies', in which kinship was embedded in economics, politics and other social relations. It is not just a question of describing the normative principles and practices of kinship or the instrumental character of kinship in social relations, but of giving an account of the symbolic structures of kinship, that is, the ideas, beliefs and values relevant to kinship relations.[9]

If the tendency of previous anthropologists was to focus kinship studies on aspects of social organisation and to limit cultural analysis to the study of religion, ritual, magic and myth (Schneider 1976: 206), this division can now be considered the cause of a false dichotomy that splits social institutions into 'instrumental' domains (kinship, economics and politics) and 'expressive' ones (religion, ritual and myth). Following this distinction, kinship is grounded in objective realities (birth, sexual intercourse and death) and religion expresses symbols based in another kind of reality, the 'society' in Durkheimian analysis or the 'infrastructure' in Marxist analyses. Because of this distinction, kinship studies have been centred on the analysis of normative and social relations organising activities

9. See the influential book by Schneider (1980) and his critical analysis of the assumptions behind kinship studies (Schneider 1984). See also Yanagisako (1985).

related to affinity and the transfer of rights. The symbolic aspects of these activities have, however, almost never been analysed accurately. Kinship has been studied mainly as a social and normative system and social structure has been identified with kinship, but kinship has seldom been analysed as a cultural system (Schneider 1976: 208). In kinship studies the principal question was: 'How do people organise themselves in order to do something?', instead of 'What does what they do mean?', and thus function has been confused with meaning.

If kinship as a principle of social organisation in modern societies seems peripheral and is relegated to the domestic and private sphere, the analysis of its symbolic language, free of organisational aspects, has a central significance. If it cannot be considered as an idiom of other basic social phenomena or as an instrument of social structure, it can be analysed as an idiom wherein a constellation of ideas surrounding descent and affinity are structured in terms of a set of symbols which refer to the group's identity and collective memory, their different ways of conceiving time and their distinct modes of combining personal, family and social time.

I.3. Family History

At the same time as anthropologists were beginning to abandon kinship as a focus of social organisation analysis, the historians began to display an increasing interest in the western family.[10] For social history, the study of the family has proved a useful vehicle for studying people, social forms and daily life in the past. The methods of historical demography[11] have produced both accurate description and rigorous analysis of family types in different periods and in different European countries.

The data from population lists of pre-industrial Europe point to a prevalence of simple households (Laslett and Wall 1972),

10. There are excellent reviews of studies on the history of the family. See Berkner (1973), Wrigley (1977) and Stone (1981). See also Anderson (1980), Mitterauer and Seider (1982) and Segalen (1986). Since the 1970s there has been an increasing interest in the history of the family. It is enough to look at journals like *Annales E.S.C.*, *Journal of Interdisciplinary History*, *Past and Present* and *Journal of Family History* to realise the relevance of family studies in historical analysis.

11. See the family reconstruction of Fleury and Henry (1976) and the system of household classification of Laslett (1972).

instead of extended ones. These data were contrary to the ideas received from the founders of European family studies like Le Play (1871). Le Play elaborated a sequence of families in Europe, from the patriarchal to the modern. The intermediary form was the stem family. According to Le Play, industrial society was characterised by an unstable family, because neolocal residence caused the decline of the sense of a descent line which enabled individuals to feel identity with a house, a name and a patrimony. Le Play opposed the unstable family to the stem family, which was related to a property, a house and a male descent line. The house was the family symbol, giving continuity through the male heir.

Inheritance was by primogeniture, and the heir was socialised in a manner which enabled him to succeed his father in agricultural production. After marriage, the inheriting son remained in the house, brought his wife to live with him, and their children were born in it. The daughters and the other sons received a dowry after marriage; the sons having the possibility of launching industrial or commercial enterprises, aided initially by family capital and with the house acting as a point of reference. If they remained unmarried they could stay at home under the authority of the heir. If farm production was extensive and the family labour force inadequate, servants were hired and were regarded as members of the household. The children's socialisation was in the hands of the family and not left to external institutions: parents, grandparents, uncles, aunts and even servants participated in it. This way of bringing up the family guaranteed the reproduction of the domestic group and at the same time guaranteed social peace, making social reproduction possible without the crises and contradictions of industrial society. For Le Play, the stem family was shattered by the Napoleonic civil code and the inheritance rule of equality of siblings. This was the cause of the dissolution of descent lines; the house lost its power to symbolise family continuity and unstable families replaced stem ones. Although Le Play's concern, as Durkheim (1915: 116) remarked, was more doctrinaire than scientific, his evolutionist theory of different family types and his monographic method led the way for studying family types in Europe.[12] Sociologists went to rural places in order to find

---

12. On Le Play, see Brooke (1970). Le Play and his disciples showed great interest in the Catalan and Basque stem family. According to Le Play (1871: 97),

family forms already lost in industrial cities. Rural family life was idealised, being considered as a place to renew social peace and local traditions. It was thought that the stem family had prevailed throughout the whole period of pre-industrial Europe and that it was still alive in some remote areas of the continent.

With the demographic data in Laslett and Wall's (1972) book, the question of the stem family could be seen to be the product of nineteenth-century intellectual nostalgia, instead of the result of an empirical analysis. The idea, so entrenched in social science, of a progressive simplification of family roles related to industrialisation and modernisation could be regarded as a sociological myth. Although Le Play's lineal sequence was empirically unsustainable, it did, however, raise the question of data interpretation in the analysis of families in the past. Discussions around the relevance of census data for the sociological analysis of family structure (Berkner 1975) started after the publication of Laslett and Wall's book. This debate raised the same basic problems about the family as arose in anthropological debates about kinship. Family life, as a set of activities in the past, seemed invisible to analysis. When its specific function was defined, it raised the same theoretical problems as in the case of kinship. If the analysis of the family was to serve as a means of understanding the past, it was not enough to break down the lineal evolutionist sequence, but necessary to account for the continuity of family forms which accompanied economic, social and cultural changes.[13]

Family life represents a totality made up of a full spectrum of activities. Census data inform us only about residence types. If we talk about continuity of simple families in pre-industrial

they 'must be imitated all over Europe', because they preserved the continuity of family lines, and they seemed to adapt to industrialisation. On Catalonia, see Le Play (1874, III: Document F), 'Caractères de la famille souche en Catalogne' and the lecture of Perier (1956). On the influence of Le Play on Spanish thought at the turn of century, see the inaugural lecture of the Marquis de Pidal to the Real Academia de Ciencias Morales y Políticas (Discursos de Recepción, 1887).

13. Although functionalist anthropology broke with evolutionism, it considered acceptable the dichotomies between societies ruled by kinship and those ruled by locality; status and contract societies; and mechanical and organic solidarity. Historians of the family seem to have evolved the same procedure for considering changes in the western family. The debate about the family is centred on the continuity or discontinuity of family forms in history. Stone (1977) emphasises discontinuity and reproduces the dichotomic scheme. Macfarlane (1978 and 1979) emphasises continuities and places himself outside the classical dichotomies of sociological thinkers.

Europe according to census lists, we equate family types to residence types and extend the meaning of residence to the whole set of family activities. But the two concepts are, as Bender (1967) argues, logically and empirically different. Family refers to a set of activities, but census lists refer only to residence. Nor do they refer to a 'domestic group', because included in this concept is a set of functions like production, distribution, socialisation and reproduction which can be inferred only from residence. In comparative analysis the confusion of family, household and domestic groups can lead to the equation of disparate structures (Verdon 1980) and lumps different social processes into the same category. As Medick (1976: 295) remarks, the proto-industrial extended family is not comparable to the peasant one. The former worked mainly as a private institution to redistribute nuclear family poverty, but the latter was a jural group which preserved property. As Yanagisako (1979: 192) observes, the Bengal family group, equivalent, from the genealogical point of view, to the western family, is grounded on different cultural meanings and norms from its western counterpart. Although it has the same residence form and genealogical structure as the western family, its different cultural processes do not allow us to incorporate it into the same family type. These abstract types identify residence with family and cannot account for local variations in the domestic cycle.

If social historians are to regard the study of the family as a key to understanding historical variation in social structure, they need a definition of the family which is not limited simply to residence.[14] The definition of family solely by residence leads to an apparent historical continuity in family organisation, which it is not congruent with the historical analysis of change and variation. Historians of the family view it as unchanging, postulating a kind of continuity that recalls the thesis of the universality of the nuclear family. As Laslett (1972) remarks, we can, in fact, see so little actual variation in the organisation of the family in human history that it is very difficult to find examples of societies changing their character in accordance with changes in the family.

Historians who have continued to study the family in terms of

14. For a critique of Laslett's typology, see Berkner (1975) on domestic cycle; Medick (1976 and 1981) on the economic functions of the family; Goubert (1977) on local variations; and Wheaton (1975) on kinship systems.

the idea that changes in the family express variations in social structure through time dismiss residence as the main element in the definition of the family and regard it as a multifunctional domestic group where residence is an effect of other activities defining the group. Members of a family group live together in order to produce, reproduce, distribute and consume. Residence is, then, an outcome of these motives. In the definition of the family as an activity group with different functions, a link is presumed to exist between collective activities and solidarity inside the group. If their members work together, there is more interaction between them and, hence, more solidarity. With regard to this multifunctional group, many preconceptions about the 'extended family of the past' have continued in the form of assumptions about a historical gradual loss of family functions in domestic groups. A 'traditional' family with a strong solidarity, as a unit of production, reproduction, distribution and consumption, becomes a 'modern' family with solely private functions and strong intra-group sentiments.[15] Family change has, therefore, been analysed in terms of the great dichotomies which nineteenth-century thinkers used to analyse social change: traditional/modern; rural/urban; instrumental/ sentimental family. Changes in family form and function have been seen as adaptations of domestic relations to social conditions, especially economic ones. In contrast to this kind of functional analysis of family change as an immediate reaction to social forces, some historians, like N.Z. Davis (1977), try to examine the consistency and tension between family life and cultural systems. Davis analyses French family life in the sixteenth and seventeenth centuries in relation to religious, political and social processes, and the dilemma between private family values and the corporate interests is considered as a creative element in the cultural system.

Posing questions on the history of the family in terms of a decline of extended family or kinship caused by western 'rationality' or social changes induced by industrialisation, has made it difficult to provide a more accurate analysis of the relation between changes in kinship and cultural systems, and also in family ideologies and social structure. Faced with the option of a family model reduced to forms of residence and a history of its continuity, or the family defined as a group whose

15. See Ariès (1973); Shorter (1975); and Stone (1977).

functions are decreasing through history, some historians have centred their analysis on the role of domestic structures in processes of production, social reproduction and formation of the labour force from the beginnings of industrialisation.[16] They have focused on the continuity and change of family social roles, the dual 'rural' and 'industrial' aspect of many families in the period of industrialisation, the seasonal migration of some family members to industrial centres and the relevance of kinship in migration and adaptation to industrial conditions. From this point of view, domestic groups are not 'traditional' units integrated and adapted to a new economic system but institutions created by the system itself in order to control the labour force. In this context labour history and family history have discovered common objects of analysis (Hareven 1982: 5).

Other historians have focused their researchers on the reciprocal effects of social and cultural processes on inner family structure. The analysis of family system caused by inheritance strategies (Goody, Thirsk and Thompson 1976), the 'bureaucratisation' of peasant households (Rebel 1982) and the 'domestication' of family life have proved the relevance of the relation between 'interest and emotion' in family and kinship studies (Medick and Sabean 1984). These studies are not about household statistics but about the character of family experiences related to norms and modes of behaviour in different times and places. The 'emotional' perspective of the history of the family, however, has considered 'interest' and 'emotion' in family life as two distinct, and also contradictory, spheres. Instead of analysing the conditions of expression of family experience and defining the specific domain where family sentiments are shaped, material interest and family sentiment tend to be regarded as two opposite ways of representing family relations in history. In this manner the classical dichotomy between 'traditional' and 'modern' becomes an opposition between a traditional family dominated by interests of inheritance and a strongly sentimentalised modern family in which private life seems to have liberated passions previously absorbed by material interests. As a consequence of this view of history, peasant families appear motivated only by material interests. Peasant marriages are regarded as a matter of dowry price and the relations between

---

16. See mainly Anderson (1971a), Hareven (1982), Levine (1977) and Medick (1981).

parents and children are seen as being dominated by the question of inheritance, without room for sentiment, as if the two spheres were completely isolated in family experience. With respect to this viewpoint, which appraises private values of kinship in the present and projects onto the past the present's public and social values, what is required is an analysis of different patterns of the 'relational idiom' of kinship and of the conditions under which different aspects of social exchange are combined into a single element. In inheritance and the gift of dowries, material goods symbolise the meaning of kinship in social relations. Family and kinship cannot be regarded as institutions prescribing norms of social action to their members, but must be seen as social practices for which social interaction determines conditions of operation and meaning production (Bourdieu 1980: 46). In the social practices of kinship, personal interest can be reduced neither to material interest nor to the satisfaction of emotional desires. The meaning of kinship is produced by different modes of interweaving symbolic with material exchanges, and it is through these different social meanings that family experiences can be expressed.

These questions have led historians to abandon the general view of the history of the family resulting from sociological theories of industrialisation or modernisation. They conduct local research in which they can account for the social and cultural elements shaping family life. In these local studies it is not enough to find stem or simple households, different marriage patterns or rates of celibacy; it is also important to put data in context and to examine whether the concepts, definitions and accepted hypotheses of social sciences are valuable in the analysis of family life in different places. This research attempts not only to represent abstract concepts in a realistic manner but also to confront real situations with these concepts in a creative way. In the face of a common-sense realism that reproduces the topics of our prejudices about the family, it is important to raise abstract questions in real situations in order to prove the power of interpretation of some of the ideas of the social sciences.

I.4. The Complex Structures of Kinship

Lévi-Strauss (1965) has described the future of kinship studies in terms of the progress that could be made in moving from the domain of elementary structures to the analysis of complex structures. He asks if we should not try to apply to complex societies the same conceptual framework that has proved so productive in the study of more rudimentary societies. While this question remains unanswered, it is pointless to perpetuate esoteric disputes about the nature of kinship. Far from providing an answer to the problems, these debates seem to end up in a cul-de-sac, the effect of which is to abandon the study of kinship as a privileged domain of anthropology. According to Lévi-Strauss, it is futile to try to discover what kinship is before deciding whether its action extends to all human societies and how it changes when kinship systems pass from simple to complex societies. One way to answer the question would be to settle the problem of the Crow–Omaha kinship systems. Lévi-Strauss argues that these systems are in a crucial position with respect to the general theory of kinship, because they are the point of union between elementary and complex structures. While the former try to transform consanguineous into affinal relations, preferring or prescribing marriage alliances inside the consanguineous circle, the latter try to turn affinal into consanguineous relatives, preferring or prescribing that consanguineous and affinal relationships be reciprocally exclusive. The Crow–Omaha systems can be considered as semi-complex structures of marriage alliances because they belong to the realm of elementary structures from the point of view of their matrimonial prohibitions defined in terms of social structure and, at the same time, they are complex structures from the point of view of their probabilistic network of matrimonial alliances. For kinship analysis, these systems have the advantage over complex structures of assigning matrimonial prohibitions to descent lines. When a line is chosen, according to Lévi-Strauss, all members are automatically excluded as possible spouses for the reference line for several generations. It is in this sense that the Crow–Omaha systems belong to the same mechanical model of matrimonial prohibitions as elementary structures, in contrast to the model of matrimonial prohibition of complex structures, defined in terms of kinship degrees rather than kinship categories. On the other hand, as far as their probabilistic network of matrimonial alliances is concerned, recurrent forms not generated by chance can presumably be found, because these systems work in small societies where, in spite of matrimonial prohibitions, it is possible to detect a fixed average of marriages at the same degree of consanguinity after several generations. When these systems work in small populations, they enable recurrent forms of alliance, matrimonial circles inside the domain of alliance with 'permanent turbulence' generated by arbitrary selection of a spouse. The solution of the Crow–Omaha problem could help us to understand the way kinship works in areas with a high degree of local endogamy and, thus, to overcome the difficulties posed by the transition from elementary to complex structures.

Lévi-Strauss's proposal, as he points out, does pose methodological problems. On the one hand, there would be data-handling problems in processing genealogies and, on the other, it would be necessary to change the traditional way of studying kinship, in order to enter into a world without commutative sets or networks with periodical structures, a world with unforeseeable events whose statistical distribution would show significant regularities. The problems inherent in implementing Lévi-Strauss's proposal were indeed difficult to overcome. Through mathematical simulation, the number of probabilities of matrimonial alliances was very high and the significance of the recurrent forms of alliance observable in these systems was also difficult to interpret. Only an analysis of the workings of a semi-complex structure in an actual society could clarify the nature of kinship and the character of the domain of marriage in complex structures. One example is Héritier's (1981) analysis of the alliance structure of the Samo, a society with an Omaha kinship system. Starting from her data she raises the question of the 'fundamental laws of kinship' – the differential value of sexes and the opposition between cross and parallel relationships as a basis of identity – and proposes some hypotheses about the 'transition' to complex structures of kinship.

Is there any continuity between semi-complex structures of alliance and the forms which can be observed in societies with complex structures? In our societies social groups are not organised by kinship criteria, and the matrimonial rules are solely prohibitions. From these two traits (definition of groups outside kinship and matrimonial prohibitions calculated by degrees of kinship), it has often been concluded that matrimonial alliances are only a question of individual strategies ordered by social considerations. It is feasible to ask, however, if kinship might have some role in considerations about the selection of a spouse, and if in our societies there might be matrimonial practices which incorporate alliance within the domain of kinship and generate the same kind of cycles and regularities as in other alliance systems. In societies with cognatic descent systems, the recognition of kindred has diffuse limits where it is possible to renew kinship links by marriages with remote consanguineous relatives. In societies without descent groups, kinship is measured by degrees and is perceived as a core from which relations scatter. Different zones of kinship are formed around this core. The outer zone is an area of remote relatives whose kinship is recognised, although the precise genealogical links are not known. It is quite possible to renew kinship by marriage with collateral relatives located in this area of the kindred and thus to begin a new alliance cycle that puts distant relatives back into the kinship core. As Jolas, Verdier and Zonabend (1970: 17) have remarked, in the peripheral zone of kindred is generated 'a set of strangers, slightly related, who could be also possible spouses'. The area from which a spouse is chosen can correspond to this peripheral zone of kindred in which one can behave with familiarity but without the duties appropriate to close relatives. Héritier (1981: 163) suggests that these zones of major contact, located beyond the core of prohibited consanguinity degrees, designate a preferential area of spouse selection in traditional societies with complex structures of kinship. Marriage with remote consanguineous relatives in the peripheral zone of kindred, located between 'too close' relations defined by the kinship core and 'too strange' ones, creates alliance cycles within complex structures of kinship, such as, for example, the cycles between patrimonial lines of dowry 'givers' and 'takers' studied by Lamaison (1979) or the phenomenon of chaining alliances analysed by Segalen (1985: 117–60).

In European societies with cognatic kinship, kindred is personal and is composed of consanguineous and affinal relationships. Relatives within the kindred are arranged in strata following the 'onion' principle, as Parsons (1954: 182) named it. If we consider kindred from the perspective of descent, we can define a kindred as a whole set of bilateral descent lines recognised by a person (Freeman 1961: 204). The bilateral principle restrains the formation of corporate descent groups based on criteria of kinship and releases a boundless development of kindred adding collateral relations and, hence, descent lines into the genealogical network.

All learned forms, the tree, the cross and the human body, used in western tradition to count consanguinity degrees and to represent kinship structure involve the idea of a centre from which consanguinity departs, depict bilateral kinship with two sides and also justify the limits of consanguinity. Civil and canonical laws for computing inheritance rights and matrimonial prohibitions created a limit to the boundless extension of kindred in the recognition of a kinship domain. An *ad infinitum* progression of kindred with an ancestor growth in each generation following the proportion of 2^n (where n equals the number of generations between ego and his ancestors) is socially impossible because of the limits of genealogical memory and because the calculation of maximum extension of descent is founded, as Freeman (1961) remarks, upon the unlikely assumption that no one would have married any consanguineous kin in the ascending generations. In this sense, marriage in the remote area of kindred is statistically unavoidable in small populations with reduced matrimonial possibilities. Its effect would involve the decrease of ancestor and, hence, of collateral relations. As Héritier (1981: 147) comments, however, the issue is not the statistical necessity of consanguineous marriages after several generations, but the likelihood of matrimonial strategies including that kind of alliance. Marriages within the confines of kindred renew kinship links about to fall into oblivion and, thus, reinforce kindred organisation. In traditional societies with cognatic systems, according to Freeman (1961), systematic marriages with relatives, reducing ancestors and collaterals, manage to consolidate descent lines and produce a much closer network of kinship relations than in societies without systematic consanguineous marriages. They are an important trait of some societies with cognatic kinship, because they succeed in securing continuity for their kindred and allow them an important role in a social life without the organisational principle of descent groups.

The relevance of marriages within the limits of kindred resides in their ability to strengthen descent lines in opposition to the dispersion of kindred. Matrimonial cycles renew initial kinship relations and transform remote consanguineous or allied relatives into close ones and their consequent redundancy permits kindred cohesion and continuity of family lines. On the other hand, the very redundancy of alliances with close kindred also explains the negative aspects of marriages with near collateral relatives (Zonabend 1981: 314). The transformation of close relatives into allied ones produces a reduction of kinship relations and a closed circuit within the kindred. These marriages, systematically reiterated over several generations, isolate families which, having a reduced kindred and several kinship positions for each relative, can die out. Matrimonial alliances within the core of kindred are not recurrent, and if they are, they must be linked to marriages outside the kindred either by other members of sibling groups or by members of the next generation. That is the condition for family continuity. Closed marriages must be combined with other open marriages in order to create an extended circle of kindred and to preserve a relation of remote familiarity with members on its periphery with whom it is possible to find a spouse and, thus, to renew the kindred. This kind of marriage inserts history into family memory, because, in contrast to elementary structures, complex ones force family groups to reproduce themselves without being identical.

The open and closed character of matrimonial alliances in complex structures is the major source of methodological problems in the analysis of traditional kindred formation and marriage practices in Europe. It is not a periodic structure repeating itself; each marriage inserts new elements which transform the kindred into a flexible and mobile structure. If there is a matrimonial preference for the external limits of kindred, however, there is also a principle of order in the supposedly arbitrary nature of kindred formation and matrimonial decisions. It is an order that, taking into account social motives for marriage external to kinship, designates within genealogical lines long cycles of marriage combined with short ones. These long cycles are compatible either with matrimonial strategies outside the considerations of kinship or with closed strategies within the limits of kinship – double or consanguineous marriages, for instance. The combination of different kinds of matrimonial strategies defines alliances of complex structures in which it is possible to find elementary forms of exchange such as closed circuits of marriages with relatives, restricted exchanges such as the exchange of sisters in double marriages and the creation of long cycles of generalised exchange. As Héritier (1981: 165) states, restricted and generalised exchange, closed circuits within consanguinity and repetition of alliances are basic modalities in elementary, semi-complex and complex structures. The central question in the analysis of complex structures in societies in which the economic or political domain lies outside the kinship idiom concerns the translation of forms of matrimonial strategies expressed in political or economic terms into the language of exchange, in order to discover the place of kinship in the alliance idiom.

II

Systems of Classification

A name is not just a piece of clothing one can put on and take off at will; rather it enfolds the individual and grows with him.

Goethe, *Poetry and Truth*

II.1. Names and Naming Ritual

When getting to know the people of a society and surveying their living space, one learns the proper names with which places and individuals are identified. These names, in spite of appearing to have different origins and to be entirely arbitrary, are not mere labels placed on individuals and places, but form part of a complex code through which reality is filtered and classified. Places as well as people can be given names, and in many cases these names can be exchanged. Families can receive the name of a house and the land they possess and work on, in the same way that people and family groups give names to living space. Toponymics and onomastics form part of the system of classification. 'Space', says Lévi-Strauss (1966: 168), 'is a society of named places just as people are landmarks within the group. Places and individuals alike are designated by proper names, which can be substituted for each other in many circumstances common to many societies.'

As we are accustomed to the official definition of our identity in written registers, we see only disorder in the various ways people orally express and exchange names, whereas in reality they are using a system of classification that is much more complex than one consisting of written lists of names. Just as in many societies an individual may change name during the course of his life according to rules which anthropologists have tried to explain, at a more microscopic, and perhaps less impressive, level this variation also occurs in what can be called the oral tradition of complex European societies.[1] An individual changes name, and therefore identity, according to the context in which he is situated and the status he holds. In the naming process it is possible to use the surname, the name of the house, the personal name, the individual nickname, a combination of names, with specific prepositions which are used as terms of reference ('wife', 'widow' or 'son' of such-and-such), similar to the 'tecnonyms' or 'necronyms' to which anthropologists often refer when speaking about systems of personal naming in exotic societies.[2]

If we try to find an order in the different forms of naming in Formentera, not only in terms of the general rules of name transmission but also in terms of the rich interplay of variations and uses that daily life introduces into naming, we might well be left as perplexed as Montaigne who on starting his *Essai sur les noms* felt compelled to conclude that 'sous la consideration des noms, je m'en vous faire icy une galimafree de divers articles'.[3] However, owing to the possibility of speaking through the names of different aspects of a culture, an ethnologist interested in the microscopic detail of the real is able to appreciate the structural complexity of this 'galimafree' and find order where there appears to be only chaos in the particular and individual name. Linguistics and logic are concerned with the

1. On the microscopic scale in our own society of phenomena that also exist in exotic societies, Lévi-Strauss (1977: 81) states: 'when we are surprised to find in the narrations of the Kwakiutl Indians that individuals change name twenty times during their lives (in a way that makes it very difficult to follow the intrigue), we realise that on our side, amongst ourselves, phenomena of the same type exist and it is simply necessary to know how to distinguish them at a microscopic scale, while in other places they appear in a macroscopic scale'. One of the tasks of anthropology in our own society is to determine the scale of phenomena already shown to exist by anthropologists in other societies.
2. A 'necronym' is the name of a person by virtue of his relation with a dead relative. For example, 'dead oldest child', when it is a name applied to a person whose oldest son has died. A 'teknonym' is the name of a person by virtue of his relation with one of his living descendents. For example, 'father of Pepe', when it is a name applied to a person independently of his relation to other kin. Our own personal names are autonyms. On this type of name, cf. the comments made by Lévi-Strauss (1966: 279) on the 'names of death' analysed by Needham (1954). On 'teknonyms' and the kinship system, cf. Geertz and Geertz (1964).
3. In this essay, Montaigne refers to the homonymy and synonymy of names; to the repetition of names in the genealogy of Christian and plural names; to the good and beautiful name and the name as significant; to the name of the house and the family name. For a discussion of his *Essai sur les noms*, cf. Compagnon (1980).

nature of the proper name, its denotative and connotative values and its place in the linguistic system,[4] philology with a historical and etymological reading of names,[5] and demography with the way in which people's names are seen as an index of the origin, stability and mobility of a population;[6] in contrast, ethnology, in being conscious of the functional multiplicity and complexity of names in a cultural system, focuses its attention on the ways in which names are used, the situations in which they appear and the functions they fulfil according to the circumstances and forms of their transmission. All this follows from the assumption that forms of classifying, ordering and naming people are not arbitrary but correspond to a certain social morphology.

Claude Lévi-Strauss has emphasised that, in addition to their identifying function, names have a classifying role. The proper name can be defined as a 'means of allotting a position in a system admitting several dimensions' (Lévi-Strauss 1966: 187). Because of their pure position they can be an indicator of class as well as an indicator of a particular determinant. Names are not only practical forms of classification, however, but are organised on the basis of a system whose meaning varies according to the way culture filters reality. The rules of name transmission in each culture order the names of individuals into a system whereby they are continually renewed through the domestic cycle which permits the succession of births to be structured. 'By its rules and customs,' in the words of Lévi-Strauss (1966: 199), 'each society, to impose a structure on the continuous flux of generations, does nothing more than apply a rigid and discontinuous grid'. Besides being interested in the nature of names, the anthropologist establishes that 'proper names are all integral parts of the system we have been treating as codes: as means of fixing significations by transporting them into terms of other significations' (Lévi-Strauss 1966: 172). In this sense a system of names – also classificatory terms, distinctive signs of position and symbols of psychological identity – appears with a structure whose systemic elements can be translated into other cultural

---

4. On the aspects of the Christian name from a perspective based on linguistics and logic, cf. Zabeeh (1968).

5. Cf. the philological research on surnames by Moll (1959).

6. It is in this way that Costa Ramón (1964) analyses names in Formentera. Cf. also the analysis of consanguinity due to isonomy carried out by Bertranpetit (1981: 364–420) in Formentera.

codes. Hence the importance of comparing the onomastic system with the kinship system. The structures which appear in the
classificatory forms of kindred and the continuity of filiation
lines, together with the independence of the conjugal family
and the importance of the house as residence and symbol of the
perpetuity of a closed household against the variability and
opening of kinship networks, can be considered as the translation to the code of kinship of the structural characteristics of
the system of personal denomination with its elements of individual identification (proper names and nicknames), elements
of classification of patrimonial lines (house names) and elements
which allow us to think in terms of reproduction and family
continuity (surnames and hereditary names). The capacity of
names to identify and classify is similar to the use which can be
made of elements in kinship relations. As a result, the onomastic system can translate the language of kinship by expressing
the forms of conceptualising and structuring a kinship system
through the names which are transmitted to descendants. As
Zonabend has pointed out (1980b: 17), the multiple facets of
social reality are inscribed in names, and it is through them that
the continuity of social reproduction and the discontinuity of
social units are contemplated.

The form of name transmission and naming ritual try to
resolve the contradiction between the social continuity of the
family and the personal discontinuity of the individual, between
his social role and his individual destiny. This opposition appears in the baptism ceremony as an expression, in the naming
of the newly born child, of the antinomy between natural birth
and spiritual birth. As Charles (1951: 12–13) has pointed out,
ceremonies which carry out the first naming of a newly born
child place spiritual things and earthly things in opposition to
each other and give importance both to relations with the
spiritual world and to the uniqueness of the person. However,
Gudeman (1972: 54), in analysing the ideological basis that
supports the institution of 'compadre', has shown that it is
based on the ideas of spiritual rebirth and spiritual paternity as
an attempt to resolve the fundamental antinomy of man as a
natural and spiritual being. From the same analytical perspective of the cultural content of spiritual kinship, Pitt-Rivers (1977:
48) has argued that, if anthropologists concerned with the status
of godfathership had taken the religious aspect seriously instead
of considering it from a purely practical point of view as a

strategy for realising political and economic interests within a network of social relations, a much better understanding of its cultural meaning within the structure of kinship would have been achieved.[7]

However, the same author (1976: 319–20) has stressed that the specific nature of relations between godfathers and godsons should never be considered as an extension or reinforcement of kinship relations which emerge at the heart of the conjugal family, because these family relations have different and, to a certain extent, opposed meanings. Whereas godparents of baptisms are considered as *propatres* in the liturgy, they are really *'antipatres' par excellence*. They do not form part of the totality of social obligations between parents and children but establish a kind of spiritual kinship related to the soul and individual destiny of the child in complementary opposition to its membership of a family group. In this sense, it is possible to think of an opposition between spiritual kinship and natural kinship. Rather than being an extension of the father, a godfather belongs to a particular rite of passage, namely the rite of baptism, and is therefore situated in a different space to the relations of consanguine kindred. If there are some rules of preference which designate some relatives as godfathers – in our case, as in many others in Europe, collaterals are preferred – they exist not to intensify closed relations between consanguine kin, but to exorcise the social obligations which emerge in kindred and to open consanguinity to individual relations outside the jural obligations of the nuclear family.

The opposition we find in the cognatic kinship system between the individual and the social, the open and the closed, the flexible and the inflexible, acquires its clearest expression in the opposition between spiritual kinship and natural kinship arising

---

7. Mintz and Wolf (1950) emphasise the position of ties of godparentship in networks of social relations which intensify and enlarge kinship relations as a whole and increase links of social solidarity. Gudeman (1972, 1975) and Pitt-Rivers (1973, 1976, 1977) have given primary importance to the ideological content of the institution of godparentship from the Christian ritual of baptism and the distinction made between spiritual kinship and natural kinship. Through the relation that emerges from the ritual of baptism, ties are established with the kinship structure. On the symbolism of baptism rituals, cf. Bloch and Guggenheim (1981). We could argue that studies on 'godfathership' ('compadrazgo') have followed the same direction as studies on kinship. Firstly, its social use has been studied, principally in Latin-American communities; then its meaning has been studied in its 'pure condition' in European societies of Catholic tradition where its instrumental use is not so striking.

from the naming ritual. This opposition is also present in the system of names between the Christian name, associated with the godfather, and the surname and house name, associated with the parents and the continuity of the family.

A person is equally an individual and a member of a group. As Van Gennep (1909) pointed out, 'when a child is given a name, it is at the same time individualised and incorporated into society', and this contradiction between individual and society is resolved through the different ways of naming a child. As surnames automatically pass to the newly born child, no ritual is necessary, and from the moment of birth they incorporate a child into its family of orientation through precise rules of transmission which mediate between the two descent lines. Surnames represent an index of continuity in filiation, and in this sense, it is possible to think of them as classifiers of filiation lines.

On the other hand, house names are social names *par excellence*: those which 'give the others', in other words, designate the island as a community and name households as units of residence which reproduce in the same space. In contrast, the proper name basically names the individual. Although it classifies the individual within the family group, it also represents the individual's place in the sibling group, and its transmission is linked to a series of norms – grandparents are generally the eponyms of their grandchildren. But the naming of a child takes place within the ritual framework of baptism which marks its spiritual birth and provides some ritual kin other than the child's parents. Thus, the surname is an official name *par excellence*, registered in written form, yet virtually unrecognised in the oral system, and transmitted to a child automatically at birth to relate it to matrilineal and patrilineal lines of descent, whereas the Christian name is an element of individual life used orally as a term of address and transmitted through a ritual which marks the differences of natural birth and establishes special ties – 'spiritual kinship' – between the participants in this rite of passage.[8]

As Van Gennep (1943: 145) points out, the name given at baptism 'assures the child an individuality which will characterise it in earthly life and secure a certain place in the after life'.

---

8. Cf. Corblet (1881: Vol. 2, 172–6) on the difference between natural and spiritual birth in the ideology of baptism.

The incorporation of the child into the family cycle is determined through its parents at birth, and the child is absorbed by filiation lines, the common family stem and the network of obligations and rights of its consanguine kin. However, its individual life has a sacred destiny to which godparents are ritually incorporated, spiritual parents who, by naming the child as an individual, are opposed to its natural parents who bring it into the family cycle.

The distinction between the individual destiny of a person associated to a Christian name, the baptism and the godparents on the one hand and the family destiny related to the surname, the birth and the parents on the other explains the belief that godparents transmit 'a moral character' to their godchildren. Rullán (1882) referred to this belief when describing the feast of godmothers celebrated in the Pitiuses Islands. Fifteen days after the baptism the mother would receive the married women of her kindred and their friends into her house, and each visitor would

> take the newly born child into their arms, cover it with kisses and endearments; always emphasising in them the good moral and personal qualities of the infant's godparents, from whom they try to see these qualities reflected to the point of passing on the same physical appearance when holding the baby to receive baptism. Thus, the natives of Ibiza are very concerned with moral qualities which require them to act as godparents for their children, and their superstition goes so far as to maintain that a godchild will be like its godparents. If there is someone of bad morals in a family, this unfortuitous circumstance will be brought into the open before the honour of becoming a godparent is bestowed. Nobody is capable of persuading simple people that the embrace given by the godfather to his godson and the handshake of the godmother at the moment of administering the baptism do not pass on all the virtues and vices of both. When a boy demonstrates an irascible disposition, commits some indiscretion or shows himself to be bright or of good character, the godfather serves as a point of comparison and takes upon himself the glory or the infamy of acts of which the guilt or merit is solely the parents (Rullán 1882: 92).

The godfather is to the 'moral' character of the godson what the parents are to his 'physical' character. What is transmitted by the parents is complemented in the person of the child by reference to the godparents. The opposition between the natural (the parents) and the spiritual (the godparents) is also clearly expressed in the belief pointed out by Haussman (1938: 134) that if, during baptism, the godmother did not hold a candle while reciting the creed, 'the child would not learn to speak well and clearly', as if the integration of a child into the culture through speech were in the hands of the godmother, in opposition to the natural birth given by the mother.

Through the proper name and the ritual of baptism, the child establishes special relations with two types of kin 'complementary'[9] to the family nucleus: according to norms of name transmission and choice of godfathers, grandparents are their eponyms (there exists an alternation of generations in the proper name against the continuity of the surname) and collaterals are their godparents ('uncles' and 'aunts' become 'grandparents', and 'nephews' and 'nieces' become 'godchildren') (see Figure II.1).

Collaterals are the first consanguine relations from which the nuclear family reaches out to the external world horizontally through individual kinship networks; and relations between grandparents and grandchildren, in representing the two points between which the vertical axis of family reproduction extends, mark the beginning and the end of the family cycle. The ritual converts consanguine kin into godfathers and eponyms and, as such, into 'complementaries' of the parents *par excellence*; into their metaphor outside the world of the conjugal family's rights and obligations. This complementarity in the system of kinship between godparents and eponyms would explain the insistence, as much in the norms of name choice as those governing the choice of kin, to respect fully the balance between two lines and to maintain the individual and open character of cognatic kinship. The tension between collateral relations of two lines united by a matrimonial alliance is resolved through the principle of equilibrium between the two 'sides'.

The rules of name transmission, in contrast to the transmission of goods, try to balance the two sides of the nuclear family, the paternal line and the maternal line. Although the

9. Complementary relations in the sense given by Fortes (1970a: 87) to 'complementary filiation' in opposition to 'unilineal descent', that is, those relations who are outside the juridical obligations of descent. As Pitt-Rivers (1973: 95) points out, 'a ritual relation is not a *fictitious* relation but a *figurative* relation whose role, far from being identical to a literal relation, is *complementary*'. Godparents are a metaphor of the parents and not their metonymy.

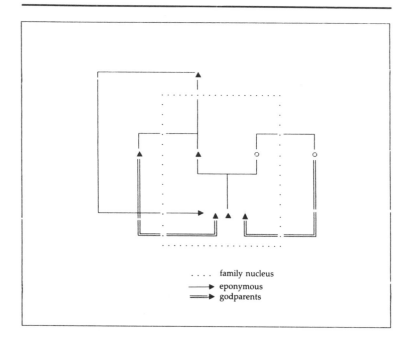

Figure II.1   Godparents and eponymous complementary to the
family nucleus

hierarchy of the paternal line is respected in the start of a series,
the subsequent alternation reproduces the undifferentiated
character of cognatic kinship. If the first child is a boy, he
receives the name of the paternal grandfather and if a girl, she is
given the name of the paternal grandmother; the second boy or
girl receives the name of the maternal grandfather or grandmother. In this way, the paternal line alternates with the maternal line until the names of the four ascendents in both lines
have been exhausted and it is necessary to look for new names
amongst collateral kin. This alternation of lines, that we find
occurs diachronically in the transmission of names, has its
synchronic expression in the choice of godparents. Thus, the
two lines appear immediately in the baptism of each child.
Godparents are chosen from among collateral relations, and for
the first child it is the father's brother (FB) and the mother's
sister (MZ) who are sought, whereas for the second child the
mother's brother (MB) and the father's sister (FZ) will be
chosen. In this way consanguine ties are transformed into ties of

spiritual affinity, and the balance between collateral relations is maintained, in opposition to the dynamic of the transmission of possessions, which may produce a lack of equilibrium favouring some siblings more than others and introducing a hierarchy between siblings.

This equilibrium between lines which appears in the norms of choosing names and godparents does not represent a perfect symmetry between lines, nor does it express exchangeability between the paternal line and the maternal line. Between the two lines there exists a principle of hierarchical opposition that refers to one of the fundamental laws of kinship: namely, the differential valency of the sexes.[10] In kinship systems, men and women are not considered as principles of identity – the pair of brothers is not identical to the pair brother/sister – but as principles of difference. Although cognatic kinship systems are considered as undifferentiated as opposed to unilineal systems, they do not start from the undifferentiation of biological consanguinity but have to establish difference and identity between consanguine kin as well as opposition between kin and non-kin. There is no absolute indifference and, therefore, no exchange of kin without taking into account their structural position. When a child is born, its identity is thought to arise through its parental lines; and although the differentiation between the paternal and maternal sides is denied by kinship terminology, it is stated in the succession of names which are transmitted in the sibling group, as well as in the alternation of lines that occurs with the choice of godfathers for each one of the siblings.

The start of a series in the transmission of names favours the paternal line and introduces a hierarchy of lines: the paternal line is to the eldest son or daughter what the maternal line is to the youngest son or daughter. This hierarchy between lines which is formed with the choosing of names is similar to the one which arises in the choice of godfathers within a collateral line: here, a godfather of an eldest son or daughter will be sought in the collateral line nearest to the father – the father's brother (FB)

10. On the fundamental laws of kinship, cf. Héritier (1981: 38): 'Crossed solidarity is never stronger than parallel solidarity; a crossed relation between individuals or groups is never the implicit support of equivalence or identity.' As the condition of this basic law: 'the different status of the sexes, or in other words, the different position of the two sexes in the framework of values, generally favours the dominance of the male principle over the female one' (ibid.: 50).

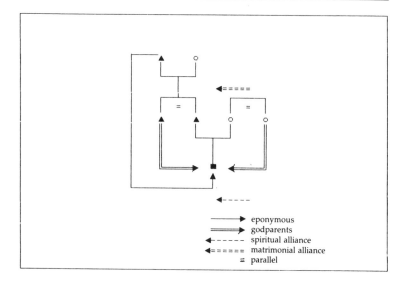

Figure II.2   Identity between matrimonial and spiritual alliance

– and a godmother will be chosen from the collateral line
structurally closer to the mother – the mother's sister (MZ); in
other words, the godparents are parallel aunts and uncles in
relation to Ego. In this case, the paternal line continues to offer a
man (structurally equivalent to the father) and the maternal line
a woman (structurally equivalent to the mother). Thus, the
meaning reproduced in spiritual alliance is the same as in
matrimonial alliance, as if affinity redoubles in the same direction (see Figure II.2).

In the case of the next (younger) child the transmission of the
name moves towards the maternal line: it is the mother's father
who transmits the name to the child. In the choice of a godfather
the terminology is reversed so that the father's sister (FZ) – the
collateral structurally different to the father – as godmother
corresponds to the mother's brother (MB) – the collateral structurally different to the mother – as godfather. In other words,
the godparents are cross uncles and aunts in relation to Ego. The
spiritual alliance reverses the meaning of the matrimonial alliance as if the spiritual affinity closes the circuit of reciprocity
and enables a balance to be established between a woman of the
paternal line, a man of the maternal line and the name transmitted through that line (see Figure II.3).

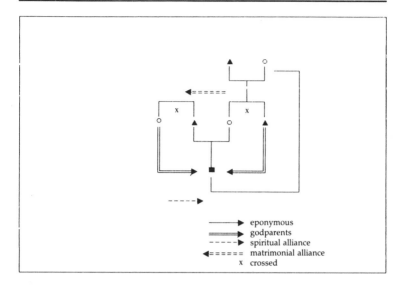

Figure II.3 Opposition between matrimonial and spiritual alliance

The initial imbalance, which prevents a man and a woman being placed on the same level and creates a difference between the maternal and paternal line, is more apparent in some of the transformations we were able to find in the general model of choosing godparents. Thus, the fact that the father's mother (FM) can be made the godmother of the eldest son and the mother's brother (MB) can be chosen as his godfather would seem to suggest that the hierarchy of generations (G^{-2} and G^{-1}) balances the inversion of sexes at the start of the choice of spiritual kin (see Figure II.4).

In the same way as the transmission of the name belongs to a register of the higher generation, to the cognitive field of reproduction through time, godparents are chosen from collateral kin, not in the past – in terms of an alternation of generations – but in the present – in terms of an alternation of collateral lines. In Formentera, it is still insisted that godparents should be young, that is, of the same generation as the parents and of the same cognitive field of collateral kin, that horizontal vector in which kindred (the world of uncles and cousins) extends to a point where all sense of kinship is lost and can only be rediscovered again through matrimonial or spiritual alliance. Kinship is fundamentally conceived in terms of the present, and the

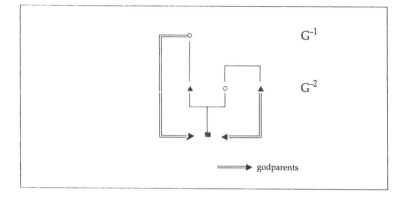

Figure II.4   Reversal of godparents choice

nuclear family lacks a profound genealogical dimension. Spiritual kinship, however, in being situated horizontally beyond the family nucleus, retains in the genealogy this line which the family may not recognise. Although there may be an awareness of kinship reaching back from living brothers, sisters and cousins, it is usually too confused to establish an exact genealogical line of distant cousins, uncles, nephews and nieces. In extending through collaterals and transforming distant consanguine relations into a spiritual affinity, godparentship redefines those lines which the genealogical memory finds difficult to trace with precision. A newly born child brings the nuclear family closer to the diffuse range of its kindred (complementary kin of the nuclear family), while its godparents redefine those kinship ties which may have faded from memory. Hence the importance given to the choice of godparents living outside the island. Here the spatial distance accentuates the distance in the genealogical relation which, if it is not to be lost, must be traced through spiritual kinship.

The retracing of distant lines can be seen clearly when relations between godparents and godchildren are renewed with the passing of generations (see Figures II.5 and II.6).

In Figure II.5, a godson of a man (who is his cousin's son) is the godfather of the son of this man (his FFBSS). The link of godparentship is reciprocally transmitted through successive births, and spiritual kinship defines the genealogical lines which, in terms of the nuclear family's consanguinity, would be lost. On being converted into a relation of godparentship, the

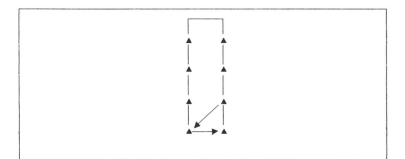

Figure II.5 Transfer of godparent and godchild relationship

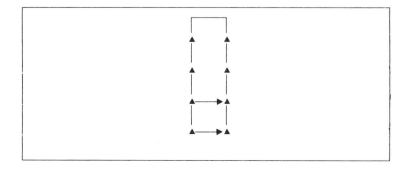

Figure II.6 Renewal of godparent and godchild relationship

distance of kinship is transformed into a distance between generations which is supposed in the godparent–godchild model.

Figure II.6 illustrates how a godfather renews his relation with his godson's son and, in so doing, strengthens ties which have become increasingly distant with the succession of generations.

The different sequences in the choice of godparents follow the horizontality of collateral kin to a point where the temporality of descent lines becomes more and more imperceptible and diffused. It would seem, therefore, that kinship centred around the family nucleus is fundamentally perceived through the collateral field (the nuclear family and its complementary kin) rather than in the cognatic terrain of filiation (from a common ancestor). As Zonabend (1978 and 1980b) has pointed out in referring to the locality of Minot, the choice of godparents from among collateral kin, instead of grandparents as occurred in the past, is coherent with the loss of genealogical depth in the family in such a way that 'today families are essentially perceived as formed basically by collateral relatives, which is necessary to preserve and hold together, due to the effect of the incessant centripetal movement of the ties of godparenthood. The main objective of these ties is to preserve in memory those lines which would otherwise tend to become distant' (1978: 670). When the people of Formentera affirm how important and convenient it is for godparents to be young, they show a preference for collateral relations which arise from ties of kinship rather than lines of filiation. Uncles are preferred to grandfathers, and godparents are considered as strong points allowing kinship relations to be traced from the family nucleus, instead of representing genealogical lines according to the model of descent which stems from a common ancestor.

II.2. Genealogies, Names and Family Memory

Maurice Halbwachs (1973) has argued that personal names are the best example of the rich and precise images preserved in the collective family memory. 'They are', he writes, 'neither general notions or individual images, and yet at the same time they name a kinship relation and a person.' Personal names are mediators between the general and the individual, between concrete, particular memories and the general position of the different degrees of kinship in a genealogy. At the same time, they are signs of a position (through the rules governing the transmission of names, they can be situated in a family genealogy) as well as symbols of individual identity. In the reconstruction of a family tree they unite 'in a single thought the image of a particular person with the idea of the position occupied by a family in exclusive terms of kinship' (Halbwachs 1973: 162). As Lévi-Strauss pointed out (1966: 215), Christian names are situated in and dominate the lower limit of the classification system and, as such, carry the action of codifying beyond the point where one would feel tempted to assign every classification to everything: the threshold after which it is no longer possible to classify but only to name.

The family memory is made up of concrete memories, of particular images and of names that designate the relative position of an individual in the family group. For this reason the oral construction of a genealogy seeks the help of Christian names to a point where genealogical lines convert into a set of names. Thus, in Formentera, a form of naming consists of reciting a sequence of names, such as, 'En Xisco d'en Joan d'en Pep', which can be extended. This serves to situate a name in a descent line in such a way that each name according to its position indicates a place at the centre of a genealogy and transforms it into the concrete representation of a given set of kinship relations. Robin Fox (1975: 141 and 1978: 73) has argued that it is possible to speak of a homology between the concept of genealogy and the onomastic system of Tory Island (Ireland), because here personal names help to fix the kinship *status* of a person (1978: 73). This relation between the name set and the genealogy may exist in Formentera, even though its genealogical memory and form of organisation is different from the Irish island studied by Fox. In Formentera there are no groups of cognatic descent; genealogies are not traced from a common ancestor; cousins are not identified with reference to the ancestor; and the relations of the sibling group are not the centre of family life.

It is, rather, the household, consisting of a nuclear or stem family living in the same house, which is the centre from which the genealogy and the recognition of kin are organised. The genealogical memory is usually not very far-reaching in Formentera; rarely does it go beyond three generations. As it is based on the house, the focus of concern would seem to be the immediate continuity of the household, and the name of the house is used to name an individual as a mark of position in a social space dominated by 'houses'. Although those who know a person and his family well can name him according to the set of names which reproduce a genealogical line, generally he will be named as somebody belonging to a house. A man may be named as 'En Jaume d'en Joan d'en Manuel d'en Carlos' reproducing a line of patrilineal descent, but normally he will be known as 'En Jaume de can Manuel' or 'En Jaume Manuel' (Figure II.7), indicating with the second name the 'house' as domestic residence but also referring to a close ancestor beyond whom kinship links are forgotten.

The name of the house acts as an amnesic mechanism on genealogical lines by transforming the series of names which they contain into a single name situated in space rather than time. In the same way as the replacement of personal names by

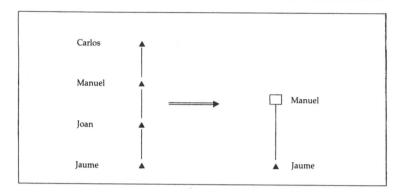

Figure II.7   Reduction of the genealogical names to the house name

tecnonymic names in Bali (Geertz 1964 and 1975: 85–94) allow a genealogical amnesia which erases all knowledge of genealogical links except those established during the life of an individual, in Formentera the use of the house as a means to name a person causes the disappearance of the ascendant line and its replacement by reference to position in the domestic space. Despite this similarity, the process of genealogical amnesia in the two cases is different: in Bali ascendants are forgotten because the people can only name descendants and the line of tecnonyms is reduced to the house of someone with a grandfather named according to the son of the son who is in the house (Geertz 1975: 86–7), whereas in Formentera kinship is not delimited by the common ascendant because, according to the system of denomination, an individual is situated directly by the name of a house, which may refer to a very close ancestor (the new 'houses' of collaterals) or continue a descent line (the old 'houses' of inheritors). In this way the name loses its concretion in genealogical time and becomes a generic name through which it is no longer possible to establish precise genealogical relations.

In the transmission of names, the families of Formentera are situated in the cognitive field of descent lines. As the names of grandparents are the eponyms of their grandchildren, the personal name is perceived in the domain of filiation. As we have already seen, an individual can be given a series of names which reproduce the male line of descent. However, rather than referring to a kinship group with a common ancestor as in Tory

Island (Fox 1963: 153) or establishing the kinship status of an individual (Fox 1978: 73), this series of names represents the permanence of the household and the reproduction of its developmental cycle. It refers not so much to the founding ancestor of a descent line but more to the permanence and continuity of a household, which is affirmed in the form of personally naming an individual. The transmission model implies an indifferentiation of descent lines (affirmation of the bilaterality of the kinship system) from the hierarchical position of the paternal side over the maternal side. This does not follow the model of double affiliation in which a man can only name his sons' sons and a woman, her daughters' daughters, as used to happen in Minot (Zonabend 1977: 265) with the consequent delimitation of the paternal side of the maternal line. In Formentera lineality disappears – both men and women transmit names through sons as well as daughters – and only a hierarchical arrangement of father over mother is affirmed in which an equilibrium is produced between women on the paternal side – who can give a name to a son's daughter – and men on the maternal side – who can give a name to a daughter's son.

This affirmation of the conjugal family over descent lines is clearly expressed in other forms of naming different from the model that preserves customs and affirms itself as the traditional one. The choice of proper name admits a greater variability than the choice of godparents and contrasts with the continuity of the surname as a 'classifier of filiation lines'. Beyond the fixed norm of the first child, the other sequences permit a greater freedom of choice, so that names can be given from outside the kinship domain. 'Other names are put forward in order for the children to affirm themselves before the parents.' If it is said that this form of naming occurs more frequently today, it is to indicate that 'custom', the past, no longer governs current behaviours. Given that tradition loses its influence and the present is never the exact representation of the past, there is always the possibility of variation. As importance is placed on individuation, a singular and original name having no relation with ascendants is chosen. The independence of the conjugal family is affirmed through the newly born child, as if the singularising role of the name were more important than its classifying role. It passes, then, from kinship register to fashion register, the chance of the birth date, taste, fate, etc., and when a name needs to be found, the wishes of the parents gain priority over the continuity of tradition represented by the grandparents.

This singularisation and variability of the Christian name, which is disconnected from family continuity, is clearly evident in the idea expressed today by the inhabitants of Formentera concerning the impossibility of replacing a dead child. If a newly born child dies when the grandparents have already given it a name, this name will not be given to any children born afterwards. The name as a singularising element cannot, then, be repeated, and this shows that a child is irreplaceable. The child does not 'remake'[11] the dead of a family group, and neither does it manifest a traditional name left vacant in the event of death. Rather than forming part of a descent group through the proper name, the child is simply introduced into the social life of the community, and the naming rite marks the beginning of the reproduction of the family cycle.

This conception that we find in Formentera of the Christian name as a denomination linked to the individual and arising fundamentally from the conjugal family contrasts with the use of the proper name as 'symbolic capital' in societies where family continuity is organised on the basis of the principle of filiation. In these types of societies, names, like patrimony, have to be preserved and transmitted, as occurred amongst the mercantile classes of Renaissance Florence (Klapisch-Zuber 1980: 100–1) which organised kinship into descent lines centred around male sibling groups. A name signified a position in a sibling group as well as a title in the lineage and could not be lost in the event of death since, until reappearing in the place occupied by a newly born child, it was simply concealed. This operation could be repeated every time there was a death followed by a birth, because the child was conceived as a

---

11. On forms of 'remaking' the name cf. Klapisch-Zuber (1980) and Vernier (1980). The appearance of modern family sentiment in Europe, centring on the couple and the child, so admirably described by Ariès (1973: 304) can be interpreted as a transformation in the structure of naming children. The Christian name of the conjugal family individualises so that the modern family sentiment surrounding the child respects its name. Its death is irreparable; the child cannot be substituted, and its name is not passed on to another. Procreation is perceived as an addition, not as a substitution. It is interesting to find that this idea of the irreplaceable dead child is relatively modern in Formentera. In registers at the end of the last century, names of newly born children replace those of dead children. These changes in the conception of Christian names are coherent with transformations in the idea of the house as a social representation of Formentera.

substitute for an ancestor instead of an addition to the family. Christian names were really the symbolic capital of family 'houses' and had to be conserved and transmitted through generations. The classificatory aspect of a name was privileged within the sibling group.

In societies where kinship centres around the conjugal family, however, the individualising aspect of the name is favoured, so that it ceases to be the symbolic capital of the family and identifies the individual.[12] Names are not given by eponyms in the sense of being continuers of filiation lines, but as being structurally closer to the child. There is a discontinuity between descent I and the formation of a couple with its descendance. The household does not form part of a descent I group, and whereas grandparents, on becoming eponyms, are situated at the end of a domestic cycle, grandchildren are the beginning of another cycle. In terms of domestic reproduction, alternate generations identify each other while adjacent generations oppose each other.

The conjugal family thinks of itself in terms of successive and alternating generations rather than in terms of descent I lines. A child which is born or about to be born has the same name as someone from the ascendant generation, because it is added to the family cycle and becomes the structural alternate of its eponym. If a child dies at or soon after birth and is already named, it has already been added to the family and, therefore, cannot be substituted by another. According to local theory, if a child dies, using its name again can cause death, so that the name identifies a child and disappears with it if the cycle is interrupted. Rather than occupying a place in the status, the child receives a name and is added to the family. As a name is already given and the individual identified with it, the eponym of a child which dies cannot be used again. Under such circumstances, different names will be necessary to continue the family reproduction. Within the family, eponyms can only be kin from the end of the domestic cycle or, in other words, kin who have reached the limit of the basic kinship group: the conjugal family. Beyond this limit other names can be found. If the nearest (the

12. In the naming system, Lévi-Strauss (1966) distinguishes between names that one takes or receives and names as indicators of the class to which one belongs. This corresponds to the difference between the idea of procreation as an addition and that of procreation as a substitution of an ancestor.

grandparents) do not serve or have already been used, the family will assure its continuity by resorting to other forms of naming.

In the baptismal registers of the beginning of the century one can find other names which were added to the proper name. These second names normally correspond to the patron of the parish where the child was baptised or to the name of the priest who administered the sacrament. They are religious names appearing only in the written registers of the parish and play no part in the oral tradition of the naming system. They were not chosen by the parents or between kindred and do not have that exclusive link with the individual contained in the first name. They were introduced into the denomination through the official request of the baptism ritual, in opposition to the community relation established by the family and the child in the same ritual. They simply introduced and classified children into the official space and time of the community and, like surnames, marked a difference to children born outside the island. It seems that the first name identified the individual and the other names only served to classify generically without entering into the system of oral denomination, in contrast to the system of identification in Renaissance Florence where Christian names classified the individual within the kinship group and second names, or 'names of devotion', had the role of individual identifiers and arose from personal decision (Klapisch-Zuber 1980: 88).

An individual is not only identified by his Christian name, the names of ascendants and the name of the 'house', but also by two surnames. Surnames hardly ever name and are never used as terms of address. They are official names *par excellence*, written in legal documents, in acts of birth, marriage and death and in municipal censuses. However, the high degree of homonymy existing among surnames makes them useless as individual identifiers. The *stock* of surnames is very small and has hardly changed during the course of this century. As Lévi-Strauss (1966: 199) has pointed out, 'some societies jealously watch over their names and make them last practically for ever, others squander them and destroy them at the end of every individual existence'. Due to the stability of its population and its lack of renewal, Formentera, like many other societies, has maintained a limited number of surnames. As these names are repeated, they cannot perform the mnemonic function of maintaining in the memory the relation of kinship between bearers of the same surname.[13] They exceed the narrow limits of the island's genealogical memory, which cannot use them to reconstruct filiation lines, although they do serve to delimit that undefined space existing between real kin and non-kin, a space which is defined by the idea that all those who have the same surname have to be kin in one way or another because they descend from the same point. This common descendance is always imprecise and corresponds to that space expressed by kinship terminology, such as distant 'cousins', a classificatory term similar in style to those examined by Morgan (1871) in primitive systems of kinship, with the peculiarity here that lines of filiation start to merge from the moment they can no longer be clearly defined by the genealogical memory.

In naming people the surname is simply a point of reference, a generic classificatory element, almost unnamed and requiring other elements for precise distinction. To carry one of these surnames merely indicates that one is a native of the island, belonging to the category of 'pagès' (peasant) and not foreign. They function as a generic frame of reference to differentiate families of the island from those that come from outside. In this sense, surnames form a closed group of names which serve to identify the families of the island, that is, families which have 'always' formed part of the relatively stable stock of population. Within this population all those who carry the same surname can be considered members of the same branch, although this does not define their kinship line. This consideration of a diffused kinship group is more important to those who have the same surname than those who do not, in the same way that all those who carry a name of the reduced *stock* of names will be differentiated from strangers and foreigners. People who spoke about this reduced number of surnames and the continuity and repetition of family surnames, as well as the diffused nature of consanguine links that become separated from surnames, presented an image of the island as a closed community to which individuals belonged by birth, that is, by nature.[14] It is an image which sees the circulation of the same blood maintained, through circuits which remain unchanged, as a substance closed

13. Maranda (1974: 24) attributes this mnemonic function to the appearance of the 'family name' in the thirteenth century.
14. The idea of 'nature' as that which is stable, the substance related to blood and the idea of 'code' as variable and related to alliance are, according to

against outside intrusion: a fixed totality of families reproducing through time to which individuals belong by birth. Associating the surname with the stem or branch family presents a principle of continuity that contrasts with other variables of the onomastic system: the Christian name as an element introducing the individual into the family group, the name of the woman as an element establishing the variability of matrimonial alliance, and the name of the house as an element separating households in the space of the island. Whereas the surname favours kinship continuity and common consanguinity, there are other aspects in the system of denomination favouring individual aspects of kinship (networks of kin and relations through matrimonial alliance).

From this latter point of view, individuals are related by kinship in many different ways which form variable kinship networks rather than stems, and with a very limited genealogical memory that makes the surname useless except as a backcloth of continuity set against the discontinuity of the kinship system. If one sees genealogical lines in this way, two people with the same surname cannot have common kinship and must belong to different families. The discrete prevails over continuity since the system is reproduced by differentiation rather than indifferentiation: it distinguishes between siblings and sexes and introduces marriage as an element breaking with continuity. Even if distant collaterals have the same surname, they are no longer considered kin, while women lose the continuity of the surname on becoming grandmothers.

As in the system of cognatic kinship where we find the idea of a common stem in opposition to kinship networks centring on Ego, that is, the continuity of descendance set against the variability of marriage (as a chance element that breaks family continuity in order to create a new family), in the onomastic system we find an opposition between the surname, as continuity given by birth, and the Christian name, as an individual characteristic given by the baptismal rite of denomination.

Schneider (1968, 1979), characteristics of kinship in American culture. Strathern (1981: 166) takes up this idea to analyse the role of the surname in an English community. The meaning of the surname does not lie in the desire of relating oneself with a group of relations in the manner of a lineage but in marking a contrast between birth and marriage.

II.3. The Name of the House

In addition to names which classify individuals generically and enter them into official lists – surnames in the civil register and 'names of devotion' in the religious register – and Christian names which identify individuals within the family group, the oral tradition includes another element basically used as a term of reference to name the individual. An individual is always considered as belonging to a household, to a house, the name of which is added to the Christian name. Thus, when someone is referred to, the Christian name will be used with the name of the household to which that person belongs. For example, a name might run as follows: 'En Joan de Can Mateu, Na Rita de Can Manuel'; so that, here, the individual is identified with a house: a unit of kinship and residence. In keeping with a form of social organisation based on houses in which social relations are mainly seen as relations between houses, individuals are not known by their Christian names, their nicknames or their surnames, but by the name of the household to which they belong. Each house has a name, and all its members are known by that name. It serves to classify individuals in relation to a household and in this way situates them within a hierarchical social structure based on the principle of house value.

The house name classifies a domestic space (a house and territorial property) and refers to a domestic group (a kinship unit) which reproduces through time in the same residence or in a house newly set up after separating from the group of origin. Residence is the fundamental element for naming these kinship units. The living space is impregnated by the families who occupy it in such a way that toponyms are used to name houses (Es Pla, Es Turrent, Sa Talaiasa, etc.) and, on other occasions, onomastics serve to name a space (for example, one estate is called Can Mateu). In this sense, the house name evokes an inscription in space at the same time as it refers to ties of consanguinity and affinity. It sustains, then, both a field of kinship and a field of residence. Thus, when the name of a house is used it refers as much to the past of the family as to the place it occupies, possesses and works on. The house as a social unit represents the physical structure as well as the family line. It can be considered as a moral person holding a property that perpetuates itself through the transmission of the name and provides a framework of reference whereby individuals are socially classified.

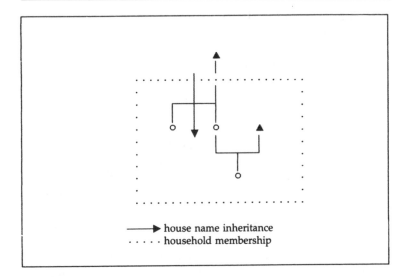

Figure II.8 Household of *Can Joan d'en Pep*

The forms by which houses are named vary considerably: the majority have Christian names, others individual nicknames referring to non-pejorative, physical or moral attributes, topographical accidents or professions. Thus, the model of naming houses seems to have recourse to different objects at the same time: individuals, spaces and professions.

The organisation of these names seems to be very varied and complex, and the informants were apparently unable to fully grasp their rules of formation and attribution. They could only indicate that 'those who name are the others'. It is the community which creates the names and produces that variability which cannot reduce the form of naming a house and the form of transmission of this name to a single norm, as if the various naming forms and the transmission of the name through family lines do not respond to a single rule.

The principle of male line superiority is not of use in explaining all house names: 'although it may seem that houses have the name of the husband, some carry the name of the female line'. The patrimonial line represented by a wife may prevail over the line of her husband, especially if he comes to live and work in her house. In such circumstances the name of the house coming from the wife's line will be maintained. In Figure II.8, the members of the household are called Can Joan d'en Pep: the

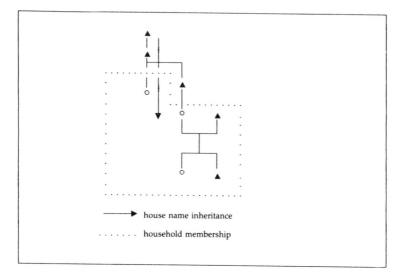

Figure II.9   Household of *Can Manuel*

husband has come to live in the house, and the name corresponds to the wife's father who is no longer alive.

In Figure II.9, the members of the household go by the name of Can Manuel. Here the husband went to live with his wife, who is an heiress to a sister of her father without descendance, and the name of the house corresponds to a founding ancestor of this patrimonial line.

A female name is given to a house not only because a woman may represent a patrimonial line to which her husband is added, but also, for instance, because a man may have emigrated to America and been absent from Formentera for some time. When this occurred, the mother's name would have been given to her children, and in this way members of a nuclear household were named (Ca na Francisca Martina, Ca na Rampuxa, Ca na Margalida Barlet, etc.). When defining his household name, the son of an emigrant will say, for instance, that at first it was 'Jerònim' because that was what his father's house was called, but that then he was given the name 'Xincho' after his mother's house since his father had been absent from Formentera for many years. In those domestic situations where genealogical estimations do not reach very far and patrimonial lines are weak, the male line needs the residence to affirm its name. If the man is absent, the name of the woman who lives permanently

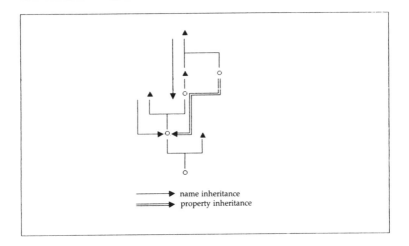

Figure II.10   Changes in the house name

in the house prevails, and the residential unit takes over from the criteria of the male line. Female house names can also emerge when a woman with children is left as a widow – 'Ca na Sofia', 'Ca sa Viuda Joana' – and, in these circumstances, without ascendance or alliance, domestic names are situated in the pure register of the residence.

It is not only property which determines a name. There are houses which have the name of the husband, even though the property belongs to the wife. In some houses the patrimonial line represented by the woman is unclearly defined, as we can see in the example illustrated by Figure II.10.

The woman received a house from a sister of her father. At that time, the household was called 'Can Forn', but when the woman married and lived with her husband in the house, it was given the name 'Can Gallet' after the husband, because it is always better that the man gives the name to the house. As a symbol of this change of name, 'new houses' are built in the style of emigrant's houses in opposition to the 'old houses' inherited by the woman.[15] When the daughter of this marriage gets married and her husband comes to live in her house with her parents, thus forming a stem household, the house will keep the name represented by the wife (Can Gallet) in accord-

15. On the type of house inhabited by the emigrant, see below, pp. 120–6.

ance with the principle of patrimonial line continuity and in opposition to the principle of male line predominance which in the preceding generation had changed the name of the house.

Some names which do not follow lines of descent are lost immediately, while others maintain their continuity through various generations, as if they were clearly defined lines in the midst of indistinct lines which rapidly disappear and give way to new names dispersed in space rather than repeating in time. Set against the perpetuity and lineality of the surname that by force of repetition through generations and extension between distant collaterals loses its capacity for classification and becomes socially useless, are those names which the oral tradition attributes to each house in order to name the domestic group and situate it in the local hierarchical order.[16] These house names indicate not so much the perennial nature of descent groups but more the presence of the household in the house and its insertion in social space.

The position secured by the family in the social hierarchy and its capacity to trace the course of a patrimonial line with precision, in sharp contrast to the short naming cycles of other lines, will depend on the extent to which the name can be maintained through generations without variation. As Cole and Wolf (1974: 9) have pointed out, the significance of this type of domestic name in situations where genealogical estimations are weak or superficial is less when we think in terms of patrilineal or matrilineal descent than in terms of the 'virtue' of each house. The continuity of the name is due to the 'symbolic capital' (Bourdieu 1980) each family is capable of maintaining and accumulating over generations rather than to the principle of descent.

In a society like Formentera, without the constant renewal of population by immigrant families, differentiation through the house name is not produced in terms of old and new houses but depends on the degree to which the vicissitudes of the domestic

16. This form of naming within a local hierarchical order distinguishes the 'name of the house' from the personal 'nicknames'. Whereas the former is situated in the social hierarchy and establishes the distance between houses, the latter is egalitarian and reduces the distance through improper informality. Nicknames 'define the people of the village as equals since they are all described in a common language of improper informality' (Antoun 1968: 169). Personal nicknames are emotionally loaded. They are a form of verbal aggression, a displacement of competitive envy (Gilmore 1982), whereas the names referring to the household are an emotionally neutral form of classification (Dorian 1970; Breen 1980; and Iszaevich 1980).

development cycle can be maintained. The constant presence of the same group of surnames for two centuries suggests that the growth in population has been produced by the families of the island,[17] and the changes in house names indicate the rules imposed by the social structure on the continual flow of generations. The continuity of the name differentiates families capable of maintaining a deep patrimonial line from others in which, as this patrimony is absent, the name can change. Whereas a name with greater temporal depth has more prestige, names indicating only the present show a situation of indigence. As a consequence, the members of a house which has been given a new name may reclaim an older name. They will say that the new name is a nickname, but that it lacks the personal and aggressive character of individual nicknames. It is merely a new name that prevails over the old family name and indicates the beginning of a new domestic cycle, as well as the insertion of the new house into the social space of the island.

This form of naming sets in motion the subtle interplay of a whole range of domestic names which, in being free from any strict rule, express the tendency towards variability and flexibility in the system of cognatic kinship, as well as setting up the dialectic between descent, alliance and residence contained in the concept of the house. Houses, as social units, are inserted in time through the commitment to alliance, and matrimonial contracts are the crucial moments that define their continuity.[18] At the centre of these social units, matrimony affords greater flexibility and variability in the transmission of the name that occurs with the perpetuity and lineality of surnames which, because they are repeated, become useless for distinguishing and classifying households. The permanence of surnames situated in the register of descent forms a relation of similarity between successive generations, whereas house names, situated in the nucleus of tension between descent, alliance and residence, order relations of difference existing between households in space.

In each matrimonial alliance either a son will be kept in the paternal house and the old name of the house continued in order to unify descent with the residence and to maintain the

17. On the stability of the surnames of Formentera, see below, p. 161, Chapter 5, note 16.
18. On marriage contracts, see below, pp. 155–6.

ideal of house continuity, or another household will be created with a new name and absorbed by a collateral from the house of origin. Names which are applied to collateral households that separate from the principal line can be composites – for example: Can Joan Mateu and Can Manuel Carlos are households originating from Can Mateu and Can Carlos – and maintain the collateral relation with the line of origin through this succession of names.

Household names formed by collaterals of principal lines change more frequently than ones arising from stem lines, so that in preceding generations successions of names and also, therefore, references to the houses from which they emerged are lost. If a new patrimonial line is created, it is given the name of whoever organises the new house – for example: Can Manuel Carlos is changed to Can Manuel – and the relation with the line of origin is forgotten. If, on the other hand, new households become dispersed and a new patrimonial line is not formed, either the changes in house name are very frequent or the reference to the original house is maintained as a real patronymic which engenders an awareness of kinship among its carriers in the area of distant kindred outside the kinship system. It can be said, for example, that 'tots els Mateus som parents' (everyone called Mateus is kin) without being able to establish a genealogical relation between them, just as it is possible to find distant kin of whom there is only an imprecise kinship knowledge.

The process of forming house names maintains the idea of a series of clearly defined stem lines from which other lines arise with different names, as if the local hierarchy between houses indicated by the degree of continuity were seen in terms of principal stem lines from which secondary collateral lines emerge. In these main patrimonial stem lines the head of the house may transmit his Christian name to the heir and successor – the eldest male child – and in so doing will create a continuous line of the same personal name which is also the name of the house. In this way, due to its link with the house, the individual name is transformed into the classifier of a patrimonial line. There is a continuity between name and classification: situated within the semantic limits of the individual is the classification of a house started by an ancestor, who founded a patrimony and a symbolic capital which were accumulated and transmitted through the generations by members of the house, identifying descent with residence through their name. Outside these stem lines, however, where names are more varied, there is more variation and alternation between personal names that are not identified with the house.

Within this system of naming houses, neither residence nor descent are the only vectors which organise names. Matrimonial alliance puts the principle of residence in tension with the principle of house descent and permits the interplay between the continuity and renewal of names. In certain moments of a genealogy, the residence or patrimonial descent may appear as the only symbol of family continuity with the same name, while in other moments variations in matrimonial alliance may renew household names that have become separated from the house of origin. In Formentera the names attributed to houses, as households, correspond not only to the idea of perpetuity that 'will unite family continuity with the implantation of a place' (Flandrin 1976: 19), an ideal related to the ideology of patrilineal inheritance that maintains a corporate group anchored in the same place from generation to generation, as shown by Cole and Wolf (1974: 240) in St Felix (Switzerland).

We do not find ourselves in a system like that existing between the *domus* of Provence (Collomp 1983: 95) where family continuity is expressed through houses named by a patronymic and representatives of diverse branches of the same agnatic patrimonial line. When the oral tradition in this system uses hereditary nicknames to name houses, these names function as a form of subdividing, homonymic branches originating from the same ancestor and classify in the same group – thus refreshing the collective memory – collateral houses emerging after various generations from the same individual. In this form of naming the hereditary nicknames of the house, rather than replacing the surname, are merely put into second place and restrengthen the genealogical memory. The name of the house in Formentera, by contrast, substitutes for the surname and, as we have seen, produces genealogical amnesia. The classification of houses in Formentera is based not only on descent, nor is it the house as residence that gives the name to its inhabitants, as if family continuity were reduced to a physical space as in the Basque country (Douglass 1969: 103–7). These house names do not correspond to the variability of nicknames which, as Pitt-Rivers (1971: 191–9 and 1977: 131–9) has described in Alcalá, can be individual or hereditary. Neither do they have the emotional intensity of personal nicknames found by Gilmore (1982) in Fuenmayor. A house name not only names a particular individual but also the members of a household and, rather than having the emotional content of personal nicknames, is semantically neutral.

In being neither individual nor family descriptions such as nicknames or external signs of the perpetuity of descent lines through the same residence, the house names of Formentera are situated between the double reference of descent and residence which, as a result of relations established by matrimonial alliance, makes the renewal of names compatible with family continuity and weak genealogical estimations compatible with the idea of a distant kinship which is recognised but not named.

II.4. Ideas about Kinship and the Language of Community

We have already seen that the house name, like the individual name, cannot be reduced to a single rule encompassing all the different practices of individual identification. The construction of the naming experience at the heart of a family is not based on a single principle of transmission governed by the descent line. From the perspective of social uses, pure bilaterality introduces us to the domain of indifferentiation and leads to a multilateral recognition of kinship as the centre of relations which expand concentrically.

From the viewpoint of social organisation we can develop a balanced image of cognatic kinship, distributed on both sides and corresponding to the representation of biological kinship. Through the transmission of status by both ascendants, no stable kinship groups are formed beyond the family. We do not use kinship groups as the basis for the constitution of political groups, and the use of kinship in the social sphere does not follow basic structural principles but, rather, the informal channels which constitute networks of social activity compatible with kinship networks. For example, it is possible to establish circuits of mutual aid among relatives during particular agricultural works. However, it is not possible to establish any principle useful in predicting the type of relatives who will enter into these circuits of mutual aid. On the other hand, neighbours can also be included in these circuits, so that, at this level, relations

regarding relatives beyond the domestic group can be equivalent to the ones maintained with neighbours.

There may be a temptation to attribute little importance to
kinship as a principle of organisation beyond the domestic
domain and to characterise cognatic kinship as an open system
in the sense that a given community allows some families to
isolate themselves while, at the same time, others maintain wide
circuits of cooperation using kinship relations. Given the negative organisational consequences of cognatic kinship and its
apparent flexibility in forming kinship networks, we are accustomed to analysing these systems as absolutely undifferentiated
and completely open since, at the moment when different
possibilities of individual behaviour are established from kinship relations, no principle is established to explain the formation of stable social groups, and individuals are not restricted to
a type of solidarity based on kinship.

This balanced image of kinship distributed on both sides and
showing a basically open character does not preclude a principle
of order within bilaterality stemming from the introduction of a
series of values into the idiom of kinship. Kinship is conceptualised in lineal terms by the house as a social representation, and
bilaterality acquires almost exclusively unilineal forms. On the
other hand, a person's kindred is divided into areas of differential density which establish a hierarchy in the recognition of kin.
The 'family' can be conceptualised in terms of multilateral ties
and with reference to the two sides of kinship, but it can also be
reduced to all the members of a group carrying the same house
name. In this case, the principle of lineal order may be introduced into the undifferentiated character of bilateral kinship
and common participation introduced into the same line of
descent, as if all carriers of the same name were descended from
the same house.

When people speak about their family in genealogical accounts, they refer fundamentally to the history of their house,
that is, the house as the representation of a patrimonial line
rather than a physical space. In oral genealogies one line is
always imposed over the others, and this introduces an order in
the history whereby the details about kin who do not follow the
history of the house are eliminated from the family memory.
Collaterals and affines of collaterals beyond the second generation are eliminated from the account, and only the direct line
representing the continuity of the house is followed. There is a

conception of kinship centred on the house in which it is considered that all the descendants share the same 'blood', derive from the same 'race'. From this principle of genealogical narration, the generic name of the house is used as a patronymic classifier of different descent lines united by a common ancestor. The homonymy of the house name would suggest that a kinship link exists between different houses and, therefore, that they are different branches which have to be united somewhere. Faced with more than one example of the same name, one can say 'venim tots d'una mateixa raça, però hem sortit des parentesc' (we have all come from the same race, but we have fallen out of kinship). 'Race' functions here as a reference to a diffuse kinship extending beyond recognised kin and presiding over the union of different patrimonial lines. In the same way that genealogical recognition of kindred extends over three generations, beyond which there is only a diffuse knowledge of kinship, the homonyms of the generic house name create an awareness of coming from a common stem, beyond kinship recognised between houses. This common generic name does not imply, however, the existence of a social group. It is simply a reference to a supposed common kinship, to participation in the same substance, the same 'race'.

When the house is referred to in terms of its continuity, the image of the stem and derived branches is imposed over the consciousness of kinship, and this image provides the possibility of conceiving the hierarchy between houses in terms of seniority. A direct stem produces the oldest houses, and the branches derived from this common stem form the most modern houses. In this way the hierarchy between houses is measured by the capacity to maintain a patrimonial line and the continuity of the name, and the identity of modern houses is conceived in terms of their relation to the totality of the central lines from which current names derive.

This identity of houses as a continuity of patrimonial lines, which reproduce themselves through generations and the participation of its members in the same substance (the same 'race'), produces a model which allows us to think of the island as a community and the identity of the people born on the island as belonging to the same locality. In the same way as the members of a house are treated as the product of generations reproducing through time, the island as a community is represented as the continuity of principles transmitted through time, and despite changes in the social structure (emigration at the beginning of the century and the effects of tourism today), there exists a rhetoric of continuity provided by the language of kinship.

The universe of mutual knowledge that prevails in the community life of the island is identified with the universe of kinship. 'All of us know each other' is equivalent to 'all of us are kin', and so apparently an image of the community prevails in which all its inhabitants participate in the same substance and the same principle of solidarity.[19]

In Formentera the adjective 'pagès' (peasant) is used to identify everything that comes from the island in contrast to everything from outside. The products of local agriculture are called 'pagesos' (peasants) to distinguish them from products coming from outside, which can be found in the food shops of the island; traditional houses are known as 'pageses' which distinguishes them from present-day constructions; the language spoken on the island is 'pagès' in contrast to other languages and other local dialects of the islands; the songs, dances and forms of native dress go by the name 'pageses' in contrast to other cultural forms originating outside the island. In short, the universe of 'pagès' defines the identity of the people born on the island and is connected with the world of tradition which distinguishes them from others. Thus, the old sailors and labourers currently working in the hotel trade consider themselves to be 'pagesos' unlike those born outside the island who are 'forasters' (foreigners). Being 'pagès', as a symbol of identity, is constructed on the fact of belonging to the same place, and the island, as a community, represents the source of differences with others. It is a symbol of social continuity based on the locality, in the same way that kinship represents continuity through common descendance and membership in the same house. Through the category of 'pagès', the substance of which the natives of the island are made is identical to the substance of which the place is made. The island as a locality is transformed into a community, and one becomes 'pagès' by being born in Formentera and participating in the same tradition. Through the category of 'house', all the descendants share the same 'race' and are made of the same 'blood', and the house as a living

19. On the relations between kinship and locality, cf. Schneider (1979) and Strathern (1982).

space is transformed into a representation of the origin of distinct descent lines. Just as people are 'pagès' because they come from the same locality, they are 'kin' because they come from the same house.

Houses as patrimonial lines carrying a name organise the universe of kinship based on descent, which we can characterise as closed, in opposition to the open networks of kinship and individual affinity through which houses are related. Simultaneously, the idea also appears of the island as a closed community that reproduces itself without outside elements and through a line of continuity in opposition to other social transformations of the island which have occurred during the course of this century. There is a static vision of the population of Formentera which omits external elements and underlines continuity. When the people of Formentera speak about the emigration to America, they present this fact as a continuity rather than a split with the past and as the condition of possibility allowing them to continue being 'pagès'.

From the perspective of the continuity of the island as a community, marriage represents its social reproduction, and the image of a closed community emphasises the importance of marrying within the island. In the model of marriage presented in the period of emigration, the return to the island to marry was valued positively. The locality giving the identity of being 'pagès' also forms the limit of the matrimonial field. At the community level, marriage is considered within the narrow limits of the island, and in terms of the continuity of a closed community, the open aspect of alliance is superseded by consanguinity. Thus marriages between kin are used to symbolise the continuity with the past in opposition to the detachment with which the present is lived.[20]

At the level of individual houses as patrimonial lines, kinship is considered in terms of the substance ('race', 'blood', 'name', 'inheritance') passed from generation to generation through marriage with someone from another house. In this sense, each particular alliance can be considered as an open one and able to create new kinship ties. However, the idea also exists that kinship extends over different places of the island to the extent

20. We are analysing here the symbolic use that is made of 'marriage' in the language of the community and not the real practices of marriage. On the distinction between the language of community and the language of locality, cf. Jolas and Zonabend (1970).

that neighbours are identified with kin, the locality with kinship. When individuals are outside recognised kin ('hem sortit des parentesc' – 'we are out of kinship'), genealogical links continue to unite people and are known as 'poc parents' (little kin); and distant kin are recognised as long as they come from the same stem. A man can tell someone about the existence of distant kin by saying 'encara som un poc parents' ('we still are a little kin') and by describing the kinship relations with reference to the house from where the common kinship emerged. On the other hand, close collateral kin can serve as intermediaries of other, more distant kinship relations united at some point by the same house. Thus a woman may refer to a man as a 'parent d'enfora' ('an outside kin') saying that he was 'fill de cosí' (the son of the father's father's brother) of her aunts (her father's sisters) and that he came from the same house. In this way an image is created in which consanguinity extends over the whole locality, and at the community level, one can say that marriage not only creates new kinship ties but also renews old ties which have become distant and almost forgotten.

In the same way that, at the level of houses, a closed image of kinship as a descent line is constructed, at the community level a closed image of kinship as an alliance relation is formed. Marriage is considered as a cycle between different families of the community and provides the idea of a population that renews itself within continuity. It is considered that in each locality of the island kinship connects with the neighbourhood and that marriages renew existing links. In the restricted circuits of the island, marriage is always related to the same point of origin. In this way, the 'race' making up the houses is identified with the 'locality' constituting different groups of neighbours and, in the last instance, with the island as a community. Marriage means to marry between kin and to renew the substance of which the people and the island are made.

If at the level of the house it is possible to say that marriage creates new kinship ties, at the community level, in so far as it constitutes a solidary totality, one can also say that marriage fundamentally renews old links which have become distant and almost forgotten. The cyclical image of marriage – whereby it returns to the same point – is not in contradiction to the opening of new kinship ties created by marriage in each house. The former is based on the supposed distant links of consanguinity which interconnect the community, whereas the latter is founded upon the new close ties created by marriage in the house.

From this double idea of kinship that, on the one hand, interconnects community ties and closes them on itself, and on the other, creates new ties in each marriage and opens houses to the exterior, it is necessary to distinguish the different areas of individual kindred groups. Each individual in his own kinship universe distinguishes between close kin and distant kin. There is a zone of close kinship that at the collateral level extends to first cousins (the second degree of consanguinity) and at the level of ascendants to grandparents. In this reduced zone of consanguinity that draws the close border of the household, godparents and eponyms are preferred, and on the contrary, marriage is prohibited, although sometimes it is practised. Whereas in this kinship area the system of classification implies a certain type of behaviour, in the zone of distant kinship kin are situated by tracing kinship links through close collaterals, without this link involving the existence of distinctive kinship behaviour. It involves a universe of known kin, but kinship is not recognised in its behaviour since this is determined by other social considerations. In being distanced from the central nucleus of consanguinity, a direct relation is established with people – kin of kin – between whom kinship is known but whose behaviour is not dictated by kinship relations. They are known simply as 'little family' that have left the zone of 'real' kinship and form the class of kin distanced from the house, little-related kin between whom marriage is possible and even desired.

By analysing the category of cousins ('cosí') we can see how the gradation of kinship is constructed from a centre. This category is divided into subclasses by means of various modifiers.[21] A modifier is used in the reference 'cosí germà' ('first cousin') to designate a close cousin on one of the two sides, the father's or mother's siblings' sons. 'Fill de cosí' ('son of a cousin') is employed to name the third grade of collaterality (FFBSS), and it is theoretically possible to multiply the modifier 'fill de . . .' ('son of . . .') as we move up the collateral stages. In terms of collaterality it is considered that kinship becomes dispersed, and distant cousins enter into the category of

---

21. On the distinction between *base* terms and *modifying* terms, cf. Schneider (1968: 117). Some *base* terms are 'mum', 'dad', 'onco', 'aunt', 'germà', 'brother', etc. *Modifying* terms are those that are used to create combined terms: 'fill de' ('son of'), 'dona de' ('wife of'), 'germà' ('brother'), etc.

diffuse kinship, deriving from closer collaterals in senior generations. These collateral relations of cousins are situated according to the descent of the closer collaterals used in senior generations to name distant kin. It is said that 'els seus padrins eren cosins' ('their godfathers were cousins') to name distant collaterals from the fourth grade.

Given the consideration that kinship is dispersed from ascendants, in the area of close kinship preference is given to senior generations, whereas kinship is thought to become weaker between descendants. The collaterals of higher generations are closer than descendants of the same generation as Ego or of a generation lower. Siblings of grandparents who form the same stem are conceived as close kin while their descendants, forming dispersed branches, are considered as situated in the area of distant kin.

Within the area of distant kin where consanguinity becomes dispersed, the term of address 'primo' is used in opposition to 'cosí' to refer to collaterals who have left the close nucleus of kinship but conserve an awareness of common descent which has faded with the passing of time and no longer allows the genealogical relation to be specified with precision. Between these 'primos' there is no social obligation derived from kinship relations, and they are situated in the external limit of kindred where relations of consanguinity are identified with the relations of familiarity and solidarity existing in the island, considered as a community differentiated from others.

The idea of a diffused kinship becoming dispersed from central stems serves to symbolise the internal structure of different parts of the island as homogeneous groups of houses related through kinship. From the point of view of individual kindred, beyond the close area of kinship there exists the category of distant kin whose exact genealogical relation is not known. From a global point of view encompassing localities, the belief in this distant and vague relation removed from kinship produces a principle of familiarity between its components and helps to maintain their identity against foreigners, so that the idea of some kinship relations being dispersed through the locality symbolises the existence of cohesion between different families.

In this local context it can be argued that marriage acquires a circular character signifying the renewal of old ties. In each locality of the island internal matrimonial circuits are established that affirm the cohesion of the place and produce the sociocentric affirmation that 'everyone becomes related by marriage' and, therefore, 'marries with kin'. This does not mean that each house duplicates existing kin relations as would be the case with marriages repeated between close kin. Rather, it involves marriage within the same locality being identified with distant consanguinity by the idea of diffused kinship. At the level of each house, marriage creates new links and, therefore, the prohibition on marrying with close kindred is maintained. At a global level, however, the cohesion of the locality is valued, and marriages are not incompatible with distant kindred.[22]

22. On marriages in the distant kindred group, see below, pp. 167f.

III

Household Forms

III.1. The Model of the Peasant Family

Thomas and Znaniecki (1927) and many later writers who have contructed a model of the family in European peasant societies[1] present an ideal type of peasant household, in the Weberian sense, as a corporate unit linked to land and patrimony in which property is attached to the family rather than the individual: 'Property essentially belongs to the family, the individual is a temporary administrator' (Thomas and Znaniecki 1927: 92). They stress the importance of the relation of the family with the land, not so much for its economic value but for its social value, a familial 'symbolic value' which marks its continuity in the eyes of the community. 'The amount of land and equipment passed on to the children constitutes the basis for the prestige accorded by others and of their own assessment of the way in which they have acquitted their tasks' (Galeski 1972: 62–3). On the other hand, the household team is the basic unit of production and consumption, and the organisation of labour is based on the members of the family. 'And since, on the family farm which has no recourse to hired labour, the labour force pool, its composition and degree of labour activity are entirely determined by family competition and life, we must accept family make up as one of the chief factors in peasant farm organisation' (Chayanov 1966: 53).

The two characteristic elements contained in this model of the peasant family – its corporate character and the domestic organ-

---

1. Besides the authors mentioned, we refer to the models of the peasant family that can be found in the pioneering works in 'peasant studies' by Galeski (1972), Shanin (1972) and Chayanov (1966). We have chosen these authors as representative of a type of analysis on the European peasant family that has directed empirical research in general.

isation of labour – are associated with the internal organisation of family authority along patriarchal lines, since 'the patriarchal feature corresponds to its functions' (Galeski 1972: 64) of organising the domestic productive unit. To belong to a peasant household means living under the authority of a patriarchal head, with a social organisation and a division of labour according to traditional family lines and the basic identification of the members with their household (Shanin 1972). The ideal of the extended family appears in relation to this patriarchalism and maintains the continuity of peasant households as units of production. Evidence of the transformation of peasant families would be their reduction to nuclear groups, as if this type of conjugal family were a logical consequence of modern society. 'There is agreement on the transition from the three-generation family to the small family consisting of parents and children' affirms Galeski (1972: 68) when discussing the changing forms of the modern peasant family.

Through the corporate character of the household, the family dominates the individual, and a 'family solidarity' is created which is manifested in 'the control exercised on any member of the group by another member representing the group as a whole' (Thomas and Znaniecki 1927: 89). In this sense, marriage represents one of the critical moments in the reproduction of the group since it is related to the peasant household structure and cannot take place following individual inclinations or personal feelings. The matrimonial norm, according to Thomas and Znaniecki (1927: 90), is based on 'respect' rather than love because the former is a relation that can be more easily controlled and reinforced by the family. Collective interest holds sway over individual emotions, and the presence of love in marriage is an indication of the irruption of an individualism which 'leads to qualitative changes in the concept of the family' (Thomas and Znaniecki 1927: 105), although these authors do admit the existence of a relative social homogeneity in this type of individualist marriage given that 'the feeling of love requires a certain community of social traditions' (ibid.: 112).

We should also point out as a typical feature in this type of family the earlier age of marriage of women (Galeski 1972: 117–18) and the pressure exerted on every member of the younger generations to get married.[2] This universality of marriage and the

---

2. This feature of the young age of marriage clearly indicates that this model

rejection of remaining single is a logical consequence of the family group being the fundamental unit in the peasant social structure. In this sense 'the family not only requires its members to get married, but also directs their choices [. . .], a logical consequence of the individual's situation within the family group' (Thomas and Znaniecki 1927: 108).

Geographical and social mobility in marriage is considered to be limited, and local endogamy becomes the marriage norm. In this way neighbourhood relations interlace with kinship relations, and the peasant community appears as a group in which kinship relations are introduced into the social structure. Social homogeneity is reinforced through kinship. In peasant communities, as Galeski points out (1972: 63), 'the uniformity of social, and usually also of territorial, origin is reinforced by ties of kinship which are very strong in the village. There are usually only a few family names in the village community. The village consists of several interrelated families (or clans).' For this reason, a village is sometime defined as a local family group (neighbour group). Kinship dominates the social relations of the peasant community and is the language through which local political relations are expressed.

All these features defining the fundamental characteristics of the classical peasant family type will inevitably disintegrate under the impact of modern individualism, as the deep divide between peasant families and modern families becomes patent. The dichotomy between the traditional and the modern has fundamental explanatory value in this scheme: the changes can only be explained in terms of the disintegration of traditional family forms. This dichotomous perspective is clearly expressed by Thomas and Znaniecki (1927: 98) when they point out that 'the organisation outlined is the traditional base of family life, yet in reality it is difficult to find in all its intensity. Family life, as it appears in published work, is undergoing a profound process of disintegration alongside certain trends and under the influence of various factors. The main signs of this disintegration are: the isolation of the conjugal group and personal individualisation.'

This model of the peasant family, from which the changes in the modern family emerge, is set in the intellectual framework

---

of the peasant family is determined by researchers and information from the East. On the high age of marriage in pre-industrial western Europe in contrast to the young age of marriage in eastern Europe, cf. Hajnal (1965).

of what we could call the Weberian conception of the rise of rationalism and singularity in the West. Fundamental to this perspective are the dichotomies through which the history of the family has generally been presented. Through notions such as 'pre-capitalist', 'traditional' or 'peasant' the family is placed in an undifferentiated starting point completely opposite to the present. Thus, ethnocentrism enters into the question, and the present is overvalued, positively or negatively, in contrast with the past. From this perspective, the history of the role of kinship and the family may be summed up as the history of the progressive loss of kinship ties, along with the functional complexity of the relations between household members, as 'economic rationalism' developed (Thomas and Znaniecki 1927: 204). The privatisation of family life is presented as a logical process in the historical evolution of the West, which is seen as increasingly dominated by bureaucratic organisations different from primary solidarity groups. Thus, its transformations and its role in society are posed in terms of oppositions (extended/ nuclear family, traditional/modern family, familism/individualism, marriage for interest/marriage for love, instrumental kinship relations/relations of mutual obligation), which are nothing more than variations on the main dichotomies used by thinkers at the end of the nineteenth century (mechanic solidarity/ organic solidarity, community/society, family organisation/ political organisation, pre-capitalist/capitalist).

As we have already pointed out (see above pp. 15–17), one of the most important results of studies on the family in the last ten years has come from research in historical demography which has resulted in the destruction of the previous sociological belief about the traditional extended family. The quantitative data to be found in the nominal lists of censuses from pre-industrial Europe clearly show a predominance of nuclear family groups (Laslett 1972) contrary to the normally accepted myth about the pre-industrial extended family provided by the pioneering studies on the family in Europe. The transition from the extended family to the nuclear family is a phenomenon that cannot be proved statistically. It can also be argued that this transition did not coincide with the Industrial Revolution. On the contrary, in the nineteenth century an increase in the co-residence of parents and married children could be observed in some industrial areas (Anderson 1971a: 223; Foster 1974: 97), while during the period of transition to capitalism there were more extended families amongst rural workers than in other population groups (Medick 1976: 308; Levine 1977: 48–57). Instead of a progressive nuclearisation of the family associated with industrialisation, we find evidence of a household composition that has been fluctuating between the extended type and the nuclear type in different periods and places, as well as between different social classes, according to changes in demographic, economic and legal conditions (Berkner 1973: 401). The extended and multiple groups existing in European peasant societies should not necessarily be considered as a stage within the evolution towards the nuclear family type. They are more likely to be domestic units shaped by different adaptive strategies to concrete social situations, and in many cases, they are temporary adaptations rather than stable structures (Löfgren 1974: 21). Thus, there has been an increasing tendency to reject sociological theories which affirm the predominance of the extended family in the past and in peasant societies – 'the great family of western nostalgia' (Goode 1963) – and which also establish a relation between industrialisation, the dissolution of traditional family ties and their substitution by the structurally-isolated nuclear family.

Alternative schemes have concentrated on the detailed study of household composition and internal organisation, in addition to creating systematic typologies of the family (Laslett 1972: 31; Hammel and Laslett 1974) which are much more elaborated and precise than the classical dichotomy between the extended and nuclear family, with which previous generations of social scientists set about explaining the changes in the family over time and its role in social relations. Rather than being regarded as an entity deserving of study in its own right, the household was seen as the product of a process starting with extended groups and finishing with nuclear groups. Even when social scientists disproved the rigid evolutionist scheme and adopted a functionalist perspective, they maintained the distinction between a traditional family with multiple conjugal units in a social structure dominated by kinship and nuclear families in a social structure dominated by economic rationality.

Functionalist anthropologists who faced evolutionist schemes defined 'the elementary family as the basic unit of the kinship system' (Radcliffe-Brown and Forde 1950: 5) but paid more attention to filiation groups and jural kinship relations than to households. The nuclear family, as a universal concept, was seen as a unit from which kinship systems were structured rather than as a residential group. Thus, households were considered as products of certain aspects of the kinship system, particularly the rules of residence and inheritance norms. The household typologies that they constructed followed evolutionist models and maintained the criteria of residence rules after marriage (neolocal, patrilocal, matrilocal) instead of focusing on the genealogical structure of the components of each household. Classifications established according to rules of residence led to clear contradictions in the light of the residential behaviour of a given society (Goodenough 1956).

The influential concept of the developmental cycle (Goody 1958) in British anthropology tried to overcome these contradictions by introducing time as a factor causing cyclical alterations in household form. Residence could not be analysed in terms of discrete rules having effect after marriage and forming different types of household, but as 'phases in the developmental cycle of a general form unique to each society' (Fortes 1958: 3). The developmental cycle was unique, and the forms of residence were considered as the crystalisation of this process in a given moment. From this perspective, normative aspects have been considered essential for gaining an understanding of household structure, and the rules governing inheritance and the fission of the family have been associated with a particular ideal type of developmental cycle. In the debate on the stem family in Europe (Austria, Ireland, the Pyrennees, the Basque country and the south of France),[3] this concept was introduced to compensate for the low percentage of stem families in comparison to nuclear families, but rather than being presented in terms of residential processes, it was defined as the fulfilment of a series of cultural ideals reflected in the juridical norms of inheritance and in the form of authority transmission within the family. The extent to which this type of family was representative evaded statistical estimation, since its frequency depended on the cultural norms of patrimonial continuity and the maintenance of the hierarchy between generations, which were considered to be fully developed throughout the stages of the stem family. This type of

---

3. On Austria, cf. Berkner (1972b). On Ireland, cf. Arensberg and Kimball (1968) and the polemic started by Gibbon and Curtin (1978). On the Basque country, cf. Douglass (1969). On the south of France, cf. Fine-Souriac (1977) and Collomp (1972 and 1983).

approach extrapolated a uniform developmental cycle and some structural principles of household composition from a synchronic description of households and the cultural ideals of a society in a given moment. It failed to take into account the situations of rapid change affecting household members and overlooked the differences in conditions of household formation dependant on social stratification. It assumed the existence of a single type of developmental cycle applicable to every family, and the contradiction consisting in the presence of a family ideal without its corresponding residential practices appeared.

Historical demographical data and the problems of interpretation that have emerged from research on households as residential units has not only compelled a break with the myth about the extended family and rigid evolutionalist schemes, but has also made it necessary to recreate the theoretical framework through which social scientists have presented the history of the family and the model of the peasant family, as well as the role of kinship and domestic organisation in different social processes. In opposition to dichotomous approaches to the study of the family, 'more empirical investigations have suggested that the family is an extraordinarily durable institution even in conditions of extreme social change and of social mobility' (Hammel and Yarbrough 1973: 162). This persistence has not only been presented in terms of household composition but also with reference to the continuity of the family's social function within the processes of social reproduction, socialisation and work. Instead of a direct relation being established between modernisation and the decline of kinship structure, it is argued that kinship relations have their own dynamic in peasant societies which do not necessarily disappear with emigration and the integration in the market economy (Yanagisako 1979: 182, and Gordon Darroch 1981: 275).

There has been a move away from the model of the stable and homogeneous peasant family set against the heterogeneity of urban families towards an emphasis on the relation between social stratification and the diversity of peasant households (Löfgren 1974: 283), as well as the interdependence of kinship and social class (Leyton 1975). In addition, the idea of the instrumental character of kinship relations amongst peasant families, in contrast to a highly sentimentalised image of the modern family, has come to be seen as a bourgeois prejudice rather than an analytical tool (Segalen 1980), and studies have focused on 'the particular features of family experience and the norms and modes of behaviour in different periods and in different classes and cultures' (Medick and Sabean 1984: 9), with specific ways of representing material interests and family emotions in territorial terms.

In preference to the study of the family within the classical theories of modernisation and industrialisation, researchers have undertaken local studies that contextualise information on family life and test the usefulness of accepted concepts and analytical relations within an ethnographic context. In this sense, the study of the internal structure of domestic organisation can be considered as a key element for the understanding of social structure, economic developments and their relation to the cultural models of a society.

III.2. Family and Residence: Morphology and Functions

In the study of the households of a society it is necessary to make an analytical distinction between family and household, two 'logically distinct and empirically different' elements (Bender 1967: 493). This distinction, which is now a classical feature of anthropology, establishes the contrast between kinship, as an element defining family membership, and locality, as an element defining household membership. The coincidence between family and household, as can often be seen in our own society, is not empirically universal. The family is a unit of kinship that does not necessarily include a residential unit, and the household is a unit of residence that does not necessarily include a relation of kinship. The reference in the family is kinship, whereas for the household it is locality, two principles of social classification and organisation that do not belong to the same universe of discourse.

The distinction between residential unit and kinship unit, between 'house' and 'family',[4] can be observed in the everyday discourse of Formentera where a universe of kinship and a universe of locality are quite evident. There is a 'familial' discourse level in which daily life is interpreted and integrated through kinship relations, and there is a 'domestic' level of

4. On the history of these two concepts, cf. Flandrin (1976: 17–28). On the different use of 'house' and 'family' in the kinship system, cf. Karnoouh (1979).

discourse in which those who live in the same house are classified. Kinship, as a social language, structures the world through
the principles that orientate family relations and, taking the
family as the model for society, brings together its separate
units. In contrast, domestic discourse basically classifies enclosed units that exclude each other. The universe of locality,
which is known by the term 'can', establishes houses as social
units. It names a unit of residence that is described in kinship as
well as in economic and juridical terms. Each house, as a
household, is defined by the individuals who inhabit it – its
identity finds expression through the name of the house – but
also by the land, animals, tools of work and additional constructions they possess. On the other hand, it is also a 'symbolic
good' that forms part of the system of representations and values
of the society with its rules governing the game of hierarchy,
prestige and power in which different households compete.[5]

The distinction between kinship and residence to differentiate
between family and household has to take into account the
universe of 'domestic activities', since in referring to households
we not only mean a group of individuals – whether related by
kinship or not – who share the same living space, but also a
totality of activities carried out by the individuals as members of
the household. These activities are not very often defined with
precision, but they are fundamentally related to the production
and consumption of food, as well as to the reproduction and
socialisation of children. Descriptions such as 'to share the same
space' and 'to live below the same roof' define households as
residential groups, whereas others like 'to work the same lands',
'to eat from the same table' sum up what households do. The
house as a household not only contains some individuals but
also performs a series of functions that establish the domestic
domain as 'a system of social relations through which the
reproductive nucleus is integrated into the medium and structure of society' (Fortes 1958: 9).

Since 'family, co-habitation and domestic functions represent
three different types of social phenomena' (Bender 1967: 507), it
is necessary in typologies not only to contrast family and household but also to make a further distinction between residence
and domestic functions, that is, between the composition of

---

5. On the house as a social representation, see below, pp. 138 ff.

households and what they do. Households have two aspects that should be treated as analytically distinct. These two dimensions we shall call *morphology* and *function*, according to whether we are referring to the residential composition of a household or to its activities (Netting and Wilk 1984: 8).

Morphological classifications have been used most in what has come to be called the analysis of household structure, and classical classifications of the family using the distinction between nuclear, stem and extended refer to morphological composition in terms of kinship relations. The standardised classifications of more recent times (Laslett 1972; Hammel and Laslett 1974) use much more precise descriptions and are based on more explicit criteria. The fundamental criterion is common residence, and descriptions focus on the relations of kinship which unite the members of a domestic group.

There are five principal categories of household: households composed of single members, households without conjugal nucleus, conjugal families, extended families and multiple families. A household with only a single member is made up of an individual who lives alone (unmarried or widowed). A household without a conjugal nucleus consists of a group of individuals who live together without any kinship relation or a group of unmarried brothers and/or sisters. A household with a conjugal family consists of a married couple, a married couple with children or a widow/er with children. A domestic group with an extended family is formed by a conjugal nucleus with or without children to which additional member/s from direct or collateral lines are integrated, but it contains only one conjugal nucleus. Finally, a household with a multiple family takes in two or more conjugal units related by kinship through direct or collateral lines. All of the household types include resident members that are not related by marriage (servants).

In this classification of households the description is based on the genealogical ties of each individual belonging to a group with respect to one person ('Ego') who often, although not always, appears in the census list as the 'head of the family'. In extended and multiple households the main nucleus is distinguished from the secondary members or units. The typology presented by Laslett (1972) differentiates the extension of ascendants, descendants and collateral relations. It also establishes the difference in multiple-family households between secondary units as ascendants, descendants and collaterals. The

criterion for this distinction is the relation of kinship between
the members and secondary units and the 'head of the family'.
In this typology the identity of the 'head of the family' is
emphasised in such a way that two households with an identical
genealogical scheme may appear with different classifications,
depending on where the 'head of the family' is situated. As the
criteria in the censuses of Formentera for deciding who is the
'head of the family' seem to be arbitrary and, what is more
important, the use of the term 'head of the family', implies a
series of value judgements about authority inside the household
which go beyond a purely morphological analysis of household
composition while introducing into the typology, at the same
time, a qualitative variable that is hardly comparable, we have
thought it more suitable to maintain the formal criteria of a
reference to 'Ego'. According to convention, therefore, and
dispensing with census indications to the head of the family, the
point of reference ('Ego') to describe the genealogy of an extended household will always be 'the male Ego' who forms part
of the conjugal unit, while in multiple extended groups the
youngest conjugal couple will be taken as the primary unit and
the genealogical description will be made from the male 'Ego' of
this unit. It would seem useful to introduce into the description
and genealogical classification of households with extended or
multiple families a distinction between patrilineal and matrilineal members or secondary units, given the importance of this
distinction in anthropological literature and the possible cultural
meaning it may have in an interpretation of percentages of
extended and multiple groups.[6]

The household is not only a residential unit but also performs
a series of activities, which are not necessarily the same for each
household in a society and which can change over time. Although
greater precision has been achieved by typologies using morphological criteria, we also need a classificatory scheme with the same
concretion and explicitness as morphological classifications to be
able to analyse what households do. For this reason, we intend to
use the activities performed in a society and the role that households play in the performance of such activities as the basis for our
criteria, rather than the inclusion of an individual in a group.

---

6. On the analysis of extended and multiple groups in terms of the type of
extension beyond the conjugal nucleus, cf. Kertzer (1977) and Netting (1979, 1981).

Households are integrated into a society through their activities, and as primary groups they carry out a series of basic activities. Domestic activities can be classified as production, distribution, transmission and reproduction. Not all of these activities are undertaken by households, nor do all households perform the same activities.

The distinction between the morphology and function of households is necessary in order to avoid drawing hasty conclusions about social structure from the exclusive use of a morphological analysis of households. If we describe household structure from a morphological perspective, we only refer to household composition according to kinship. The persistence of a certain type says nothing about its social functions. In order to speak about what households do, we require additional information from sources other than morphological typologies. It is necessary to set these typologies within the context of the social system to which they belong; since census lists only offer information about residential groups and the predominance of a particular form, they cannot show us anything about the functions of these groups.

Where morphologies coincide, household functions may vary. An absolute correspondence between morphology and function cannot be assumed. Thus, groups with identical morphology may carry out various functions, and the same functions may correspond to different forms. In this sense, it has been pointed out that morphological typologies can hide important functional variations and fail to reveal completely different principles of organisation. Amongst land-owning families, the house is a stable centre of domestic activities in its fundamental capacity as a unit of production, whereas amongst non-landowning peasant families, the house is a force of centripetal organisation. It is not a unit of production but rather a base of operations (Löfgren 1974: 29).

On the other hand, the persistence of extended household types amongst peasants and workers in rural industries indicates nothing about its functional identity. There are fundamental differences in the legal, material and institutional determinants of the two groups. The existence of the extended family amongst the workers of rural industries was the result of increasing pauperisation, rising demographic pressure and poor living conditions, as well as secondary poverty stemming from the family life cycle. In contrast, the classical stem family of peasants was formed essentially to preserve family property (Medick 1976: 307–8).

We can say the same about the existence of extended households in Formentera with regard both to peasant landowners and emigrant sailors. The former have a way of conserving their family property which has its legal foundation in the institution of single inheritance and the house as a unit of production, whereas the latter undertake temporal adaptations aimed at redistributing the poverty of the nuclear family through kinship relations. Rather than representing the survival of traditional family forms, emigrant households are the result of principles of social organisation which differ from those of landowning peasant families. The house is neither a unit of production nor a unit of work, and domestic organisation has its physical basis in the emigration of men. The household is an operational base that can split up, without following the classical domestic cycle of the peasant stem family, and come together again with the construction of a new house when the emigrating member returns.

In addition, from a functional point of view, there is a difference between a household with an extended family emerging as a temporary arrangement for the maintenance of an aged ascendant or as a means of providing initial economic help for a young couple, and one that is a phase in the developmental cycle of a stem family. In the latter, the same household passes through various phases in its developmental cycle following the principle of patrimonial continuity, whereas the former type arises from temporal extensions which do not necessarily repeat cyclically and which are not governed by the principle of continuity.

In discussing the significance of peasant stem families, the distinction between morphology and function can help to clarify many questions. In general, those who have defended the importance of the stem family in different zones of Europe, in spite of its low statistical presence, have given more attention to the functions of the household than to the explicit criteria of residence. In these cases the residence is considered as an epiphenomenon of the kinship system and the social structure. In his definition of the stem family, Le Play turned away from the consideration of residence to concentrate on the domestic authority of the family head, which rested with the man in the oldest generation (Wall, Laslett and Robin 1983: 19). In this way it was possible to describe the stem family without necessarily implying common residence.

Descriptions that see the stem family as a cultural ideal in the sense of its privileged position within the kinship relations system of a society, because it contains a series of relations which are valued positively by the society (Wheaton 1975), or that relate the stem family to indivisible inheritance (Berkner 1976; Berkner and Mendels 1978) hold an image of the stem family that is defined by the function of transmission rather than by residence. In the stem family cycle, this represents the continuity of a patrilineage in the same house and with the same patrimony. The stem family, in this case, is seen as an attribute of filiation lines rather than as a residential group, and residence is considered as an epiphenomenon of family continuity, the spatial expression of familial groups organised for the production and transmission of goods.

The ambiguities present in definitions of family type in which functional features of the household are mixed up with residence and the apparent contradiction in the importance of a family type that only finds its spatial materialisation in some households of a society can only be eliminated by considering residence in its own right (Verdon 1980: 122) and by adopting an operative definition of group.

In morphological typologies, households are defined as residential groups, and no other type of process that could define the group is prejudged. The processes of production, distribution, transmission and reproduction should be analytically distinguished from the process of residence, even though they appear united within the household. An analytical point of view avoids superimposing these processes and creating multifunctional groups that evade comparison with each other. A stem family defined as a residential group is, at the height of its growth, composed of the paternal conjugal family and the family of one, and only one, of their children (Verdon 1979: 91). The processes of transmission and continuity of patrimonial lines which are often associated with the stem family are analytically different to the processes of residential groups.

III.3. The Structure of the Residential Group (1857–1955)

Morphological typologies of the household provide detailed descriptions of the genealogical relations of household members which enable us to establish comparisons within a society at

Table III.1 Population and households in Formentera

Year	Population	Households
1857	1.632	300 (267 computed)
1925	2.728	576 (567 computed)
1930	2.925	597
1940	2.931	646
1955	2.778	689

different times. With these typologies set in the relevant social and cultural context, it is possible to gain an insight into the different functions of households in situations of social and economic change. We can seek to explain the causes of permanence and change in the size of extended and multiple families, as well as the conditions necessary for the creation of stem families.

In order to detect changes and continuities in the morphology of households in relation to the social context, we have chosen to focus on a time period of one hundred years (1857–1955) using the censuses of 1857, 1925, 1930, 1940 and 1955. The population and number of households in these years are given in Table III.1.

The repopulation of Formentera in the modern era began at the end of the seventeenth century and was carried out mainly by natives of Ibiza. As can be seen in Figure III.1, there was a gradual population growth which reached its height in 1930, until a new period of growth started in 1960.

The population was distributed over the whole island without any real nucleus. Although it had three centres defined by the parishes of Sant Francesc Xavier, Sant Ferran and El Pilar, as a whole the population was dispersed.

In the evolution of the population we should stress the importance of temporary emigration, which was practised by a large part of the island's male population (Vilá Valentí 1950: 421). Young men would go to work temporarily in South America and the West Indies and later return to Formentera to settle there permanently or wait for further seasons in South America until their final retirement on the island. This temporary emigration can be detected throughout the nineteenth century, reaching its highest level at the end of the nineteenth century and during the first third of the twentieth century, when the censuses indicate a high

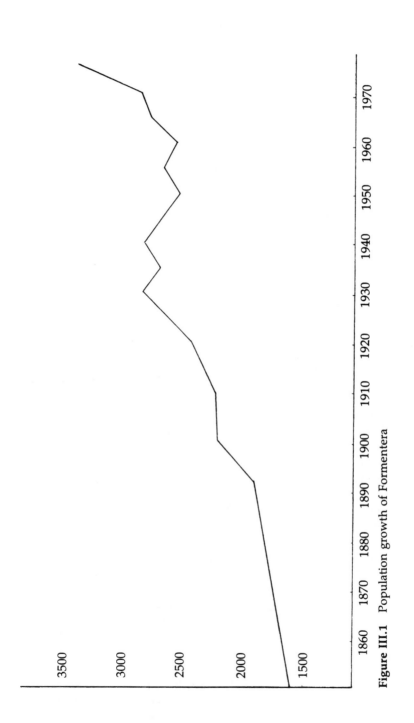

Figure III.1 Population growth of Formentera

proportion of 'sailors'. As Habsburgo Lorena reported at the end of the nineteenth century (1890, II: 462):

> One can say that, out of the island's adult and young male population, roughly two-thirds from the *low* part and a third from the *high* part of the island are sailors, but although they appear as such in the register of licencees, or men of the sea, in Ibiza, not all of them really are sailors or do not sail on a constant basis even though they may have an aptitude for sailing and the authorisation to do it. The majority of them usually look for jobs on national ships trading with South or North America or with the Spanish West Indies and continue sailing for a period of seven to ten or up to twelve years with relatively long interruptions, after which they return with as many pesetas as they have managed to save from their earnings to settle down in their native country for the rest of their days as farm labourers or fishermen or as both at the same time, unless they prefer to take up quarrying, the manufacture of coal or the buying and selling of the Island's products.

In the 1940s and 1950s most emigrants travelled on Spanish ships that sailed around the Mediterranean instead of heading for South America as in previous times. In the 1960s this type of emigration was interrupted, and the migratory process was reversed with the appearance of tourism and the creation of new work opportunities.

Although the phenomenon of emigration was mainly temporary, part of the population did emigrate permanently, as suggested by the negative migratory balance from the end of the nineteenth century until 1955, excluding 1925. During this period, there was a rapid decrease in 1930, and the highest negative migratory balance was recorded between 1940 and 1950 (Bertranpetit 1981: 86).

Some informants indicate that many men went to America and never returned. They distinguish between those who went to Cuba to find work felling trees and making coal and those who went to Montevideo. The former, whose work involved little skill, would nearly always return, whereas the latter, with skilled work, would never return to Formentera.

During this period of intense temporary emigration by the people of Formentera, an important transformation took place in the distribution of land property. On returning to the island, temporary emigrants bought land, built houses and set themselves up as 'pageses' with a self-subsistence domestic property.

According to what the old people say: 'They bought the land after making a trip to America. When they returned they bought a piece of land. Afterwards they made another journey and bought more land.' The large holdings are divided up and title to the land is distributed in such a way as to form small domestic properties with houses as units of residence and production dispersed throughout the island. Comparing the land surveys of 1879 and 1957 (Bisson 1977: 136), we can see that there was a considerable increase in the number of small properties (up to 20 hectares, with a marked concentration of properties of 5 hectares), while the number of properties of more than 20 hectares decreased. In 1879 there were 288 owners of land between 0 and 20 hectares occupying a total surface of 1,332.66 hectares, whereas in 1957 there were 1,027 owners of land between 0 and 20 hectares occupying a total surface of 3,828.14 hectares (Table III.2).

The image of property distribution given by Habsburgo Lorena is very different to the one we have now. He observed (1890, II: 389) that

> Property is not so divided in Pytiusa menor as in Pytiusa mayor, Mallorca and Menorca, thus it covers a surface area of 11,529 hectares, according to the results of triangulation, inside which territorial statistics estimate the existence of no more than 387 farm holdings giving an average size of 29.79 hectares, a figure notably higher than in the rest of the Baleares Islands and four times greater than in the whole of Ibiza.

This image of property distribution on the island was completely changed by the temporary and permanent emigration of its population. The labour force available for the large farms diminished, and temporary emigrants, as a result of the paid work undertaken during part of their lives, were able to buy up land which they could exploit through the work of the family and by directing their lives towards a 'subsistence' economy. They built new houses and intensified the dispersed habitat of the island.[7]

---

7. On the appearance of a new type of house as a consequence of emigration, see below, pp. 120–6. On the appearance of small family properties as an effect of emigration, cf. Brandes (1975: 73).

Table III.2 Landowning distribution in Formentera

Hectares	Landowners Number	%	Extension Ha.	%
Year 1879				
0–5	197	52.6	338.57	6.1
5–10	47	12.5	334.64	6.1
10–20	44[1]	11.4	659.45	11.9
20–30	33	8.8	788.16	14.3
30–50	33	8.8	1,280.28	23.2
50–70	10	2.6	569.57	10.3
70–100	4	1.0	343.53	6.2
100–150	3	0.8	308.53	5.6
150–300	2	0.5	376.68	6.8
300–500	1	0.2	495.83	9.0
Year 1957				
0–5	782[2]	71.2	1,394.82	19.2
5–10	140	12.7	997.53	14.3
10–20	105	9.5	1,435.79	20.5
20–30	36	3.2	884.45	12.5
30–50	21	1.9	834.91	11.9
50–70	8	0.7	468.32	6.7
70–100	3	0.2	242.27	3.4
100–150	2	0.1	287.22	4.1
150–300	1[3]	–	244.49	–
300–500	1	0.09	426.41	6.1

[1] Including the lighthouse section.
[2] 292 owners have less than 1 hectare.
[3] The salt-pan has been excluded.

III.3.a. Household Composition

Table III.3 sums up the composition of households in Formentera between 1857 and 1955. One of the features of household composition in this period that should be highlighted is the consistently high proportion of households with only one conjugal nucleus in relation to groups of an extended or mutiple type. In every year of the period under examination, nearly two-thirds (57 per cent in 1940 and 1955, 63 per cent in 1930) of households were of the conjugal type, while approximately one-third (29 per cent in 1955, 30 per cent in the years 1857, 1930 and 1940, and 33 per cent in 1925) were of the extended and multiple type. The other two types represented between 7 per cent in 1925 and 1930 and 8 per cent in 1857, with a slight rise to

Table III.3 Structure of households (1857–1955)

	1857		1925		1930		1940		1955	
1. Solitaries	16	(6%)	28	(5%)	29	(5%)	53	(8%)	71	(10%)
2. No family	6	(2%)	13	(2%)	14	(2%)	33	(5%)	31	(4%)
3. Simple family households	165	(62%)	338	(60%)	373	(63%)	371	(57%)	387	(57%)
a. Married couples alone	15		33		35		27		48	
b. Married couples with child(ren)	121		237		269		250		275	
c. Widowers with child(ren)	7		12		17		18		3	
d. Widows with child(ren)	22		56		52		76		61	
4. Extended family households	47	(18%)	113	(20%)	117	(19%)	146	(23%)	130	(19%)
a. Lineal										
Patrilineal	18		32		27		39		33	
Matrilineal	6		10		12		21		19	
Bilineal	1		–		1		–		1	
Indeterminate	–		–		–		3		2	
b. Collateral										
Patrilateral	8		23		20		24		31	
Matrilateral	2		10		9		17		14	
c. Lineal and collateral										
Patrilineal	10		32		41		37		26	
Matrilineal	2		6		7		5		4	
5. Multiple family households	33	(12%)	76	(13%)	64	(11%)	43	(7%)	69	(10%)
a. Lineal										
Patrilineal	10		17		14		12		22	
Matrilineal	1		5		6		5		10	
b. Lineal and extended collateral										
Patrilineal	20		46		34		24		29	
Matrilineal	–		5		5		1		–	
c. Collateral										
Brother	1		2		4		–		7	
Sister	–		1		–		1		–	
Other collaterals	1		–		1		–		1	

13 per cent in 1940 occurring at the expense of the nuclear type.

During the same period the proportion of households of an extended type was higher than the proportion of multiple type households. In 1857, 1925, 1930 and 1955 the proportion is two-thirds of extended type households to one-third of multiple type households and in 1940 the proportion of multiple type households fell to one-quarter of the total number of the island's extended and multiple families.

A comparison of these figures with household composition in other European communities highlights the high proportion of extended and multiple families in relation to nuclear families.[8] According to available information, Formentera shows a strong similarity to the south of France, the centre and north of Italy and the Alps and a sharp contrast with the north of Europe and England. We are in what has traditionally been considered an area with one type of stem family.

III.3.b. Types of Kin beyond the Conjugal Nucleus

In the formation of multiple and extended households one can obtain a detailed description of composition by indicating the type of kin that do not form part of the central conjugal nucleus. By this we mean kin living in the same house and related to the conjugal nucleus through consanguinity or affinity.

Through the genealogical description of extended or multiple households, we can distinguish kin according to the direction of extended lineal and collateral lines and according to the distance between distant and close kin. These two distinctions of direction and distance we can, in turn, subdivide into patrilateral or matrilateral according to whether the kinship tie with the conjugal nucleus is through a man (the husband, H) or through a woman (the wife, W).

The extension is of a lineal kind when kinship ties are traced

---

8. In comparison to the tables presented by Laslett (1972: 61, Table 1.3; 1977: 20–1, Table 1.1, 22–3, Table 1.2, 24, Table 1.3; and 1978: 92–3, Table 6.1) Robin, in his monograph of Elmdon (England) (1980: 28, Table 11, and 223, Table 59), finds a high percentage of conjugal families (76 per cent in 1861 and 68 per cent in 1964) in contrast to a low proportion of extended and multiple type families (13 per cent in 1861 and 7 per cent in 1964). Brandes (1975: 109) found in Becedas (Castilla) in 1970 that only 10 per cent of families following our classification were of an extended or multiple type. A proportion of 30 per cent of extended and multiple families can be considered as an indication that the presence of kin beyond the conjugal nucleus is important in household composition.

through the consanguine ascendants or direct descendants of the conjugal nucleus, such as the father (F), the mother (M), the father's father (FF), the father's mother (FM), the mother's father (MF) or the mother's mother (MM) of one or both of the spouses who form the conjugal nucleus, or the children of the son (S Ch) or the children of the daughter (D Ch) of the spouses who form the elementary family.

The extension is patrilineal if the line of ascendant kinship is in the name of the male spouse (H) or if the descendant line is through the son (S). The extension is matrilineal if the ascendant line is from the female spouse (W) or through the daughter (D) of the elementary family.

The extension is of a collateral type when the kinship ties are traced through sibling ties with one or both of the spouses forming the elementary nucleus, such as the brother (B), the sister (Z), the brother's son (BS), the brother's daughter (BD), the sister's son (ZS), the sister's daughter (ZD) or the brothers of a relation in the ascendant line such as the father's brother (FB), the father's sister (FZ), the mother's brother (MB) or the mother's sister (MZ). The collateral extension is patrilateral if the kinship tie is established through the male spouse (H) of the elementary nucleus and matrilateral if established through the female spouse (W).

Affinal kin are present when there is a primary term of alliance (H or W) in the chain of terms describing ties of lineal or collateral kinship with one of the spouses of the elementary nucleus. Linear affinal relations are the husband's father (HF) or mother (HM) where the husband's 'Ego' is feminine (W), and the wife's father (WF) or mother (WM) where the wife's 'Ego' is masculine (H). Collateral affines are the wife of a brother (BW) or the husband of a sister (ZH) of one of the two spouses of the elementary nucleus, the wife's brother (WB) or sister (WZ) where the 'Ego' is masculine, and the husband's brother (HB) or sister (HZ) where the 'Ego' is feminine.

Regarding distance, relations that are close to the conjugal nucleus will be defined as those relations whose description goes through only one transition in the ascendant or collateral line in relation to the 'Ego' of the elementary nucleus (for example, F, B, M, Z of the husband or wife) or one transition in the descendant line in relation to the children of the conjugal nucleus (for example, SS, SD, DS, DD). Those kin whose genealogical description requires more than one transition either in the direct line or the collateral line in relation to the conjugal nucleus

Table III.4 Extended lineal households

	1857 W	1857 H	1925 W	1925 H	1930 W	1930 H	1940 W	1940 H	1955 W	1955 H
F	9	–	4	–	6	3	2	3	2	2
M	7	5	24	5	18	4	35	11	31	15
FF	–	–	1	–	–	–	–	–	–	–
FM	–	–	–	–	–	1	–	–	–	1
S Ch	–	–	1	–	1	–	1	–	–	–
D Ch	–	1	–	–	–	3	–	4	–	1
SW & S Ch	2	–	–	–	2	–	1	–	–	–
HM	–	–	–	3	–	–	–	1	–	–
HF	–	–	–	2	–	1	–	2	–	–
WM	–	–	1	–	–	–	–	–	–	–
M & WM	–		–		–		–		1	
F & WM	–		–		1		–		–	
D Ch & S Ch	1		–		–		–		–	
Not deter.	–		–		–		3		2	

will be considered as distant (for example, FF, FM, BS, ZS, FZ, FB).

Tables III.4, III.5, III.6 and III.7 show the distribution of kin resident in extended households (III.4, III.5, III.6) and multiple households (III.7) during the years studied. Relations are distinguished through the man (H) and through the woman (W). A distinction is also made between lineal groups in close, distant and affinal lines, collaterals in close lines, as well as lineal and collateral relations present in the same household. In multiple households we distinguish between lineal groups, lineal and collateral, distant and close, as well as multiple groups in which the secondary conjugal nucleus is established through the collateral line.

The observation and comparison of the tables highlights the centrality of the elementary nucleus in the households of Formentera. The number of kin present in the household becomes smaller as we move away genealogically from the conjugal nucleus. The first ascendants in the direct line (FM) and the first collateral relations (BZ) predominate in extended and multiple households. Amongst the extended groups existing in 1857, about a fifth were extended with a close relation, a proportion rising to two-thirds in the other years. Amongst the multiple groups, four-fifths had only close lineal and collateral kin in all the years studied.

Table III.5 Extended collateral households

	1857		1925		1930		1940		1955	
	H	W	H	W	H	W	H	W	H	W
B	4	1	2	–	3	2	1	–	7	1
Z	2	1	11	5	7	3	15	6	15	4
Sib	–	–	2	–	2	–	1	–	3	–
FB	–	–	–	–	1	–	–	–	–	–
FZ	–	–	1	–	2	–	3	3	2	3
MB	–	–	–	–	–	–	–	–	1	–
MZ	1	–	2	2	–	–	–	2	–	1
Sib & FZ	–	–	–	–	2	–	1	–	1	–
Z & F Sib	1	–	1	–	–	–	–	–	–	–
BS	–	–	1	–	–	–	–	–	–	–
ZS	–	–	–	–	1	1	–	1	–	–
ZD	–	–	–	–	–	–	1	–	–	–
ZD & ZDD	–	–	–	1	–	–	–	–	–	–
MZ & Z Ch	–	–	1	–	–	–	–	–	–	–
BW & B Ch	–	–	–	–	1	–	1	–	1	–
FBS	–	–	–	–	–	–	–	–	1	–
WB/HB	–	–	–	–	–	1	–	2	–	1
WZ/HZ	–	–	1	2	1	2	1	3	–	4
WB & WFZ	–	–	1	–	–	–	–	–	–	–

The marked presence of close lineal and collateral kin is in keeping with the norms of patrimonial transmission involving co-residence of the married heir and his parents, and it is also appropriate to the cultural norms regarding the care of elderly parents and the maintainance of single siblings in the house.

The equal proportion of masculine and feminine lineal ascendants (M, F) in 1857 is particularly noticeable, if we compare extended lineal groups (III.4) and collateral groups (III.5), a feature contrasting with the other censuses which found a higher proportion of feminine (M) ascendants and feminine collaterals (Z). These censuses also showed a higher proportion of distant collateral relations and affines than in 1857. Temporary emigration during these years increased the residential mobility of young men who worked as sailors outside the island, while women stayed within the household. In the families of emigrants, the lineal and collateral extension followed the logic of family aid and the redistribution of needs through kinship rather than the logic of patrimonial transmission. Lineal and collateral kin were attached to the simple conjugal unit when this type of extended residential form seemed useful and

Table III.6 Extended lineal and collateral households

	1857		1925		1930		1940		1955	
	H	W	H	W	H	W	H	W	H	W
F&B	–	–	2	–	4	–	1	–	–	1
F&Z	2	–	2	1	3	2	2	1	–	2
M&B	1	–	2	–	5	1	4	1	4	–
M&Z	4	2	14	1	11	–	20	2	10	–
F&Sib	1	–	1	–	4	–	–	–	–	–
M&Sib	1	–	3	–	7	–	7	–	5	–
F&FZ	–	–	1	1	1	–	–	–	1	–
M&FB	1	–	–	–	–	–	–	–	–	–
M&FZ	–	–	–	–	2	–	–	–	1	1
M&MZ	–	–	1	–	–	1	–	1	–	–
FF&FZ	–	–	–	–	–	–	–	–	1	–
M&FM&Z	–	–	1	–	–	–	–	–	–	–
FM&Sib	–	–	1	–	–	–	–	–	–	–
F&B&FB	–	–	1	–	–	–	–	–	–	–
F&B&FZ	–	–	–	–	–	1	–	–	–	–
F&Z&FZ	–	–	2	–	–	–	–	–	–	–
F&Sib&FZ	–	–	–	–	1	–	–	–	–	–
M&B&MB	–	–	–	–	–	–	–	–	1	–
M&B&FZ	–	–	–	–	–	1	–	–	–	–
M&Z&MF	–	–	–	–	1	–	–	–	–	–
M&Sib&FB	–	–	–	–	2	–	–	–	–	–
M&Sib&MZ	–	–	–	–	–	–	–	–	1	–
M&B&FZ	–	–	–	–	–	–	–	–	1	–
M&B&MZ&MFZ	–	–	–	–	–	–	–	–	1	–
M&B&MZ&FM	–	–	–	–	–	–	1	–	–	–
M&Z&BW&BD	–	–	–	–	–	–	1	–	–	–
M&Z&BS	–	–	1	–	–	–	–	–	–	–
M&WZ	–	–	–	–	–	–	1	–	–	–
HM&HSib	–	–	–	–	–	1	–	–	–	–
HF&HZ	–	–	–	1	–	–	–	–	–	–
HM&HZ&HZS	–	–	–	1	–	–	–	–	–	–
HF&HFZ	–	–	–	1	–	–	–	–	–	–

necessary. The formation of these extended households was a flexible process that, despite its morphological resemblance to households of landowning peasants, may be due to different factors. Whereas the extension of peasant households can be seen as an instrument for conserving land and followed the logic of the inheritance system, extended and multiple households in families of sailors and emigrants were a means 'for redistributing the poverty of the nuclear family through the kinship system' (Medick 1976: 308).

Table III.7 Multiple households

	1857 H	1857 W	1925 H	1925 W	1930 H	1930 W	1940 H	1940 W	1955 H	1955 W
F&M	9	1	16	5	14	6	12	5	22	8
F&M&B	5	1	10	1	8	1	7	–	9	–
F&M&Z	9	–	14	1	8	2	4	1	6	–
F&M&Sib	4	–	19	1	14	–	8	–	6	–
F&M&FM	1	–	–	–	–	–	–	–	–	–
F&M&MM	–	–	–	–	1	–	–	–	–	–
F&M&B&FF	–	–	–	1	–	–	–	–	–	–
F&M&Z&FF	–	–	–	–	–	–	1	–	–	–
F&M&B&FM	–	–	1	–	–	–	1	–	–	–
F&M&Sib&MM	–	–	–	–	–	1	–	–	–	–
F&M&Sib&FM	–	–	1	–	–	–	–	–	–	–
F&M&FZ&FM	–	–	–	–	–	–	–	–	1	–
F&M&FSib&FM	–	–	–	–	–	–	–	–	1	–
F&M&B&FZ&FF	–	–	–	–	1	–	–	–	–	–
F&M&B&FF&FM	–	–	–	–	1	–	–	–	–	–
F&M&B&MF&MM	–	–	–	–	–	–	–	–	1	–
F&M&Z&FF&FM&FZ	1	–	–	–	–	–	–	–	–	–
F&M&MZ	–	–	–	–	–	–	1	–	–	–
F&M&FZ	–	–	1	–	–	–	2	–	1	–
F&M&B&FZ	–	–	–	–	–	–	–	–	2	–
F&M&Sib&FZ	–	–	–	–	1	–	–	–	1	–
F&M&Z&ZD	–	–	–	1	–	–	–	–	–	–
F&M&Sib&ZD	–	–	–	–	–	–	–	–	1	–
FB&FBW	1	–	–	–	–	–	–	–	–	–
F&FBD&FBDH	–	–	–	–	–	–	–	–	–	1
F&FZ&FZH	–	–	–	–	–	1	–	–	–	–
F&M&HM	–	–	–	–	–	–	–	–	–	1
WF&WM	–	–	1	–	–	–	–	–	–	–
B&BW	–	–	–	–	–	–	–	–	1	–
B&BW&B Ch	–	–	–	–	–	–	–	–	1	–
B&BW&M	–	–	–	–	–	–	–	–	1	–
Sib&BW&M	–	–	–	–	1	–	–	–	–	–
Sib&BW&BS&M	–	–	–	–	2	–	–	–	–	–
Sib&BW&F&M	–	–	1	–	1	–	–	–	1	–
Sib&BW&B Ch&F&M	–	–	1	–	–	–	–	–	–	–
Sib&BW&F&M&MZ	–	–	–	–	–	–	–	–	1	–
Sib&BW&F&M&FZ	–	–	–	–	–	–	–	–	1	–
B&BW&B Ch&F&M&MFZ	–	–	–	–	–	–	–	–	1	–
B&BW&BZ	1	–	–	–	–	–	–	–	–	–
Z&ZH&Z Ch	–	–	–	–	–	–	1	–	–	–
Z&ZH&ZS&F	–	–	1	–	–	–	–	–	–	–

Table III.8 Patrilineal or matrilineal extended and multiple
households

	1857		1925		1930		1940		1955	
4. Extended	48		113		117		146		128	
	H	W	H	W	H	W	H	W	H	W
	39	9	88	25	88	29	107	39	93	35
5. Multiple	31		75		64		43		69	
	H	W	H	W	H	W	H	W	H	W
	30	1	64	11	53	11	37	6	58	11

Amongst multiple households we should draw attention to the presence of secondary collateral conjugal units, particularly in 1930. They consisted of multiple groups formed by married brothers who, being frequently absent as sailors, adopted this form of residence temporarily instead of a household structure that reproduces over time according to variations in the family cycle. The apparent similarity of these multiple groups with the classical *frérèches* of some European peasant families exists only in form. They represented temporary strategies of household formation that do not conform to any ideal model of residential conduct; neither did they derive from any general principle of household organisation. They were, rather, the consequence of a series of individual decisions made within the framework of available resources and social necessities of different families.[9]

In extended and multiple groups, extension through the patrilineal line clearly predominates over the matrilineal line (Table III.8). During this century there has been a noticeable change in the proportions of patrilineal and matrilineal extensions. The proportion of extended and multiple groups of a patrilineal kind ranged between about four-fifths in 1857 and 1925 (87 per cent in 1857 and 80 per cent in 1925) and three-quarters in 1930, 1940 and 1955 (78 per cent in 1930, 75 per cent in 1940 and 75 per cent in 1955) in relation to matrilateral extended and multiple groups.

Amongst extended and multiple groups there was a rise in the proportion of patrilineal kin in groups of a multiple type (97 per

9. Bell (1979: 109–12) also points out that this type of formation of extended and multiple families was a consequence of the temporary emigration of peasants to the south of Italy.

cent in 1857, 85 per cent in 1925, 83 per cent in 1930, 79 per cent in 1940 and 84 per cent in 1955) in contrast to the proportion in extended groups (81 per cent in 1857, 78 per cent in 1925, 75 per cent in 1930, 73 per cent in 1940 and 70 per cent in 1955). On the other hand, the presence of patrilineal kin was also more evident in multiple lineal groups with collateral extension. It is interesting to note the persistence of extension by the paternal line throughout the period studied and, more significantly, the fact that temporary emigration had no influence in changing the type of kin that were added to the conjugal unit, in contrast to the experience in other places of Europe. Netting (1979: 45-50) pointed out, in his observations of an Alpine village, a change of emphasis from extension through the paternal line to an extension of an undifferentiated kind due to the temporary emigration of the men. 'It is possible', he writes (1979: 50), 'that the spouses of men who, as paid temporary workers were absent from the village, played an important role in the agricultural enterprise and gained the freedom to seek the work and company of their own relations.' In Formentera, however, the seasonal paid work of men became the principal element of household subsistence and provided the foundation on which most family agricultural units were created. The absence of the men did not allow greater freedom for women to look for residential arrangements with their relations.

III.4 The Domestic Cycle

The censuses provide a static picture of household composition at a particular time. However, it is necessary to take account of the fact that a household passes through different phases in time. It is a unit of production whose principal characteristic is its variability during the life cycle of its members.

Fortes (1958), in introducing the concept of cycle into the analysis of households, pointed out that the study of social structure had achieved a great advance by isolating and conceptualising the time factor and affirmed that the analysis of households was suitable for introducing dynamic elements into structure. The development factor is intrinsic to household organisation, and to ignore it can lead to a serious misunderstanding of data. It involves studying the household as a process (Hammel 1972) instead of as a static unit in a given period. Individuals go through various types of household composition during the course of their lives, and these domestic variations within the same family type can be obscured in the static approach to household composition. The majority of individuals can be part of stem families during their life cycle without this necessarily being reflected in the list of habitants (Wrigley 1977: 73). The presence of a high percentage of nuclear families in a given moment does not necessarily mean that the type of domestic cycle is nuclear. It is important to follow individuals through their domestic cycle in order to find the dominant type of household in a society.

In the analysis of household types using censuses the proportion of extended and multiple families is rarely higher than 50 per cent. Normally in Europe it stays between 10 and 30 per cent. Societies with a social and cultural context in which we would expect families of an extended and multiple type to be relatively important rarely have more than 30 per cent of this type. Berkner (1972b) has pointed out that a frequency of twelve multiple type households out of every one hundred households of all types is sufficient to indicate the existence of stem family domestic cycles which only reach a maximum limit of development in short periods of time owing to the mortality of the older generation. As well, it has been indicated that the formation of multiple families is inhibited by demographic forces, so that an incidence of multiple groups as low as one out of twenty can indicate that it exists, if there is evidence from other sources that this type is of particular importance in a society's system of kinship relations and if this system contains types of kinship relations to which the society gives special value (Wheaton 1975: 611).

Various explanations have been given for the low proportion of extended and multiple household types (Berkner 1972, 1975; Goody 1972; Wheaton 1975; Segalen 1977) based principally on the introduction of the concept of the developmental cycle in the analysis of household forms. Rather than having a static composition, extended families pass through different phases according to demographic, economic and cultural conditions that affect the duration of co-residence between two matrimonial units and different types of kin.

Fortes (1958) makes a generic distinction between three phases in the evolution of a household: extension, dispersion and replacement. Following this scheme, we can make a hypothetical characterisation of extended families through different phases of

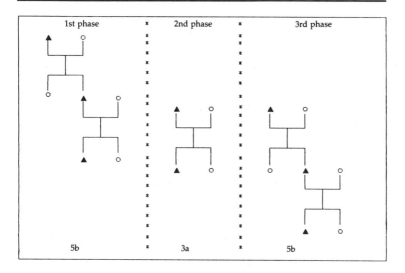

Figure III.2 Developmental cycle in multiple households

development. In the first place an extended or multiple household is formed when a married son or daughter remains in the paternal house; this conjugal nucleus reproduces, the co-resident parents die and a household of an elementary type is formed; then a new extended or multiple household is formed when one of their children marries and lives in the same house as the parents (see Figure III.2).

III.4.a. Household Composition and Age of Ego

One way of controlling the phases of the domestic developmental cycle is to distribute residential types according to the age of Ego. An age distribution of this kind provides a precise image of the temporal aspect of household reproduction and allows us to consider the global results according to which the proportion of conjugal household types is higher than the proportion of extended and multiple types, insofar as this is evident in the different phases of the domestic cycle.

We have distributed the types of household with conjugal, extended or multiple family according to the age of Ego as it appears in the census lists of 1925, 1930, 1940 and 1955 (Tables III.9, III.10, III.11, III.12) in intervals of ten years, from less than 25 up to more than 65. As previously indicated, we always

Table III.9   Household composition according to the age of Ego
Year: 1925

	≤ 25	26–35	36–45	46–55	56–65	66 ≥
Nuclear						
(a & b)	6	46	51	72	60	35
Extended	5	31	20	34	14	5
Multiple	14	30	23	8	–	–

Table III.10   Household composition according to the age of Ego
Year: 1930

	≤ 25	26–35	36–45	46–55	56–65	66 ≥
Nuclear						
(a & b)	10	52	55	66	72	50
Extended	3	30	34	24	21	5
Multiple	7	26	24	7	–	–

consider the Ego of a multiple group to be the male who forms the youngest conjugal nucleus and the Ego of an extended group to be the individual who forms the conjugal nucleus. If we take into account the convention we have established concerning the age of Ego, the proportions between households of a conjugal, multiple and extended type during the initial age of formation of the conjugal nucleus (in our case up to 35 years) can reveal the relative importance of domestic cycles with a growth limit of an extended or multiple type in the totality of households.

In all the lists studied (1925, 1930, 1940 and 1955), if we limit the age of Ego to 35 years, the proportion of extended and multiple households exceeds the proportion of groups of a simple type: in 1925, 39 per cent were conjugal families and 61 per cent extended and multiple; in 1930, 48 per cent were conjugal and 52 per cent multiple and extended; in 1940, 40 per cent were conjugal and 60 per cent multiple and extended; in 1955, 48 per cent were conjugal and 52 per cent extended and multiple. This proportion corresponds to the first phase of household extension when a son and daughter marries and continues living in the house.

Considering the age interval of Ego between 36 and 45, there

Table III.11   Household composition according to the age of Ego
Year: 1940

	≤ 25	26–35	36–45	46–55	56–65	66 ≥
Nuclear (a & b)	2	36	67	63	58	51
Extended	6	31	44	31	26	18
Multiple	1	19	17	6	–	–

Table III.12   Household composition according to the age of Ego
Year: 1955

	≤ 25	26–35	36–45	46–55	56–65	66 ≥
Nuclear (a & b)	9	58	80	77	51	48
Extended	2	24	44	39	12	9
Multiple	4	41	17	6	–	–

was a slight rise in the proportion of conjugal type families in
relation to the extended and multiple type: in the lists of 1925, 54
per cent against 46 per cent; 1940, 52 per cent against 48 per cent;
and 1955, 57 per cent against 43 per cent; with the exception of
1930 which maintained a slightly higher proportion of the extended and multiple type in relation to the simple type, 51 per
cent against 49 per cent.

From 46 onwards in the age of Ego, the proportion of households with a conjugal type family is clearly higher than the
extended type: in 1925, 73 per cent were simple and 27 per cent
extended and multiple; in 1930, 77 per cent were simple and 23
per cent extended and multiple; in 1940, 68 per cent were simple
and 32 per cent extended and multiple; and in 1955, 72 per cent
were simple and 28 per cent extended and multiple.

From 56 onwards in the age of Ego, groups of a multiple type
disappear in the four censuses studied, while the extended
groups dominate. This corresponds to the fact that the secondary units of multiple groups are lineal as opposed to collateral,
as well as to the importance of collateral extension to conjugal
nuclei of single siblings who continue living in the house.

The lack of consistency in the proportion of households of a
multiple and extended type should be emphasised. Up to 25 in
the age of Ego, the proportion of multiple types exceeded the

Table III.13   Developmental cycle of multiple households

Year	Cycle no.					
	1	2	3	4	5	6
1925	5a*	5b	5b	5b	5b	5b
1930	5a	5b	5b	5b	5b	5b
1940	5a	4c	5a	5b	4c	4c
1945	3b	4b	5a	4c	3b	4b
1955	5b	5b	5b	4b	3c	3b

* The nomenclature is derived from Table III.3

extended type in the lists of 1925, 1930 and 1955, while in 1940 the proportion of extended types was higher. In contrast, between 26 and 35 in the age of Ego, the proportion of extended types exceeded the multiple type, except in 1955. Between 36 and 45 in the age of Ego, the proportion of extended types was higher than the multiple type in all the lists except in 1925. From 46 onwards in the age of Ego, there were always more extended types than multiple types, until these disappeared. This discord in the proportions of extended and multiple household types indicates that not all households necessarily followed a homogeneous developmental cycle and that, often, the appearance of multiple and extended groups was due to temporary adaptations in family needs rather than to the result of the extension phase of the domestic cycle.

III.4.b. Phases in the Domestic Cycle

As a concrete illustration of the variability of households within extended and multiple type families depending on the phases of the development cycle, we have chosen a series of examples of multiple type groups at the start of the cycle and followed them over a period of 30 years (1925–55), indicating the type of residential group to which they correspond in each chronological interval (Table III.13). The groups chosen started their domestic cycle in 1925 and finished in 1955. This period of thirty years is the time required for these families to reproduce, taking into account that the average age of marriage in the period between 1950 and 1959 (the end of the chosen cycle) was 29.32 for men and 24.4 for women (Bertranpetit 1981: 211).

Cycle 1 began in 1925 with a phase of a multiple type (5a). The

1925–1940

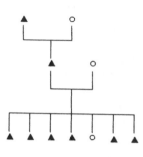

Household: 5a
Ego's profession: farm worker
Ego's father's profession: farm worker

1945

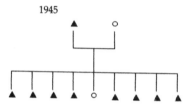

Household: 3b
Ego's profession: farm worker

1955

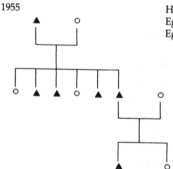

Household: 5b
Ego's profession: farm worker
Ego's father's profession: farm worker

Figure III.3 Cycle 1

difference of age between the father and the child was 29 years. The household continued to develop and maintained the same type of multiple family until 1940, then in 1945 it changed to a conjugal type (3b) and ten years later converted into a multiple lineal and collateral type (5b).

Cycle 2 started with a multiple phase (5b) and in 1940 was reduced to an extended lineal and collateral phase (4c). In 1945 the lineal kin of the older generation disappeared causing the household to change to an extended collateral type (4b), and in 1955 a new cycle began with the marriage of one of the children which transformed the household into a multiple lineal and collateral type (5b).

In Cycle 3 the multiple type remained throughout the developmental cycle only varying with the presence of collaterals. In this case the household reproduced through a daughter, and the difference of age between the two members of the two generations was 26 years, whereas in the preceding examples it was 30 years. We should also point out the long life of the older generation which permitted the existence of a multiple group of three generations in 1955.

Cycle 4 started out in multiple form in 1925 with the presence of collateral kin (5b). After 20 years it converted into an extended and collateral type (4c) and in 1955 was an extended collateral type (4b), later to become a multiple type with the presence of collateral relations in 1960 (5b).

In these domestic cycles used to illustrate the phases through which a family group passes, it is necessary to take into account that the conjugal phase (3b) only appears in one of the cases, and the phases with less temporal depth are those which last for less time. An aspect that should also be considered is the presence of single siblings resident in the house, which makes the cycle in the phase of contraction an extended collateral type (4b). On the other hand, the homogeneity in the type of cycle of these families is due to the fact that all of them form part of the class of farm owners. They adhere to the principle of patrimonial indivisibility and the continuity of the patrimonial line. However, this type of homogeneity in the developmental cycle cannot necessarily be generalised to describe all the households of Formentera. The conditions of social reproduction vary according to the class to which households belong, and the family development cycles which households follow have different degrees of extension and complexity. This raises the question of whether all the multiple groups in the years under examination participated in the same type of domestic organisation and whether identity in relation to morphology implies identity in relation to functional structure.

A look at the course of domestic cycles starting as multiple in

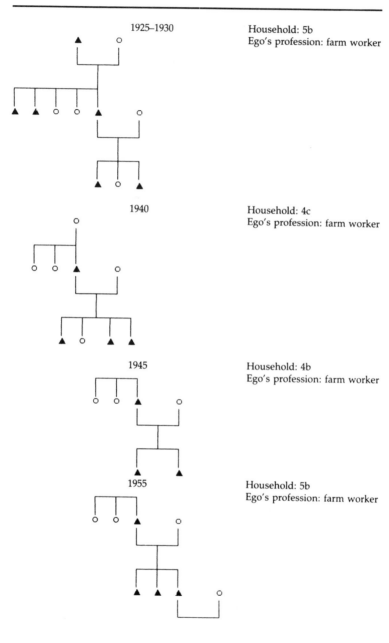

1925–1930

Household: 5b
Ego's profession: farm worker

1940

Household: 4c
Ego's profession: farm worker

1945

Household: 4b
Ego's profession: farm worker

1955

Household: 5b
Ego's profession: farm worker

Figure III.4 Cycle 2

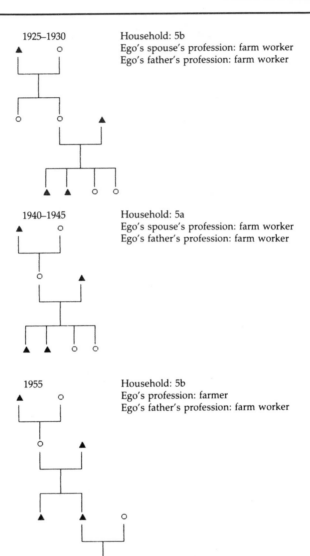

1925–1930   Household: 5b
Ego's spouse's profession: farm worker
Ego's father's profession: farm worker

1940–1945   Household: 5a
Ego's spouse's profession: farm worker
Ego's father's profession: farm worker

1955   Household: 5b
Ego's profession: farmer
Ego's father's profession: farm worker

Figure III.5   Cycle 3

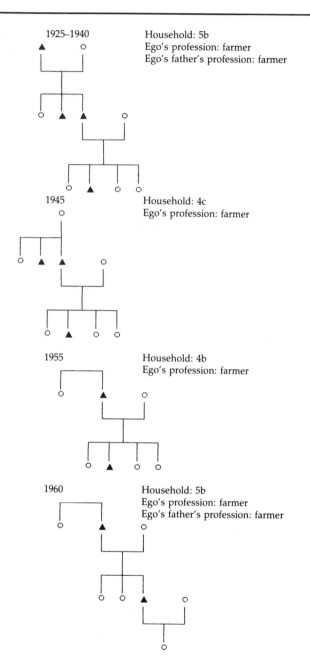

1925–1940
Household: 5b
Ego's profession: farmer
Ego's father's profession: farmer

1945
Household: 4c
Ego's profession: farmer

1955
Household: 4b
Ego's profession: farmer

1960
Household: 5b
Ego's profession: farmer
Ego's father's profession: farmer

Figure III.6   Cycle 4

1925 in families of temporary emigrant sailors shows that, instead of following the process of renewing a multiple type composition over time, households lost individuals to such an extent that their complexity disappeared and they converted into elementary type groups.

In Cycle 5 the initial phase was of a multiple type (5b), and following this in 1940 it converted into an extended lineal and collateral type (4c), later to develop into a conjugal type (3b and 3c).

Cycle 6 started with a multiple type phase (5b) with all the men of the household except the older generation described as sailors and absent. It later transformed into an extended lineal and collateral group (4c) with the men described in the same terms, until in 1955 it converted into a simple household with the men classified as farmers.

In spite of the cultural and juridical importance given to the stem domestic cycle with its maximum limit of development in families of a multiple lineal kind including the presence of single collateral relations, we cannot affirm that this cycle was experienced by the whole population of Formentera, since it was limited to land-owning farmers. There were other multiple and extended groups, principally among sailors and temporary emigrants, which were formed in a logically different way than that of patrimonial transmission and paternal house continuity. They were formed from conjunctural family needs as temporary adaptations rather than cycles maintaining residential continuity.[10]

III.4.c. *Transformations in Household Composition*

We have followed the courses of household development during a short period of five years between 1940 and 1945 in order to detect possible changes in their morphology. Our analysis focuses on all the households of a multiple, extended and conjugal type appearing in 1940 and indicates their transformations in 1945 (Table III.14).

The multiple and extended groups show a high degree of variability, whereas the conjugal groups remain constant. Half

10. This lack of homogeneity in family cycles has caused some authors (Sieder and Mitterauer 1983: 341) to speak of 'courses of family life' in preference to 'cycles of family life', since the concept of 'cycle' implies a certain regularity in the sequence of domestic phases.

1925–1930

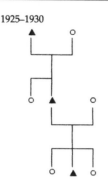

Household: 5b
Ego's profession: sailor
Ego's father's profession: sailor

1940

Household: 4c
Ego's profession: sailor

1945

Household: 3b
Ego's profession: day worker

1955

Household: 3c
Ego's son's profession: day worker

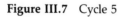

Figure III.7   Cycle 5

1925–1930

Household: 5b
Ego's profession: sailor
Ego's father's profession: sailor

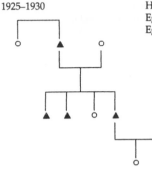

1940

Household: 4c
Ego's profession: sailor

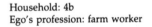

1945

Household: 4b
Ego's profession: farm worker

1955

Household: 3b
Ego's profession: farm worker

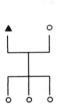

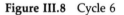

Figure III.8   Cycle 6

Table III.14 Changes in households between 1940 and 1945

1940		1945		
		1. Solitaries	5	(1.50%)
		2. No family	4	(1.25%)
3. Simple	318	3. Simple	271	(85.00%)
		4. Extended	24	(7.75%)
		5. Multiple	14	(4.50%)
		1. Solitaries	6	(5.00%)
		2. No family	1	(0.75%)
4. Extended	124	3. Simple	31	(25.00%)
		4. Extended	82	(66.00%)
		5. Multiple	4	(3.25%)
		3. Simple	12	(28.50%)
5. Multiple	42	4. Extended	8	(19.00%)
		5. Multiple	22	(52.50%)

of the multiple groups and two-thirds of the extended groups maintained the same form in contrast to four-fifths of the conjugal groups.

The greater variability of extended and multiple groups corresponds with the opinion of demographers in which the low frequency of extended families is attributed to demographic constraints and the short time of the maximum extension limit in this type of families. However, it is necessary to take into account that these demographic constraints are overdetermined by different causes of a social and cultural kind which are not necessarily homogenous and that the way they operate is the same in the formation of households. The formation of extended and multiple households in Formentera does not always present the same structural principle. They can arise from a stem domestic cycle related to patrimonial transmission or from a temporary and flexible arrangement of families of sailors, wage labourers and small landowners. This last type presents a higher variability than the former ones. Its complex composition is less durable and lacks uniformity in the developmental cycle of domestic groups.

By 1945, out of the 42 multiple households whose existence had been recorded in 1940, twelve had transformed into nuclear groups, eight into extended groups and the remaining 22 were still of a multiple type.

Amongst the twelve households that transformed into nuclear groups, there were four groups in which the conjugal nucleus separated from the youngest generation. In two the conjugal collateral nucleus was segregated (in one the conjugal nucleus of the sister and in the other the conjugal nucleus of the brother's wife). In the remaining six the conjugal nucleus disappeared from the oldest generation.

The existence of different ways of producing elementary types from multiple groups indicates that a significant part of the multiple households (in this case half) did not follow phases of development limited by demographic constraints and by the principle of maintaining patrimonial continuity represented by co-residence in the paternal house. They were, rather, forms of temporary residence maintained at the start of the marriage cycle, later to separate into independent residential units. As a whole, in multiple households that had transformed into elementary groups and did not follow the stem domestic cycle, the profession of farmer never appeared, whereas in those that followed the cycle, maintained the multiple phase or changed into extended groups, the profession of farmer or farm worker was the most common.

The multiple groups that transformed into extended groups, as well as the multiple groups that maintained the same form, present a high degree of homogeneity in the principles of their transformation and variations in their internal composition.

Out of the eight multiple groups that transformed into extended groups three were of a lineal type (5a) and converted into extended lineal groups (4a). The remaining five were of a multiple lineal type with collateral extension (5b) and transformed into extended lineal and collateral groups (4c).

The 22 multiple groups continued with the same type of internal genealogical composition. There were six multiple lineal groups (5a) in 1940 which were still the same in 1945, and there were eighteen multiple lineal groups with collateral extension (5b), out of which fourteen maintained the same genealogical composition and two became multiple collateral and lineal groups (5c).

Out of 31 extended households transformed into conjugal groups, only twenty followed the principle of order in the developmental cycle of losing the members of the oldest generation and the collaterals of Ego. The remaining groups did not follow this principle of transformation. In two households the collateral relations of the generation inferior to Ego (ZD and WZD) disappeared. In three households a new conjugal couple was formed with one of the children who remained in the house and the other young and old members of the previous extended group left. In the six remaining groups the conjugal couple of the youngest generation departed.

The four households that changed from extended to multiple were homogeneous in their principle of transformation and followed the order of the stem domestic cycle. Every one was formed with the marriage of a young member of the house who continued living with all the members of the original extended household.

In two of the six extended households that transformed into solitary groups a member of the oldest generation remained in the house. In another two a member of the intermediate generation stayed and in the remaining two a member of the oldest generation.

The household formed by kin without a conjugal nucleus was the product of the disappearance of the mother and the male children of an extended collateral group which left an uncle and his nephews living in the same house.

A series of variations in the genealogical composition is evident amongst the 82 households of an extended type which maintained the same morphology.

Out of 51 extended lineal households (4a) 50 kept the same form and only one transformed into the lineal and collateral type (4c), when one of the children married and resided in the same house and the mother of the father disappeared.

Of the 22 extended collateral households (4b), there were nineteen that maintained the same genealogical structure and three that transformed into the lineal and collateral type (4c). Two of these three were households in which one of the children married and the residence continued with the same members as in the original extended collateral group. The other transformed into a lineal and collateral group when the mother of Ego went to live in the same house.

Of the nine lineal and collateral groups (4c) only one maintained the same genealogical structure. There were five groups that transformed into extended collaterals (4b), four of which lost members of the oldest generation and a collateral relation and one in which the conjugal nucleus of the youngest generation left the house and a brother of the mother entered the group as co-resident. The remaining three converted into extended lineal groups when the collateral relations no longer lived in the same house.

The 24 conjugal families that transformed into extended groups experienced a number of different changes. One conjugal family without children (3a) converted into an extended collateral (4b) when the husband of the preceding family disappeared and the son of the mother's brother with his wife and children went to live in the house.

Three conjugal families with children (3b) became extended lineal groups (4a). In one of these, a child married, and the father and brother disappeared. In the other two, a member of the oldest generation was added to the conjugal nucleus (in one it was the wife's mother and in the other the husband's father).

Three conjugal families with children (3b) transformed into extended collateral groups (4b). In two of these a collateral relation of one of the members of the conjugal nucleus was added (in one the wife's sister, WZ, in the other the husband's sister, HZ). In the remaining family a son married and stayed in the same residence as one of his siblings, while his parents and another sibling left the house.

Three conjugal families with children (3b) became extended lineal and collateral groups (4c). In two of these a child married, the father disappeared and the mother and the siblings of the new conjugal nucleus remained. In the other family the mother and a sister of Ego went to live in the house.

Three families formed by a widow with children (3d) transformed into extended lineal and collateral groups. One was joined by the wife's mother. In the other the daughter's daughter was added. In the third the daughter married and resided with the mother and her husband.

Two families formed by a widow with children (3d) transformed into extended collaterals (4b). In one the son of the wife's widowed mother (BS) was added and in the other the wife's widowed mother disappeared, her son remained and the daughter of her mother's sister (MZD) joined her husband.

Eight families formed by a widow with children became extended lineal and collateral groups (4c). In five of them a son married and remained in the original residence. In one it was the daughter who married and continued living in the same residence. In the other two a widowed mother went to live with her son or daughter.

One family formed by a widower with children transformed into an extended lineal and collateral group (4c) when one of the children married and remained in the paternal residence.

The fourteen families of a conjugal type (3b) that developed into multiple groups, showed a higher degree of homogeneity in their transformations. There were five that transformed into multiple lineal groups (5a) when the son who lived with his parent married. In three of them the line of extension is through the woman and in the other two through the man. The remaining nine converted into multiple lineal groups with collateral extension (5b) when one of the children married and went to live with the other members of the original conjugal group. Seven of them extended through the man and two through the woman.

The five nuclear groups that transformed into solitary groups were formed on the disappearance of one of the members of the conjugal family without children (3a). The four groups of kin living together without forming a nuclear group came into existence as groups of co-resident single siblings following the disappearance of the two members of the previous conjugal nucleus or as a result of the disappearance of one of the members of a conjugal family without children and co-residence with a collateral of the youngest generation (a nephew).

From the detailed description above of the different changes in household types it is evident that the highest degree of variability in the form of transformation is found in the transition from an extended to a conjugal type, and in the opposite direction of this transformation. In contrast to this variability, we find a high degree of homogeneity in the transition from an extended to a multiple type and in the opposite direction.

It is the conjugal household type that showed the most diverse fluctuations according to social circumstances and family needs, whereas the most complex groups followed a principle of regular transformation.

The symmetry of the two forms of transformation between two contiguous types of family (Mult.↔Ext. and Ext.<=> Conj.) should be contrasted with an asymmetry in the two opposed poles marking the two limits of the conjugal household: the multiple type and the conjugal type (see Figure III.9).

The form of transformation from the conjugal to the multiple type was marked by a high degree of homogeneity, whereas in the reverse direction it showed a high degree of variability.

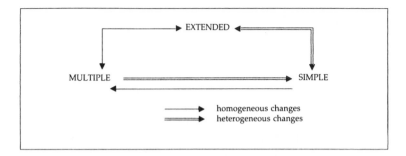

Figure III.9   Forms of change in the developmental cycle of
households

Multiple families were formed from elementary groups following the principle of expansion of the domestic cycle but did not
follow the same principle of reproduction. It should be taken
into account, however, that this homogeneity in the transformation of elementary groups into multiple groups includes a
principle of internal disorder. Amongst the fourteen elementary
groups that developed into multiple groups there was no hierarchical principle of age for children (older/younger) or sex
(masculine/feminine) governing the order of transformations. It
is just the growth of the elementary family. This would explain
the conjunctural character of the social conditions of formation
of multiple groups from elementary groups as well as their rapid
disorganisation along different routes.

The model of a single developmental cycle seems inadequate
for explaining the diversity of transformations in the households
of Formentera during these years. They did not always follow
the same principle of domestic reproduction. The house as a
kinship unit was not a regular and continuous group but rather
showed great flexibility both in its composition and in its transformations over time.

The conditions of multiple and extended family formation
were not homogeneous. Some multiple and extended forms
were temporary modes of residence – either because one of the
children married and remained in the paternal residence for a
time before forming a new elementary household or because the
extension converted into a form of helping the parents in old
age. In other cases, among land-owning farmers, extended and
multiple families could represent an element of prestige for the

head of the family and corresponded to the principle of patrimonial continuity.

During the years in which we have looked at transformations
in household composition, there were, as we have already
pointed out, important changes in social structure and in the
distribution of property in Formentera. The temporary emigrants who returned from South America created a positive
global discourse in which the house was seen as an independent
unit of domestic residence in opposition to the hierarchical
models of the old owners, who gave importance to the house as
a patrimonial unit. They valued the elementary family and
permitted the independent house to become the central point of
the kinship system. They constructed new types of houses after
their journeys to South America (see below, p. 120) as a symbol
of the formation of a new, economically viable type of domestic
organisation. These new houses became an important element
within the family system of perception. An informant's statement that 'the men went to South America to build a house'
expresses the economic and residential independence of the
new families that were formed with the resources emigration
provided. If extended or multiple families were created, they
had a temporary character that expressed a form of order of the
family economy at a certain moment instead of reflecting principles of patrimonial succession.

The new class of small landowners who gained their resources through emigration gave no importance to the institution of the single heir and undivided patrimony. The
inheritance was divided amongst the siblings, although preference was given to the brother or sister who 'looks after the
parents' in old age.

The alternatives in forming multiple and extended families
were more varied between them than among the old land-
owning farmers. Each married man tried to establish his own
independent house. If he achieved this, when his children
became adults he would try to retain some of them in the house.
They, on the contrary, would also look for a form of independent residence. When the conjugal couple had reached old age
or one of them had died, either they would have a son or
daughter, married or single, to look after them and to whom
they would leave the largest part of the small inheritance, or
they would seek to share the residence with some of the children who had formed a new household.

These different options explain the heterogeneity evident in the mode of formation of extended families, as well as the lack of any hierarchical principle in the formation of multiple families, and the fact that many of these, far from forming part of a complete cycle of household development, only had a temporary character.

IV

Ways of Living: Past and Present

La maison-structure sociale et la maison-construction se répondent l'une l'autre.

C. Lévi-Strauss

IV.1. The Domestic Space

The house as a construction, as inhabited space, bears witness to a certain type of social formation that conditions the way in which domestic relations are understood and lived. The structure of the household, its distribution of roles, its internal hierarchy and its integration in the community are reflected in the position of its rooms and in the movements and habits of the actors who are distributed and move in its space. Society inscribes its own structures, its relations of production, its social relations and its fundamental symbolism in the built space of houses. As a microcosm, the house gives a reduced image of the outside world. Domestic space is ordered and transformed by the social and cultural forces that determine the model of family life.[1]

Changes in the internal structure of households, as well as changes in the relation that these groups have with the community and with the outside world, acquire visible shape in the structure of rooms and in the way they are used by their inhabitants. Ways of living are expressed in the forms of inhabitation and changes in life style involve a series of transformations in the house of a domestic unit.

Historians as well as ethnologists[2] have pointed out that the

1. On the house as a microcosm and reduced image of the world, cf. the excellent analysis by Bourdieu (1972b) on the house in Cabila.
2. Cf. the analysis undertaken by Elias (1982: 60–90) on room structure in courtly aristocratic society contrasted with bourgeois society. Collomp (1978,

process of privatisation of the western family has been reflected in different forms of domestic space distribution that indicate new ways of defining the frontiers between the public and the private, intimate life and the life of relation, masculine space and feminine space, the space of each generation. The places where one can eat, sleep, work and relate socially are expressions of the internal dynamic of family life, of its hierarchical structure, of the values that shape its form of life and of the family mechanism that is imposed on the social whole. Their references to the habitation structure of aristocratic family life in the *ancien régime* and to the transformations undergone by the houses of peasants and workers contain the dominant idea that different spatial structures reflect different forms of organisation of family life, as if each separated space and each new habitat in the use of this space represented a transformation of the household's internal and external frontiers. These different forms of family organisation are differentiated by the redistribution of internal hierarchies and by the form of incorporation in the social fabric rather than by the size and composition of households. Such changes in domestic organisation are not evident in the information offered by census lists but appear in the different customs of families and the modes of relation between their members. Groups of similar size and composition can conceal very different forms of relation between household members and different household functions. Only if we manage to integrate domestic functions with the composition of a household's members can we speak of a given domestic structure and of the house as a social formation.

The domestic space, with its transformations and ruptures over time, is an extremely appropriate element for enquiring into the changes in the forms of family life and household functions. In studies on the transformation of the family, the old sociological model of the progressive nuclearisation of family life has prevailed, particularly amongst historians. As community life disappears and converts into a relation between abstract

---

1983: 53–80) on the forms of living and family structure in the Provençal *domus* of the eighteenth century. Zonabend (1980: 27–47) on the experience of domestic space in Minot. Du Boulay (1974: 15–40) on the structure of the house and household relations in a Greek mountain village. Segalen (1980: 43–84) on the relation between family, domestic space and community. Löfgren (1982, 1984) on the process of privatisation and the change in room structure in the Swedish middle and working classes.

subjects, the family encloses itself, and family sentiment appears while, at the same time, more divisions are created in various areas of domestic life. The transformations of the family can be presented in a simplified form as a process of self-isolation involving a series of spatial divisions, as well as the appearance of new attitudes and feelings amongst its members. Typical of the modern family is a new family feeling towards the children, new forms of activity in the private sphere and a new discipline in the family group. In short, what Elias (1978) called 'the civilizing process' in domestic customs involves a past in which, to use the words of Ariès (1973: 460), 'social density leaves no place for the family' and a present in which private life is clearly separated from public life and in which the family withdraws into itself and needs clearly differentiated spaces within a dense domestic life.

This model of family transformation inherited from classical sociology cannot be presented as a purely lineal process that leads inevitably to the privatisation of the modern family in an ever more complex world, its progressive loss of functions thus bringing it into a state of 'structural isolation' (Parsons 1943) in industrial societies. Rather, it involves the analysis, in concrete situations and limited time periods, of the complex cultural processes that lead to changes and adaptations in family life and the social fabric. In no way do we intend to present the modernisation of family life as a progressive process from a supposedly traditional situation; our aim is rather to contextualise the different processes of family life in concrete situations. From this perspective, domestic life, with changes and transformations in its internal frontiers, develops into a complex phenomenon with diverse meanings according to each situation.

In Formentera, the processes that lead to changes in domestic life and the relations each family maintains with the rest of the community can be uncovered by analysing the different house types on the island. This involves following the discourse of informants when they speak about the different types of houses they have seen and the different household forms they have lived in, analysing the organisation of family memory from the distribution of domestic space and contrasting the changes and transformations undergone by the different types of houses as well as the meanings attached to different types of family relations.

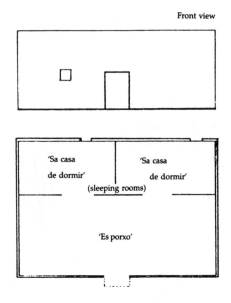

Figure IV.1   'The old houses'

IV.2. The Houses of Emigrants

When enquiring about houses, about forms of living in the past, about differences and continuities in the ways domestic relations were lived, one element that clearly defines the forms of habitation in the past stands out in what informants say: the emigration of sailors to America at the beginning of the century. This element explains the change in the typology of houses in Formentera: 'Before, there were few houses; they were small and flat.' It is an element that is used to mark a point of discontinuity with the past and is clearly expressed in the changes in rural housing introduced by the emigrants. There is a type of house that is considered to be the oldest – 'ses cases velles' ('the old houses') – belonging to the remotest past, that is associated with a form of life that impelled men to emigrate. It is a past form of living that, far from being idealised, is associated by informants with scarcity of space and density of domestic relations. 'Hi havia poques casas i érem molts a cada casa' ('There were few houses and we were many at each house'). This type of house had a rectangular ground plan with a flat roof made of clay, coal and seaweed supported on rafters of *savina* over which planks of the same wood were placed ('es Tegell'). It had only one door through which the light and air could enter during the day. The entrance of the house was protected by a branch of pine held firm by two sticks. The façade usually had a small square hole which served as a window, closed by a wooden hatch. The kitchen was normally on the outside, but if it was inside the house, it was situated to one side of the main rectangular floor. These houses were simple and adapted to the natural environment. Their construction did not require the investment of large sums of money nor the importation of materials. In order to build a house 'es reunia tot el veïnat i feien une paredada. Tallaven troncs de savina per fer el texell. Posaven algues i argella. Es trispol era de terra. Era important una bona cuina per fer-hi foc' ('the neighbours got together to make a wall. They cut trunks of *savina* in order to make the roof. They put in seaweed and clay. The floor was made of soil. It was important to have a good kitchen'). Many of these houses lacked chimneys, and the fire was made on the floor.

These houses of a parallelepiped form, with large walls and flat roofs, normally faced south and could grow around the main rectangle, 'es porxo' ('the porch'), with the addition of new parallelepipeds at the back or another floor on top. The sleeping rooms – 'ses cases de dormir' – served as bedrooms and, at the same time, were used as food stores, granaries and cellars. They were not spaces clearly differentiated as bedrooms. They had other domestic uses, just as other places in the house could be used to rest in, such as the bank of masonry situated along the inside wall of the porch or outside during hot summer nights. In Formentera, there were few houses with an extra floor; those that existed were owned by the most important landowners, and houses with only one floor predominated. Spelbrink (1936: 204) counted 14 two-storey houses and 572 houses with only one floor. This is supported by the observations of Gilbert (1845: 268): 'The inhabitants live in isolated hamlets with very small houses'; and Habsburgo Lorena (1886): 'They resemble the houses of Ibiza but are generally lower, smaller and more miserable.'

These small houses were precisely the type of domestic space from which emigrants broke away. From this moment, according to the discourse of informants, windows seem to open, space diversifies and houses multiply. In this period 'se feren moltes cases noves' ('many new houses were built'). Construction techniques changed; new materials not to be found on the island were needed, and the labour of skilled workers had to be called on. 'Una casa la feia un mestre. S'home ajudava, però es necessitava un mestre, un especialista. Per fer ses bigues i ses portes es necessitava un carpinter. Ses bigues se feien de fusta de pi de Formentera. Ses portes, de fusta que venia de fora. Sa teula venia d'Eivissa.' ('A house was made by a mason. The man of the house helped him, but it was necessary to have a mason, a professional. It was necessary for a carpenter to make the rafters and the doors. The rafters were made of wood of Formentera. The doors were made of wood that came from outside the island. The roof tile came from Ibiza.') The main difference between old and new houses pointed out by the informants is that the roof had to be obtained from outside the island. The innovation of the double-sloping roof is regarded as the most important change and the sign of transformation from a past when houses had flat coverings made from materials of the island with the unspecialised help of neighbours. In addition, the windows were much larger than in the old houses, which only had small squares cut in their façades, if they had windows at all. The new houses had two windows situated on each side of the front door, which was protected by a covering made of branches that had a less provisional character than before. To the right there was a room that served as a food store or as a bedroom for the children. They were no longer called 'ses cases de dormir' but 'quartos' ('rooms'), a name indicating that these rooms were more integrated into the house as a whole and that domestic functions were more differentiated than in the old houses. Finally, on the left was the kitchen which was clearly separated from the porch (Figure IV.2).

This new type of house built by emigrants was gradually established as a homogeneous model in the scattered habitat of the island and gave rise to an original style that was clearly different from the rural houses of Ibiza. It became an ideal and, at the same time, a criticism of the past. With all that is represented in the symbols of an epoch and in the affirmation of a social group, it gradually superseded the old house of rectangular floor and flat roof. This old structure became a sign of backwardness or a lack of resources necessary to change one's way of domestic life. Thus, new houses were sometimes erected beside the old ones, which were converted into auxiliary struc-

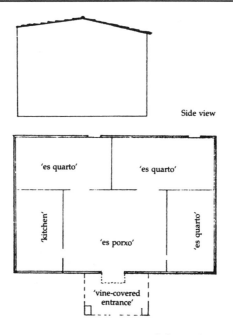

Figure IV.2 The houses of the emigrants

tures in which to keep farming tools or used as store houses. Those who inherited an old house would transform it by building a new roof, enlarging the windows, dividing its space and arranging a new kitchen. Only a few old houses were maintained as symbols of a very distant past and of these, in some cases, only ruins remain, mostly beside important two-storey houses on properties where some of the land was sold.

Each emigrant constructed a house with the profits obtained from his voyages as an expression of his capacity to control resources independently. 'Molt eren els qui anaven a America, Feien una temporada o anaven a Cuba a tombar madera, i els hi donava per fer-se una caseta.' ('There were many who went to South America for a short time, or who went to Cuba to cut wood; from this they made enough money to build a small house.') These sailors built houses on pieces of land that were either inherited or bought. 'Es varen fer la meitat de ser cases des sous que guanyaven a Cuba i per aquells llocs que anaven els homes. Se n'anaven allà, estaven dos, tres anys, lo que fos, i venien aqui amb cinc-centes o mil pessetes i feien sa casa i es casaven. Aixi hi ha haver, jo pensaria, una bona meitat de sa illa.

Era sa base per casar-se.' ('Half of the present houses were made with the money our men earned in Cuba, or in the other places they went to. They went there, they stayed for two or three years, or whatever, and they came back with five hundred or a thousand pesetas and built houses for themselves and got married. About half the island did that; that's the way they went about getting married.')

With the proliferation of new houses, the importance placed on the construction of a house by each married man gives an indication of the increasing significance of the couple at the centre of domestic life. Kinship and neighbourhood ties beyond the conjugal nucleus continued to exist, but the couple were independent, and a new family feeling developed around the new houses built by emigrants. Usually, they constructed half a house with a roof of only one slope, and after further voyages this would be enlarged into a house with a double-sloping roof. This new mode of construction prevailed as an expression of the changes that were occurring in the social and economic structure of the island, changes which prompted travellers and visitors to speak of a certain cosmopolitan air on the island in this period.[3]

These changes are not perceived, however, as part of an abrupt transformation in contrast to changes in the present. The past seems to be situated on a kind of *continuum* along which there has been a rhythm of adaptation to economic changes. In the discourse of informants, the present is a time of ruptures and radical changes. As a consequence of tourism and the economic transformations of the 1960s, the rhythms of change accelerated and introduced a new rhythm of life which was considered 'faster', since time is appreciated by its productive value. It was a fractured time in which past rhythms of family and social life disappeared and abstract relations between individuals predominated. This orientation in the memories of the informants in no way means that there was an absence of important changes in the past. The emigration of sailors rad-

3. This is described in the following terms by Chamberlin (1927: 253), who was somewhat surprised by the appearance of the people in comparison with the people of Ibiza: 'There is no doubt that the people as a whole are much better looking and much more cosmopolitan. I had expected to discover the opposite, but one need not look very far for the reason why this is so. It is the influence of travel, thus practically all the men in Formentera have been, or are, on board a ship. Every man is a sailor and every sailor knows the world.'

ically changed the distribution of land property and caused the old share-croppers and day-labourers to become small land-owning farmers.[4]

This type of temporary emigration of sailors created the possibility of the emergence of small family farms, and at the same time, it was the condition for the survival of a peasant domestic economy orientated towards family consumption, since the wages earned by the emigrants helped to maintain the households to which they belonged. The real reason why the emigrants left was not to gain new occupations in other societies but rather to improve their position in their own society. They were wage workers during part of their lives and had other means of resources in the 'subsistence' activities of the small family farms.[5]

The scattered habitat model already existing on the island intensified with the construction of new houses by emigrants who, without large amounts of capital, returned to their land and became small land-owning farmers or maintained family properties. As Bisson (1977: 151) points out, in referring to the type of settlement in Formentera, 'the profits gained as sailors has accelerated the tendency towards dispersion since each return from a voyage is accompanied by the construction of a small elementary house, isolated in the centre of a small plot on a part of the land belonging to the parents'. The voyages of the sailors enabled them to become 'pagès' and, in this way, to maintain a subsistence domestic economy. The working of the land and its cultivation to produce the household's food requirements was to become a viable alternative and, at the same time,

4. On these changes in the distribution of property and in household functions, see above, p. 85.

5. Wallerstein et al. (1982: 438–9) point out that if we consider the household as a 'common fund of income' created by the world capitalist economy, we can distinguish between the following income categories: a) salaries (in our case the earnings of sailors and emigrant workers during part of their lives); b) possessions of consumption produced from subsistence activities (agricultural work on the family property, hunting, fishing); c) income from the small-scale sale of products in the market (animals, eggs, fruit or dressmaking products); d) rent for the use of land, animals, money, etc; and e) income received without the immediate exchange of work and commodities (presents, aid). The first factor is not necessarily the main source of income during the whole cycle of households situated on the periphery of the capitalist system. The temporary emigration of sailors laid the foundations for the continuity of a 'subsistence' economy amongst peasant families in Formentera and conditioned the integration of these households into the periphery of the world capitalist system.

a family ideal. Household identity became fundamentally
'pagesa' ('peasant'), and in this sense, the houses of emigrants
symbolised a continuity with the past. Rather than marking a
radical break with the old forms of living and inhabitation, they
made household survival and perpetuation possible. The rectangular plan of the house was maintained, and the porch
continued as the centre of family life. There were changes only
in some external elements and in the functions of domestic
space which became more differentiated. The increase in this
type of house – 'Més de la meitat de las cases de Formentera es
feren en aquesta època' ('over half of the houses of Formentera
were built at that time') – and the transformations of construction techniques were a critique of the hierarchical structure of
houses in the past and an affirmation of the viability of a peasant
domestic economy.

IV.3. Continuity: The 'Porxo', Multifunctional Space

The two house types discussed above have a common element
that marks a continuity in structure: 'es porxo', a multifunctional
space where the principal relations of domestic life were established and where contact was made with the outside world. It
was a space where visitors would be received, where young
men would come to court the girls of the house, where evening
gatherings would be held with neighbours and where the wife
would spend most of her time weaving, sewing and preparing
food.[6]

It was an austere space with no decorative elements in which
each object could generate a variety of meanings, since the
functions of the 'porxo' were determined by the activities that
took place within it rather than by divisions of space. Feminine
space during the day, it converted into a space dominated by the

6. Descriptions of the porch stress its multifunctional character. Cf. Habsburgo Lorena (1886–90, 1: 40): 'The centre of domestic life and its most characteristic element for the inhabitant of Ibiza is without doubt the *multifunctional*
main living room of his house.' Spelbrink (1936: 247): 'It is "the room for
everything" and serves every domestic end. It is used as a room to work in, as a
living room, and as a place to cook and eat.' Vilá Valentí (1950: 436): 'The
fundamental part of the house is the "porxo" [. . .] In the "porxo" the daily
household life of the inhabitants of Formentera is carried on. There they eat,
there they chat with family members, there they prepare and arrange their work
and business.'

man during evening gatherings. A space where the daily domestic activities were carried out, it became the setting for the presentation of the daughters to the young men who would come during the time of 'festeig' ('courting'). Domestic space *par excellence*, the 'porxo' was the symbol of family life equally for what it concealed as for what it allowed visitors to see. Not only was it a space where daily activities were developed, but it was also converted into a space representing the value of the family. All the wealth of the house was there: its tools of work, water jars and food provisions. It was not only a closed space where the intimate life of the family developed, but was also a focal point of social communication. The main events of the family cycle were performed there. Thus, it was equally suitable for showing off a baptised child as for placing a dead family member for all close relatives to see for the last time. As a space in which to receive relatives and kin, it reinforced the sense of community between neighbouring households.

There was no differentiation of spaces, but there were strict norms of interaction between the people of a household. Differences in generation and sex provided the foundations on which norms of conduct were created. Each act was ordered according to a hierarchy, and strict norms governing relations between sexes and generations were established. Informants give an image of a past in which there was a strict observance of certain rules: respect of young people towards their elders and a strong division of sexual roles. Authoritarian fathers and the separation of women from men are two images that emerge from the past.

Respect between generations was one of the essential normative elements in the organisation of domestic conduct: 'Els fills tractaven de vós als pares. Els fills entregaven el jornal als pares.' ('Children addressed their parents with respect. Children gave their day's wage to their parents.') It is also one of the basic elements through which the abrupt change to the present is seen: 'Ara ja no és així, tot s'ha retgirat.' ('Nowadays it is not as it was before. Everything has been altered.') The distance between generations that introduced hierarchical frontiers served to organise the life of the past within the open space of the 'porxo' where there were no physical divisions. In this way – through the hierarchy of generations and attitudes of respect towards family members – what was not arranged in space could be recuperated in time. Family relations of the past were placed within the close context of the 'porxo', without producing in this shared room the kind of promiscuity that apparently caused so much scandal among observers of rural life at the beginning of the century.[7] Hierarchical relations ordered the attitudes and decisions of household members. 'Quan un home es casava i portava a viure la dona a casa dels pares, els qui regentaven la finca eren els pares. Mentres ells podien valdre's per si mateixos, mentres ells podein sortir de sa casa, mentres podein anarn eren ells els qui decidien. Per costum, perquè els homes per edat i per experiència es creien que anaven millor.' ('When a man got married and took his wife to live in his parents' house, the farm was managed by his parents. While the parents could cope on their own, do the work and get about, it was up to them to make decisions. These were our customs; we believed that older men, who had more experience, would do things better, and that young people should respect older people.')

The division between sexes appears to have been more marked in the past than in the present and is another of the essential elements explaining the changes. In the words of one forty-year-old man, 'De sa casa se'n cuida sa dona. Ens casos excepcionals s'homo pot ajudar. Ara va canviant i es reparteix més, però tota sa vida això havia estat feina de ses dones.' ('The wife takes care of the house. In exceptional cases the husband can help her. Nowadays all this is changing and the housework is more shared than it was before, but that was all the time a work of women.') The emphasis given by the mother of this man to the separation existing between husband and wife during her childhood would suggest that the ideal of a shared intimate life in the sense of the modern conjugal family did not exist in the past and that another type of family privacy was organised in which the separation of sexes played an important part.

7. Cf. Segalen (1980: 56) on the differences in attitude towards conjugal life of peasants and their bourgeois observers. The latter group could not help making negative judgements about the interior organisation of peasant houses that were so different from the ideal of the bourgeois house. Cf. Navarro (1901: 102) for a contrast of the exterior beauty of peasant houses with their interior squalor: 'The houses of the peasants are worth much more on the outside than on the inside [. . .], they are so spotlessly white as to gladden the heart and conjure up images of welfare, peace and happiness; yet, when one approaches them and, above all, when one sees inside, the image not only disappears but turns into one of disgust. The inside of these houses could not be, in general, more untidy, dirty or uncomfortable.'

The universe of the woman was the house; her presence there was necessary for the survival of the household. She looked after the household animals (the hens, the pig and the goat), made bread, fetched water, washed the clothes, cooked the meals, weaved the wool and took care of the children. The space of the man, on the contrary, was outside the house. The man had to go out; he could not always remain in the house. He was excluded from the house in the same way that the woman was confined within it. When both of them had to go out, they would always walk separately on the way, one behind the other, as if the only place they were allowed to be seen together was the house. There was an exterior world that was typically inhabited by men, the world of agricultural work, of public life or emigration, that was opposed to the closed interior world of women represented by the house. In this opposition between outside and inside, it was as if the men always had to be seen, while the women were hidden. Even during summer nights when men could sleep outside, the women and children would remain inside. It was the young men who would go out and start organising groups along the way. 'Un sortia de casa seva, feia un 'uc', un altre el responia, d'aquesta manera s'anaven entenent els uns amb els altres i es trobaven a un lloc junts, anaven al poble, a qualque banda.' ('One would leave home, and make the special sign call; another youth would respond. In this way they communicated with each other and arranged to meet in a particular place, and then go on to the village or to some other part of the island.') At dusk a group of this kind would go to a house in which there was a single woman to establish a mock relation with the house, as if through the solidarity of the male group they were trying to break the protection given to the young women by the domestic domain.

The presence of a man outside his house always indicated a clear relation and intention, whereas the presence of a woman always appeared obscure as if it could not be seen or contained various meanings. In this sense, the masculine and the feminine were opposed as the visible and the invisible, the clear and the dark, the exterior and the interior. The work of the man was public, whereas the work of the woman was concealed within the house. Relations between men were always seen, whereas relations between women were protected within the domestic domain.

In a community where everyone knew each other, women,

maintaining their characteristic obscurity towards strangers, made possible the existence of a family world enclosed around itself, intimate and dark in the eyes of outsiders. At the same time as they prevented the family interior being seen, they created its intimacy. They were the necessary condition for the existence of an enclosed family space protected from external influences. The boundary between the interior and the exterior, the closed space of domestic life and the open space of public life, that characterised the opposition between masculine and feminine established a domestic space that made possible the protection and representation of family life.

When the man entered the house, the domestic space assumed a different social purpose to that maintained during the day by the woman in her continual relations with neighbour women. Two types of relations of different order were exemplified. The man saw the domestic sphere as a place structured in a complex way and was limited by the need to represent the house. His relations were visible and controlled, whereas the woman carried on her relations within the context of daily domestic activities as if they could not be seen clearly and were non-existent. In this sense, women had more freedom and were able to gain more detailed information about everything that was happening. There was constant gossip between women and a continual game between secrecy and curiosity. One woman, who had lived outside the island during her childhood, stated that, 'no es poden tenir amigues' ('it is not possible to have friends') and defined friendship as the ability to tell secrets without these spreading publicly.

Between neighbouring women there was a continual flow of information that penetrated the secrets of houses. They discussed and appraised domestic events. Their gossip and conversation would show affection, hostility or irony towards the actions of others. In this way they spread and controlled a certain type of information about the family life of others which the men were incapable of obtaining. This could be clearly seen in the engagement of daughters. It is said that women married their daughters, that they had the information to evaluate the houses with eligible husbands and that they devised a subtle network of strategies to marry their daughters.

In contrast, men were situated on another level, simply being present and endorsing the results of this series of feminine decisions.

The women, due to their invisibility, their secret world and the fluidity of their communication, made possible the game between intimacy and family representation.[8] In this sense, the 'porxo', with its obscure and clear parts, its sides of shadow and sun, its interior and exterior parts, its feminine and masculine presences, was the family space *par excellence*. It was the place for daily domestic life, for intimate life and for family representation. Not only did it provide a space to live in, but it also made visible the value of the household.

The division between the sexes and the meanings associated with them shaped this double game of intimacy and representation that took place in the 'porxo'. The marked separation between the male and the female organised the self-enclosure of family life and at the same time the way it was presented to the outside world. Yet, this division between the sexes eventually came to be broken by a new form of family privacy. The domestic space was reorganised; new divisions were created, and the 'porxo' lost the multifunctional character it had had in the past as a daily space and a space of representation. Its meaning drained away as it was filled with new objects. Families organised a new relation with the outside world, and family time broke its link with social time.

IV.4. The Break in the Present: Family Time and Social Time

When questioned about modes of family life and forms of living, the informants continually refer to the past, to 'un temps en-darrera'. Their discourse on domestic life is organised through the recollection of a coherent and ordered past that always remained the same and its contrast with a present in continual disorder and change. It would seem that the radical break between 'then' and 'now' has distorted modes of domestic life to such an extent that they can only be expressed correctly by

8. The observations on the secret made by Simmel (1977, I: 378) are, I believe, relevant in this respect: 'The secret offers, so to speak, the possibility for a second world to emerge alongside the evident world and for this to be strongly influenced by it.' In this sense, women, as the condition necessary for secrecy, offer to household life a second world of intimacy, the world of the family interior that exists behind but is never completely expressed in the evident world outside family representation.

referring to the past. 'Now' is the place of evidence, of daily practice and, therefore, of the unsaid. If mentioned, it is only to deny its expression except as a refutation of the past. In the present, individual strategies predominate over the coherent norms of the past. When informants refer to inheritance, they present a normative and juridical model set in the past that breaks completely with the practices of the present, as if family conduct in the present, a time of disorder, incoherence and chance, were reconstructed from a stable, normative and ordered past.

The coherent model, of a normative type, is only presented as something of the past. This 'temps endarera' ('old times') situates us in a closed system based on custom – it is the time of tradition. However, the present is always a game of strategies, of actions that are governed by social interaction rather than customs.

We have already shown that the family has undergone a series of profound transformations during this century which are reflected in the form of inhabitation and the structure of rooms. We have observed the changes in the distribution of domestic space as well as the continuity of family life symbolised in the porch. An over-insistence on this last aspect would arise merely from following the discourse of informants, whose family memory seems to be situated in a kind of continuum that follows a rhythm of ordered adaptations until the 1960s when the change occurred and the processes of adaptation were broken. The family present then becomes a broken line lacking anchorage in the social life of the community. On the contrary, the way of living and the form of family life in the past combined the enclosure of the household with the opening of other houses, the intensity of family relations with the strength of ties between households, the intimate and separated space of the house with spaces of collective relation. In short, family time came together with social time, whereas in the present families seem isolated and have lost the homogeneity that made it possible for them to communicate with each other. In this split between family life and social life, collective relations have disappeared and the majority of communal parties, dances and festive gatherings are now only memories intermixed with re-collections of emigrants in the minds of older inhabitants. Social space has been neutralised and invaded by foreign elements, while households, having lost every possibility of expansion and relation through the language of tradition, have closed in on themselves.

In the discourse of informants about the island this duality is clearly evident. On the one hand, they give an image of solidarity and cohesion in the island – 'Tots som iguals' ('we are all equals'), 'tots nos coneixem' ('we know each other'), 'tots som pagesos' ('we are all peasants') – and, on the other, an image of dispersion and individualism. Since 'temps endarera' the mind has been taken over by 'selfish individualism' and by 'aquesta espècie d'ambició que ens ha agafat a tots' ('this sort of ambition that dominates us'). Relational life has deteriorated. There used to be spaces of communication; there was life in the village; there were festivals; the people would meet; it was easy to establish contact with others; neighbours would share communal tools of work and help each other with farming tasks. In the present, however, there has been a dispersion of and breaking away from habits and customs. Now people stay at home, watch television, go out in their car and get bored alone.

Without doubt, this contrast between the past and the present has something to do with a nostalgic view of the past and with the creation of a world of traditions, customs and norms beyond time. The break with the past is often expressed by the older inhabitants in the sentence 'He viscut dos móns' ('I have known two worlds'). This division between two systems of antithetical values cannot be explained by nostalgia; neither is it simply a transformation from a system of traditional life to a system of modern life. We have already seen how important changes have occurred during the course of this century that have been reflected in ways of living and different forms of defining domestic space. Rather than appearing as a radical break in the family memory, however, the events of this history are perceived as transformations and adaptations of one form of life that remains 'pagesa'.

The emigration to America at the beginning of the century should be seen as supporting rather than breaking away from traditional forms of life. The return of the emigrants strengthened the culture and made possible its continuity. They became small land-owning farmers with a domestic 'subsistence' economy that would be unfeasible today in light of the radical change in situation that occurred. 'Abans havíem d'anar a l'Havana, ara tenim l'Havana aqui' ('Before, we had to go to Havana; now Havana is here'), as one women described the change.

New economic opportunities opened up on the island that broke away from the type of peasant economy oriented towards family consumption, as represented by emigrant houses.

If the work of emigrants created the conditions for gaining access to the land and for maintaining a domestic 'subsistence' economy that could yield most of the products consumed in the house, tourism has broken away radically from this situation. There has been an opening towards the outside world and, at the same time, an increase in the dependence on economic decision-making centres. The homogeneity of social structure, as well as the collective forms of social communication, has disappeared.

Economic differences have increased, and the lack of solidarity between nuclear families has intensified. Just as the break with traditional sociability has caused the withdrawal of the nuclear family into itself, social density has been fading away before the family. A new individualist family spirit has replaced the sociability of the past. Affective exchange and social communication have retreated amongst kin since they are no longer guaranteed outside the family. As traditional festivals bringing the people of the island together have disappeared, individual family ceremonies have gained importance. The most important ceremonies are those which mark the cycle of an individual within the family. Baptisms, communions and weddings are limited basically to relatives and age groups and acquire an ostentatious character in front of the guests and the rest of the community, whereas death is celebrated with more discretion amongst neighbours and the kindred circle.

The emergence of a new type of social cohesion in which formal relations (professional groups, political parties, sports clubs) predominate over informal relations (kinship, neighbourhood, clientelism) has caused traditional channels of social communication to break and an image of socially isolated families lacking communication to appear. The more social groups participate in social changes and integrate into economic forms, the more isolated and individualised and the less homogeneous they become.

With these changes in family life, a new type of house appeared, and the population became progressively more concentrated. In these new houses, situated around the two important population centres of Formentera, a diversification of spaces occurred. The kitchen acquired an autonomy of its own and became the centre of domestic life: it is the meeting place for eating, the place for daily domestic activities and also the place to receive neighbours, friends and relations on their daily visits. It has its own entrance at the back of the house and serves as a point of indirect access to the house.

The large room (which is no longer the 'porxo') has lost its role as the multifunctional space of the house and has become an unoccupied space of purely potential reception with no specific function; thus it lacks the rich interplay of functions that the 'porxo' had.[9] The main room is merely an ostentatious decoration where objects defining the life of a typical modern family have been put. As these objects filled up the 'porxo', its characteristic meanings drained away. No longer do families sleep, work, eat or receive each other in this place. The main door of the house giving access to this room is always closed (one enters by the kitchen door). It has converted into a cold space, merely a necessary object of consumption with no meaning in domestic activities. Its meaning lies simply in what it contains and not in its use.

In the same way that social interaction between families has been losing intensity and converting into an abstract relation between individuals, the main room has been transforming into a space unintegrated in the house, into which it is practically impossible to enter and live since it represents exclusively the external family models to which present-day households are trying to adapt.

It is not a comfortable refuge from the increasing rationality, neutralisation and anonimity of exterior space but a place where one finds the signs of modes of life imported from outside. An increase in the social capacity to use these signs and to handle new styles of domestic life implies an increase in use of the room as the scene of social ostentation. But, on the contrary, it remains closed practically throughout the year. These houses cease to have the homogeneity that characterised the houses of emigrants.

In these new houses the rooms clearly differentiate generations.

9. On the appearance of this empty room that is merely an abstract space of representation, cf. Zonabend (1980a: 40) who explains the introduction of bourgeois family models in peasant life. Also, cf. Löfgren (1984: 54–8) who discusses the split between the place for receiving – a space of representation – and the kitchen – a space of daily life – amongst the Swedish working class at the beginning of the century and their resistance to a more rational use of domestic space proposed by rationalist architects.

Domestic life is split into different spaces that separate the components of the household and, at the same time, modify the norms of family conduct. Both the distance between generations and the division between the sexes have changed in meaning. Children have acquired more independence from their parents, and women are no longer confined to the house or separated from the men. The whole interplay of hierarchies between generations and between the sexes that took place in the 'porxo' lacks meaning in this new room that has merely become the setting for the disintegration of domestic functions. Intimate family life and domestic representation, which were combined in the 'porxo', have been radically separated. The room is never used and only seems to symbolise the possibility of a relation that never actually takes place. The family has separated from the outside world, taking refuge in the house where this room has become a space of abstract relation as forms of community sociability have disappeared. This empty room expresses the split between the world of intimacy and the world of family representation that can no longer enter the scene of community life. The interplay between secrecy and exterior representation ceases to have meaning, becoming merely a reflection of consumption capacity.

These new houses, in so far as they symbolise a new form of life, the adaptation to new economic activities and the break from the idea of domestic self-sufficiency represented by the houses of emigrants, were to become models for others. The old houses scattered over the island were to undergo a radical transformation; the 'porxo' began to lose its uses and meanings and gradually developed into a unidimensional space of representation in which the meaning of social communication was completely lost. Its use was no longer clear as it lost its role at the centre of family life. The model of enclosed family life was imposed throughout the island. The old houses, devalued as domestic spaces, gradually became objects of speculation in response to tourist demand. Many were sold, and their inhabitants moved into new houses near urban settlements. Paradoxically, the houses they left acquired great value as objects of aesthetic consumption precisely because they have all the characteristics of what has been called the popular architecture of the Mediterranean. Thus, tourism came to define the aesthetic value of these living places, while excluding the former inhabitants who gave them full meaning.

The isolation of the family combined with the disintegration of traditional forms of relation, the split in what we have called family time and social time, has its counterweight in a specific form of affirming the collective self-identity. Another discourse unfolds that brings together what technology, modernity and the outside world would have dispersed. The adjective 'pagès' is applied positively to all the cultural products of the island and 'ser pagès' ('being a peasant'), continues to be a positive affirmation of one's values. As a result of the emigration to America, 'ser pagès' became a real possibility and the best way to run the domestic economy, whereas with the economic and social changes produced by tourism, it became an ideology affirming the collective self-identity against an encroaching outside world.

When home-grown agricultural products become hard to sell in local shops owing to competition with products from outside and when 'tothom té un tros de terra per cultivar, però ningú no pot viure de sa terra' ('everybody has a piece of land, but no one can make a living from that land'), the products cultivated by the family group are valued positively and clearly distinguished from the products of outsiders. Thus, 'ser pagès', becomes a form of collective affirmation and a way of finding a mode of social communication in response to the split with past forms of life and the invasion of foreign standards of life. In this way, the system of values maintains its stability, and there is no absolute split with the past.

The split with the past is clearly evident at the level of family discourse and the discourse of individual personal experiences, yet we can argue that, at the level of collective discourse, time is recovered. The past reappears and affirms its continuity with the present. Through the continuity of 'pagesos', tradition is affirmed.

V

Household Reproduction

V.1. The House As Social Representation

We have already pointed out the importance of the house in the system of naming and identification of the person. The house, in Formentera, can be considered as a unit through which its members are socially classified. Social relations are fundamentally perceived as relations between houses, social units that determine the character of their members and their introduction into the social structure. The universe of houses is the framework within which social relations are organised and within which the hierarchy is ordered according to the patrimony of houses, as if society were classified into houses which, in turn, structure themselves into social classes.[1]

The house is not only a building or the totality of material possessions that surround it and are related to the family name; it is also the 'symbolic capital' that each family has accumulated during the course of its social history and that is projected in the patrimonial space. It is not only the totality of goods possessed at a given time, but also the insertion of the house within the social history of the community. It is the form of its introduction in the social fabric of other neighbouring houses and the different perceptions they have about their past. The house as a social representation is a balance between the ownership of patrimonial possessions and the prestige that the family has to maintain within the community. Its continuity is guaranteed by the differentiation in each sibling group of one of the sons who becomes the heir and on marrying remains in the paternal house. 'Es casava i es quedava a casa' ('He married and re-

---

1. On the concept of the 'house' as a unit of kinship, cf. the interesting reflections by Lévi-Strauss (1983, 1984). On the importance of the house in the Catalan system of kinship, cf. Iszaevich (1979, 1981).

mained at home'). The heir 'estava casat a casa' ('was married at home').

Only one son, usually the first-born, is the successor to the house – he receives the name of the house – and inherits the most important part of the patrimony. 'Aquí en so sistema antic es fa hereu. S'hereu té la meitat i part amb s'altre.' ('Under the old system, we nominated an heir; he would inherit half, and part of the other half. It is the duty of the heir to take care of his parents and the others living in the house.') The perpetuation of the household through a universal successor and principal heir should not be considered as the exclusive result of applying the principle of unilineal transmission, as if households were lineages in the sense of groups of unilineal descent.[2] Neither primogeniture nor male-line predominance over the female line are the only vehicles for the succession of the house and the principal inheritance of patrimony. Transmission to a daughter or youngest son is not an exception to a formal rule that is traced through a single line of descent, but follows the logic of the perpetuation of the house as a social unit of kinship in which the principle of lineality inevitably unites with residence. In order to be successor and heir, it is necessary to live and work with the parents as well as share the responsibilities of the house. 'S'hereu té s'obligació de cuidar-se des pares i de sa gent que hi hagi a casa.' ('The heir has the obligation of taking care of his parents and of the people who live in the household.') In this sense transmission to a son is the definite state of shared existence rather than the result of applying a principle of unilineal descent.[3]

2. On the use anthropologists have made of the notion of lineage as a group of unilineal descent in contrast to the use historians have made of lineage as a 'house' or 'patrimonial agnatic line', cf. Goody (1983: 222–39).

3. Concerning the predominance of common life over the principle of descent in the transmission of the house inheritance, cf. Yver (1969: 39–41). When explaining the exclusion of children who are given dowries, he states: 'This exclusion cannot be explained without considering the family and its patrimony from a community angle. The term "family", in fact, mixes up two different notions. One considers the succession of generations in time and organises the transmission of patrimony from one to the other: it is, if I may use the expression, the notion of *lineage*. The other, which we can call the notion of *house* (*menage*), considers, in a given moment, the domestic community existing between members of a same home; to this community of life there corresponds a *community of possessions* and out of this comes, on the day of its dissolution, the right of the participating members to share a patrimony that is, to a certain extent, already theirs. The community notion of the house and family patrimony is more likely to cause the exclusion of the children who are given dowries,

The juridicism implicit in many concepts of inheritance causes the continuity of houses to be discussed as if these were groups of unilineal descent. The complex strategies that families resort to in order to perpetuate the house and transmit the patrimony are reduced to formal single rules when the continuity of the house is established on the principle of universal succession that maintains its name and a fundamentally bilateral inheritance.[4] One of the sons is preferred as successor to his parents in the house, and the most important part of the patrimony is passed on to him, but this heir is obliged to surrender the legitimate ('legitímas') claims of the other siblings whether they be men or women. In fact, instead of a single juridical norm of unilineal transmission, we find a flexible adaptation of family strategies, in which diverse factors enter into play, that decide who will be the successor and how the partition of patrimony is to be carried out. In each domestic cycle the succession has to be decided, and this decision is not the application of a principle of unilineal descent but rather the result of a definite state.

Since a father works mainly with one of his children, he will try to keep this son in the house, while the others gradually separate from the family community. The transmission is made in exchange for the obligations that the heir undertakes with regard to the older generation – caring for the parents forms part of the inheritance conditions – and with regard to his siblings, the payment of dowries and legitimate claims is the other condition of inheritance. Thus a gift made in 1876 by a father to his heir is made in these terms: 'Desiring to reward his son [. . .] for the services he is doing and will continue doing in the future he grants him the aforementioned property, after his death and the death of his wife [. . .]'. The father imposed on the heir the

which, on the contrary, would be disapproved by the notion of "lineage".' The same idea of sharing in the house in relation to the principle of lineal descent was used to explain primogeniture in a community of stem families in Quebec. Cf. Verdon (1973: 108): 'Primogeniture (transmission to the oldest child) is not a principle of lineal transmission; it is rather a principle that is more in accord with a definite state. Given that the father works with his oldest son/s more than with his youngest son/s, he tries to keep him or them with him.' Concerning the Japanese *ie* ('house' in the sense that we use it), Kakane (1964: 28) points out that 'it is the house, rather than ties of descent, that provides a framework of organisation within which individuals are classified.'

4. The distinction between succession and inheritance was made by Maine (1861). Cf. the use that Augustins (1982) makes of this distinction in order to classify the forms of household perpetuation in European peasant societies.

obligation 'to satisfy the legitimate claims of the donor's sister [. . .] and those of his other two sons, brothers of the donee [. . .]' (Archive of Notarial Protocols in Ibiza). The inheritance was transmitted *post mortem* so that the heir stayed under the father's authority and the real control of the patrimony was kept in the hands of the older generation until the last phase of the domestic cycle. The hierarchical relation between father and son organised domestic relations. The historical domestic universe of houses with an heir is remembered as fundamentally hierarchised and the changes that have occurred in the present are seen as a loss of the older generation's authority. Conflicts of descendance (father–son) and of affinity (mother-in-law/daughter-in-law) are characteristic of this type of domestic structure.

Rather than arising from the application of an exclusive principle of descent, the heir was the product of a definite state created by a complex family strategy that structures the sibling hierarchy in each generation. The main consideration in the practice of inheritance that assured the perpetuation of the house and the transfer of its possessions was not the rule as such but its use in the context of each domestic cycle. In marriage contracts, when a new phase in the family cycle began, the choice of a future successor was left to the discretion of the contractors. A contract of 1888 (Archive of Notarial Protocols in Ibiza), which we take as an example, established that

> the future consorts, shall make *inter vivos* gifts, reserving the usufruct during their lives of half their present and future possessions in favour of the male children of this marriage, and in the absence of male children of this or any other marriage, the same gifts shall be given to the female children of this marriage, reserving in both cases the right to choose the child they think best as heir and donee, authorising each other to verify what is to be given by the other if one of them dies before indicating it, and in the case of both dying without designating it, from that moment the heir and donee of all their possessions shall be their oldest male child or, in the absence of one, their oldest female child, but in all cases without prejudicing the right of the surviving spouse to remain usufructuary of the possessions of the deceased while widowed.

Through such juridical formulas in marriage contracts the future sibling group was ordered hierarchically according to the principle of differences in sex and the order of birth, even though the latter was subordinated to the will of the parents, while the former depended on biological chance. These two conditions were in keeping with the flexibility of cognatic descent and introduced an arbitrary element into the system of the perpetuation of the house that enabled it to function without interrupting its continuity for biological or social reasons.

Although the succession of the house was unilateral, the inheritance of the patrimony was bilateral. The other brothers had a right to part of the patrimony. The sisters received it mainly in the form of dowries when they married, and the brothers received their legitim. The means of the heir determined whether this part was paid in cash, kept in full or whether the patrimony was increased. The family strategy of succession was aimed at keeping one married son in the house, preserving the authority of the older generation and maintaining intact the land that defined the patrimony. It was intended to concentrate the property in one pair of hands and exclude the other siblings, while paying them dowries and legitims. The siblings excluded from the succession were mobile elements of the house that had to leave or remain single within it.

The married heir lived with his parents in order to carry through the succession of the house and the formation of a stem of family continuity. In this sense a relation between universal succession and the stem family could be established. This type of household perpetuation created continuity through what can be called patrimonial lines, lines of descent that are traced by following the residence and the transmission of property and that have their social expression in the family group that we call a household.[5] These patrimonial lines are a compromise between the stabilisation of some possessions identified in one single member of the sibling group and the mobility of the other siblings. Emigration and remaining single were alternatives to the formation of stem families, and through the creation of a hierarchy in each sibling group, they left an opening for the mobility of excluded male siblings, who became emigrants, and sisters, who had to seek integration into other houses through marriage.

5. We do not consider household perpetuation from the viewpoint of descent groups but rather on lines of patrimonial descent in which the patrimony and common residence are the determinant factors of succession. The relation between undivided inheritance and the stem family was the main theme of the study by Le Play (1871). On the analysis of this relation, cf. Berkner (1976).

Various authors have related the system of inheritance and succession to the rate of emigration and the number of people remaining single (Habakkuk 1955; Bourdieu 1962; Berkner and Mendels 1978). In peasant areas with a basically domestic economy, a system of indivisible inheritance and universal succession encourages high levels of permanent bachelorhood, above all among women, and high rates of emigration among men. In Formentera the number of people remaining permanently single is substantial, and the majority of these are women. In the period between 1872 and 1978, of the people over fifty years of age who died:

> the percentage of single men rose from 3.5 to 7.9 while in contrast for women it increased from 15.6 to 34.8, both unusually high levels. The selective emigration of men, many of whom never return to the island, is one of the most characteristic trends of the population studied and has had a very important regulating effect on it. One of its consequences is the existence of women who can not marry (Bertranpetit 1981: 196).

The emigration of non-inheriting brothers and a high percentage of permanently single women are two of the predominant characteristics of this type of society where the house operates as the unit of kinship.

Remaining single was an alternative that enabled the patrimony to be maintained intact since the house immediately recuperated the legitimate claims of the siblings excluded from the succession. The rights of single sisters while they stayed in the paternal house were specified in local juridical customs. When an heir was established, his obligation to give dowries to his single sisters when they married was clearly pointed out, as was the right they had to live in the family house while they were still single and did not claim part of the inheritance. This was the habitation right of single sisters[6] that was specified

6. On the customary law of habitation for single sisters, cf. Costa Ramón (1958: 31): 'Here she is respected and can live without the risk of being thrown out of her home. . . . She participates in the communal work of the farm and eats with the heir of her legitim, the favourite cousin, who is usually her god-son. On other occasions the right of habitation is conceded under the condition that the one who is favoured does not claim her legitim, but in these cases the right of maintenance, care and assistance is included, "in health and in illness", and she eats with the heir "at his table and in his company". And, lastly, the right to habitation and the right to food are put together as a substitute for the legitim.'

through the following formula: 'she is allowed to live in the paternal house while she remains single or is waiting for her legitimate claim, with the use of a room that can be shut with a key, access to the porch, kitchen and oven, and permission to eat any fruit available on the property'. If not only the residence right of the sister was specified but also the obligation that the heir had to maintain her, then another formula was used which insisted on the sister's contribution in the work force: 'letting her live in their house and company and supporting her in every way necessary, until she marries or requests her legitimate claim, assigning for her accommodation a room of the house that can be shut with a key, obliging her to work while being maintained by her brother in tasks suited to her sex'. In the same way that the dowry made possible the circulation of women in exchange for their initial deposit and assured their position in marriage, the rights over inheritance of single sisters permitted them to stay in the family house and secured their position in relation to the heir without being totally excluded. On the other hand, the capacity of the inheriting brother to give them dowries, pay their legitimate claim and maintain them in the house was an indication of the social status of the house and its capacity to take part in social interaction.

The high percentage of single people transformed the gifts from an uncle/aunt to a nephew/niece into an important element in strategies aimed at the preservation of patrimonial lines. They were gifts from collateral relations to the principal patrimonial line, like the one given in 1876 by Francisca Ferrer Verdera, a single, seventy-year-old inhabitant of San Francisco living at Cape Berberia, who gave to her nephew (BS), 'a small plot of land situated in the parish and part of the property of Can Pep den Andreu Lluquí' (Archive of Notarial Protocols in Ibiza). The same meaning was behind the gift given by Antonio Mayans Marí in 1895 to his nephew (BS) who had been named heir a year before, and the sale to this heir in 1911 of the 'legitim that corresponds to him on the farm of Can Talaiasa'. These gifts were a way of strengthening the principal patrimonial line by returning to the principal heir the possessions of immediate collateral relations distanced from the house. Spiritual kinship, in creating an individualised relation between collateral relations, played an important role in these inheritances and sometimes became the preferred vehicle for gifts. 'Si el padrí no es casava, els seus béns anaven al seu fiol. El padrí es considera

com un familiar més pròxim per assumptes d'herència. Si no hi
ha fills, fiols. El fiol és sempre un grau més de parentesc.' ('If a
godfather never got married, all his property went to his godchild. When it comes to inheritance, the godfather is the closest
relative. If there are no children, there are godchildren. The
godchild is a step closer related.')

The system of universal succession of the house, which tried
to maintain the patrimony in one pair of hands, often could not
be put into practice. The stability of houses had to confront the
constant risk of speculating with the patrimony, attracting good
dowries and placing each child in the social hierarchy according
to status. There were houses that undertook important economic activities – buying land, attracting the possessions of single
collaterals, giving dowries to the daughters and creating secondary patrimonies for the children who left the house – whereas
for other houses with domestic production mainly orientated
towards 'subsistence' activities, the payment of dowries and
legitims could become a problem of constant investment. In
such cases households were forced to ask for loans under
guarantee of the property or else sell land under the condition
that they could buy it back for the same amount, another loan
formula in which the buyer's profit was gained from the land
and the seller had to return the amount borrowed if he wanted
to recuperate that part of the farm he had sold.

The *retroventa* (selling back) contracts that we find in family
histories at the end of the nineteenth century are the cancel-
lations of loans made in exchange for the ownership of land. In
1882 Vicente Juan bought back a part of his farm, Can Pins de
Can Parra, that 'he sold to Francisco Mayans with authority to
redeem it when he so wishes'. The redemption had to be
undertaken in the month of July, 'leaving the harvest for the
buyer'. The same year the farming couple José Tur Serra and
María Escandell Suñer bought 'a portion of field land on the
farm of Can Juan Gall' that belonged to José's wife and sister
who had sold it twelve years before under the condition that
they be allowed to buy it back. At the same time they borrowed
the same quantity that the portion of land cost them 'to improve
the farm' (Archive of Notarial Protocols in Ibiza), under guarantee of the property.

The contraction of debts and the buying of land established
the capacity for social reproduction in these peasant families and
marked the structural limits in which each house was situated at

the end of the nineteenth century. Only the most important houses could maintain the principle of indivision, giving dowries to the daughters, paying the other brothers or else creating new patrimonies in secondary collateral lines, whereas others were left with the alternative of losing interest in the inheritance to non-successors or else dividing the patrimony into equal parts and consequently losing the power of the house and putting at risk the means of its survival.

The poorest households divided the property equally among the children. Thus, in 1876 one farmer living on Cap de Berberia, Vicente Ferrer Serra, 'leaves his three children Vicente, Antonio and María as equal heirs of his farm Can Vicent Sort' (Archive of Notarial Protocols in Ibiza) which 'contains the previously mentioned parts to be used as they wish'. In such cases the house ceased to be the unit of domestic production, and the patrimony that the father could transmit was so small that the line of descent through one son lost its significance. In the same way that the indivision of patrimony could be established for the houses of farmers as an economic requirement demanding the maintenance of a viable production unit, farmers with houses whose land ceased to be the principal unit of production dispersed their patrimony, and the value of their land became commercial. Instead of the father working with one of the sons, whom he would try to keep in the house, his sons worked outside, and the solidarity of the sibling group acquired more importance than patrimonial lines that placed siblings in a hierarchy according to differences in age and sex. The sons acquired greater mobility and independence from the house, and the differentiation of the whole sibling group in relation to the father could no longer be sustained. Under such circumstances patrimonial lines lost importance, at the same time as the authority of the father disappeared. In this sense we can say that a process of nuclearisation among the poorest houses existed alongside the patrimonial lines of landowners' houses. The father could leave his children a piece of land on which to build a house and thus establish an independent household on marrying. In such cases it was a sister or a group of single sisters who inherited the house from the parents.'Si els pares tenen una casa i hi ha una allota que no s'ha casat, que és fadrina, li deixen sa casa.' ('If the parents have a house, and there is a daughter who isn't married, a spinster, they leave her the house.') The process of transmission was, thus, reversed, and the continuity of the house was interrupted. On the other hand, from these divisions groups of neighbouring households emerged that were, at the same time, related, and the solidarity between siblings was expressed through the formation of houses with little land to work and that needed other subsistence activities to compensate for this scarcity of land.

Some lines of non-inheritors became 'majorals' ('farm managers') of other properties; others became wage labourers and worked in the extraction of salt or else did craft work such as weaving. Their children were more mobile than those of the landowners, and from a very early age they worked outside the house as shepherds or servants in other houses. Collaboration between siblings became more important than the division of the sibling group into the heir and successor, on the one hand, and the remaining siblings, on the other. In this way, a rather precarious domestic economy was maintained that provoked emigration on a large scale at the beginning of the century. This temporary, and sometimes permanent, emigration became a fundamental element for regulating the domestic economy and maintaining the subsistence of houses.

In Genealogy V.1 we can see how strategies of succession and inheritance maintained a house and its patrimony intact, until at the end of the nineteenth century the patrimony was divided between three siblings, the succession of the house was made through work as farm manager on another property and afterwards through the work of the brothers as sailors in South America.

In 1775 Esperanza Ribas (1) made her husband Pedro Guasch (2) owner and usufructuary master, 'maintaining my name and not marrying the heiress' Catalina (3), and leaving the other two daughters 'the value of a donkey'. This heir married Antonio Serra (4) of Can Blai in 1784 and brought the possessions inherited as the dowry. They named their son José (5) as heir, and he married Catalina Mayans Serra (6) in 1807. In the marriage contract his father handed over half of all his possessions and the mother all the possessions she had received from her mother. In this marriage contract the newly married couple named a future heir and successor to whom they would pass on two-thirds of their possessions and put at his disposal the remaining third. In 1833 the child heir of this marriage, Vicente (7), married Catalina Tur, who in the marriage contract gave her present and future possessions to one of their future sons. Ten

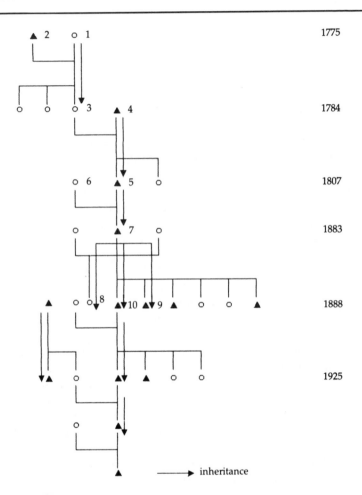

Genealogy V.1

years after this marriage his father increased his patrimony by buying the property of Can Simon from an owner of the neighbouring island of Ibiza. However, the patrimony maintained and accumulated by the father was not transmitted undivided when the son made his will in 1888. He was left as widower of his first wife with whom he had had a daughter, Catalina Serra Tur (8), and remarried Esperanza Marí Riera, with whom he had six children, José (9), Vicente (10), Catalina, María, Rita and Juan. In accordance with the marriage contract made with his first wife, he gave half of his possessions to the only daughter of that marriage (8), and the other half of what he owned was shared between two of his sons, José (9) and Vicente (10). The latter had inherited from his father the title of 'majoral' (farm manager) on a farm in the parish of San Francisco. In this way he succeeded his father and maintained the name of the house, although the patrimony was dispersed amongst three children. The heirs of the second marriage had to pay part of the legitimate rights of a brother of their father who had been left without payment when the father died, and they also had to pay part of the legitimate claim of their sister Catalina, who had not been covered by the dowry that the parents had given her on marrying. Vicente, ten years before the will of his father, had married María Ferrer Mayans, daughter of Jaime Ferrer Mayans and María Mayans Marí, sister of a principal heir and successor of Can Talaiasa in the parish of Pilar – one of the most important patrimonial lines of the island[7] – who was to be the godfather of his sister's daughter. From the point of view of the female line, this marriage with a 'majoral' and future heir of a small divided patrimony is hipogamic and clearly expresses the anisogamic chains of the non-inheriting women in principal patrimonial lines. On marrying, the wife of Vicente received from her house a dowry of five hundred pesetas in 'clothes and jewels', and afterwards she received the rest of her share of the inheritance in the form of a wood next to the main property. Thus, in this society structured hierarchically according to the wealth of each patrimony, the main lines married their daughters into less important houses, a policy of matrimonial alliance through women that permitted them to maintain relations of affinity with other houses while giving up minimal dowries and putting the households receiving their women in the position of debtors to the principal patrimonial lines.[8] The married couple

7. On Can Talaiasa Habsburgo Lorena (1886–90, II: 421) states: 'Can Talayasa is the largest and most important property and house in the Mola. It is owned by the Mayans family that also became the wealthiest and one of the most respected families of the region, a family that was, so to speak, constituted in a patriarchal fashion since it had the peculiarity that the sons of the head of the family never became independent from their paternal authority. They married and continued living in the house with their wives and offspring. The grandsons married and also stayed in the house like their parents, a practise that was continued from generation to generation. Today the family is, and has been for a number of years, made up of 22 individuals, and the head, the first-born child of Bartolomé Mayans Ferrer, who was head of the family in the period of Biot (1807–8), is 90 years old.' It should be taken into account that not all the houses of Formentera have this type of multiple structure. See above, pp. 86–8.

8. On this form of anisogamy in matrimonial alliances between houses in a

Vicente and María had five children (two men and three women) of which the two men emigrated temporarily to South America. We find one of them, Vicente, in the 1925 census list, married with four children (out of the six he eventually had during his married life), with the profession of 'sailor', absent at that time and classified as resident in the same house as his parents. Despite the lack of patrimony, the stem structure of the family was maintained, with one child succeeding his parents and carrying on the name and continuity of the house precisely as a consequence of that temporary emigration that permitted the subsistence of small landowners. However, the internal domestic structure was to be different from important patrimonial lines. The emphasis in the succession of the house was put on the 'care of the parents', and they lost authority in the domestic domain. On the other hand, the construction of new houses during this period permitted new families that resided with the older generation to be more independent. In the case that concerns us, a new house was constructed next to the old one, and here the young married couple and the old took it in turns to live up to the present day.

In Genealogy V.2, the preservation of a house established in 1845 as a collateral line of a principal patrimonial line was achieved through the permanent emigration of the male children, the permanent celibacy of the daughters and transmission to a granddaughter through a complex system of intermediate transmission between siblings. Juan Tur Juan (1) and Rita Ferrer Tur (2) married in 1882 and, following the policy of preserving the patrimony and naming a future successor, made a marriage contract that anticipated the appointment of an heir. The wife married at the age of nineteen, younger than the average age of marriage, and had nine children: five men and four women. The policy of preserving the house could not follow the line of transmission to one son, since the one that had been named as successor by the father died young and the other male siblings emigrated to South America, while the daughters remained single in the house. From 1925 to 1945 we find in the census lists the same type of household composition: a widowed mother and four single daughters. The two oldest sons died 'without leaving descendants', and the emigration of the other brothers

socially stratified structure, cf. Augustins (1977: 470) and Iszaevich (1979: 159–70).

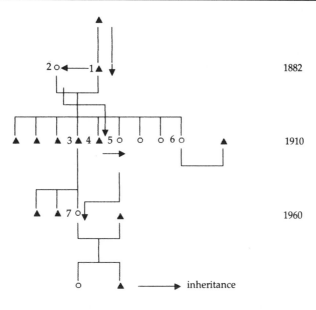

Genealogy V.2

became permanent. Only one of the brothers (3) did return from his emigration to South America, but he settled on Ibiza where he married and had three children (two sons and one daughter), the only descendants of this large sibling group which was gradually reduced by emigration, death and celibacy until the continuity of the house was put into question. The only son with descendants (3), who had settled down outside the house, was to be excluded from the succession and died before his mother made her will. When the widowed mother eventually made the will in 1950, at the age of eighty-nine, there only remained four daughters and two single, emigrant sons that 'had been absent in South America for more than thirty years', and the whereabouts of the youngest son was not known. Of the daughters one (6) had left the house against the wishes of the family to marry and live without descendants with the man who had cared for the land when all the sons had emigrated and only women remained in the house. The options of inheritance were restricted to the single son (4) that lived in South America or the single daughters that lived in the house. In the will the mother named her emigrant son as the heir. A year afterwards this brother conceded power of attorney to one of his sisters (5), so that she could accept the inheritance in his name. Despite the combined effect of emigration and celibacy, we find in the 1955 census list that the group of single sisters, all older than fifty, were still living alone in the house. Five years later the sister (5) who had received the inheritance in the name of her brother called her goddaughter (7), who had married in Formentera, to live in the house giving her the inheritance as well as the legitimate claims corresponding to the sisters living in the house. In this way, a traditional form of seeking the continuity of the house was followed by resorting to a married niece who lived with and looked after her aunts, thus forming an extended collateral residential group. Despite the identity of the residential form, however, the domestic structure of patrimonial lines of the past changed. Family decisions rested with the conjugal nucleus who, by selling some land belonging to one of the aunts, made improvements to the farming land and completely transformed the room structure of the old houses following the conception of domestic space that the emigrants had introduced when they married in Formentera. The celibacy of the women and the emigration of the men maintained the continuity of this house against the dispersion of the patrimony amongst siblings, even though this policy, that was restricted to the number of marriages, put the descendance of the house at risk. The continuity of this house was only saved, apparently at the last moment, by a complex strategy of inheritance whereby it was passed on to a group of single sisters who turned to a collateral relation, the daughter of their brother, in order to assure their descendance.

V.2. Patrimonial Lines and the Conjugal Fund

Patrimony has been one of the key elements used as a structuring principle in the analysis of marriage alliances in European peasant societies.[9] It is not so much the exchange of women but more the transmission of patrimony and the interplay between dowry and inheritance that have permitted the regularities of marriage alliance to be analysed.

The defending, enriching and transmitting of the patrimony result in unilineal descent in many complex systems and the

9. Cf. principally Bourdieu (1972a) and Lamaison (1979).

repetition of marriage alliances in other – elementary and semi-complex – kinship systems. The patrimony, considered as 'symbolic capital' (Bourdieu 1980: 191–207) that is put at stake in each marriage alliance, gives an order to the totality of particular marriage choices.

We have already stressed the importance of the house in Formentera as a social unit and as a kinship unit. The house is, at the same time, a system of identification – the name of the person is the name of the house – and a principle of social classification – the society is classified into houses and structured into social classes. It is also the unit of kinship, understood as the moral person, that carries out different marriage strategies and directs the choices of spouses between houses situated within their own sphere of matrimonial compatibility.

With the institution of an heir, the principle of unequal inheritance in the sibling group and the principle of patrimonial indivision assure the continuity of the house and result in patrimonial lines of descendance that structure the indifferentiation of cognatic descent. The patrimonial principle organises the lines of descendance of each house. And despite the undifferentiated type of descent, oral genealogies do not follow an ordered balance between the paternal side and the maternal side. The continual intertwining of the two lines seem to produce imprecision in the genealogical memory, and the diffuse range of kin made possible by the system of kinship terminology does not exist in oral genealogical narratives. One line always acquires more importance and is remembered with more precision than others. Oral genealogies have an order because they reconstruct the history of the house and follow the paths of patrimonial transmission that are governed by the principle of hierarchical asymmetry between the male and female sex and between the order of age within a sibling group.

These principles organise patrimonial lines that can be considered as units of marriage exchange ideally traced through the succession of men that carry the same name and continue the same house. They are the units that are formed on inheriting and giving each house to descendants and on entering the game of alliance.

The lines of patrimonial descendance are combined through marriage or by giving a daughter or sister, who takes a dowry with her, or by receiving a daughter or sister from another line, who also brings a dowry. Since the inheritance of the patrimony ideally maintains the continuity of the line of male descendance, the dowries of women pass back and forth between lines. In this sense the dowry can be considered as a symbolic value that becomes a mediator of marriage alliances, circulating between kinship units and assuring the principle of exchange between lines. It expresses metaphorically the transfer of the woman to another line and is an indication of matrimonial compatibility, as it symbolises the capacity that each house has to give or receive a woman. The size of a dowry indicates the hierarchical level at which a woman can be situated in the narrow marriage circuits of the island, since it condenses the symbolic elements (prestige, honour) and the economic elements (the transmission of possessions) on which the order of alliance between houses is based.

The dowry and the inheritance are not two isolated elements in the process of transmitting possessions and in the formation of marriage alliances. The dowry given to a daughter when she marries, as well as the inheritance a son receives, forms part of the diverging devolution of property which is characteristic of peasant families and is coherent with their system of bilateral kinship. Giving a woman a dowry is a way of transferring the family possessions to a daughter at the moment of marriage. Rather than all the family property remaining in the hands of a single male heir, part of it is passed on to the daughters who marry. This transmission of family possessions to daughters was made ideally in the form of movable possessions (jewels, clothes and money in cash) with the aim of conserving intact the lands of the patrimony, as is formulated in some wills of land-owning families of Formentera, when they specify that part of the inheritance of the daughter had already been handed over in full in the form of a dowry – 'to their daughter they leave the dowry that has already been handed over in the form of her legitim' – or when the daughter, on receiving the dowry, surrenders all her rights over her share of the dowry. In this case it was specified that the dowry was 'received from the parents in the form of both legitims' and the daughter renounced her rights over it. In other cases the dowry was only considered as a part of the inheritance, and the other part was received by the daughter on the death of her parents – 'to their daughter they leave the property of . . . and the dowry that has been handed over to her'.

The male inheritance and the dowry that was taken by the woman – 'so that she may more easily bear the responsibilities and honours of marriage', in the words of one marriage contract at the end of the century – provided the basis for the formation of a 'conjugal fund' (Goody et al. 1976) that determined the social reproduction of each house. The constitution of this conjugal fund was a crucial moment in the process of the couple's formation since it constituted the material and symbolic foundation that made possible the continuity of the house. It served to maintain the *status* of children in relation to other members of the community; so marriage was the fundamental mechanism for maintaining the position of the house within an economically stratified society where ties of affinity indicated the ambit of social relation in each house.

The conjugal fund created in marriage was regulated meticulously by the marriage contract – 'el espolits' according to the common juridical tradition of the Pitiusas[10] – that was normally made before the marriage ceremony. This settlement was a pact through which the family was organised. It was, as one local lawyer stated (Costa Ramón 1958: 43), 'the economic and family constitution in the majority of peasant families'.

The pacts and conditions made in marriage contracts should be put in the contexts of the matrimonial alliances of houses, the process of creating ties of affinity, and the cultural role attributed to men and women in the constitution of new conjugal units. It is not necessary to separate the purely economic aspect of the marriage contract from the structural conditions of an alliance or from the symbolic themes that govern the formation of a married couple. Marriage contracts define the nature of conjugal possessions, regulate the whole process of a family cycle and are the testimony of alliance according to which the family has to organise. As indicated by juridical tradition, marriage settlements were constituted by a series of pacts that had 'a patrimonial or economic appearance, but there is no doubt that they go beyond this, considering that their conditions not only decide the destiny of certain possessions or objects, as occurs in civil law, but also lead to the structuring of the family' (Lalinde Abadía 1965: 23). These pacts shaped the formation of the conjugal fund (betrothal gifts, dowries, 'escreix', economic rules

10. On the 'espolits', cf. Navarro (1901: 137–40), Costa Ramón (1958: 43–53) and Cerdá (n.d.). Taking into account that the structure of marriage settlements is identical to the structure in Catalonia, I have also consulted Fontanella (1916), Maspons i Anglasell (1907), Faus i Abadia Condomines (1902), Lalinde Abadia (1965) and Puig and Roca (1979).

of marriage, etc.) as well as the future continuity of the new family cycle (inheritance in favour of future children). The marriage settlements of the Pitiusas were, in the words of one observer at the beginning of the century (Navarro 1901: 137), 'a mixture of contracts' and consisted fundamentally of three parts:

1. The constitution of the dowry in favour of the future wife.
2. Gifts in favour of the future husband.
3. Conditions between the future spouses and in favour of future children.

The dowry of the woman would be established first. As indicated in a contract signed in 1884 in Formentera, the parents of the contractor's bride promised to give her a dowry: 'the consorts [. . .], as parents of the contractors and present at the writing of these documents, promise to hand over to their daughter by way of a dowry, clothes, jewels and cash to the value of 377 pesetas and 36 cents'. A quarter of this dowry was brought by the mother and three-quarters by the father of the bride.

The dowry was considered as a form of female inheritance, so it was handed over 'in payment of the legitim' that corresponded to the daughter.[11] This inheritance was, however, made in the form of movable possessions (jewels, clothes and cash) rather than landed property (lands, houses, etc.). In contrast, the productive elements of the household were transferred to the bridegroom. In the marriage settlement used as an example, the widowed mother gave the lands and the houses to the heir. In this case it was the second son because the oldest son had died: 'to the aforementioned son, reserving the usufruct during her life, she gives everything that is or may be rightfully his as a result of the intestate death of her son Manuel'.

The opposition between movable and immovable possessions that appears in the donations of marriage settlements clearly expresses the structural conditions under which a new conjugal couple was formed. The social unit of alliance was the house, which had to overcome the contradiction between continuity and family fission that every marriage involved. In this sense there is an emphasis on the unity and continuity of the house-

---

11. On the dowry as a form of inheritance and a type of divergent transmission, cf. Goody (1973a: 17; 1976).

hold, which was secured by the son through the patrimonial possessions he received, in opposition to the mobility of the woman, who moved away from the house where she was born. In the social fabric formed from marriage alliances between houses, female dowries were the mobile links that interlaced with the immobile lines of male inheritance. In opposition to the continuity of patrimonial lines represented by the man, the woman represented mobility in marriage and circulated in the same way as her dowry.

The mobility of the woman in opposition to the immobility of patrimonial lines was clearly expressed throughout the process of formation of a conjugal couple. In the 'festeig' young men in groups moved and occupied the exterior and public space of the society. In contrast, the young woman remained within her own domestic sphere and did not move from the house. In this way she symbolised the matrimonial compatibility of her family, on whom she depended for protection from the outside world. At the moment of marriage the meaning of their movements was reversed. The woman, as daughter, received the movable possessions as a symbol of the prestige of her house of origin, and the possibility of moving them away from the house enabled her to marry. The jewels that formed an important part of the dowry expressed the public value of the marriage alliance. They appeared with the future wife as an exterior sign of the movement towards another patrimonial line.[12]

The dowry defined the limits of the group of origin of a woman who ceased to belong to her domestic sphere and could no longer reclaim the share of the legitim that was rightfully hers as daughter. It symbolised, at the same time, her entrance into her husband's house and the creation of a new domestic

12. On the mobile possessions contained in the dowry, principally clothes and jewels, cf. Navarro (1901: 140): 'A woman's dowry very rarely consists of property or cash: nearly always it is made up of clothes and jewels, these being a collar with cross, reliquary or medallion more correctly called jewel, and pairs of buttons, their number depending on the wealth of the donors: buttons used to decorate the cuffs and even the sleeves of the fiancée's dress. I have never seen documents in which the rings given by the fiancé or his father to the future spouse are counted. The poorest wear a simple collar with a small cross; those with a somewhat better position wear a double turn in the necklace, which is also thicker, and maybe a small medallion. And the richest wear a necklace with three turns, the first around the neck, the second on the chest, and the third hanging further down. The cross which is large and ornate goes on the last turn, and the reliquary which is also sizeable goes on the middle one. Thus the whole chest from the neck to the waist is covered by jewels that are generally made of standard gold and do not have stones of any kind.'

space in its patrimonial line. The future husband received the dowry from his future wife, and as a daughter of the other house, she was given possessions by him as a kind of indirect dowry. This gift was considered as an increase on the dowry – the 'escreix', according to Catalan juridical tradition, to which the solicitors of the Pitiusas referred when they wrote 'they made it a rise or *increase*' ('creces'). This increase in the dowry was clearly specified in deeds because of the virginity of the future wife – 'as she is a virgin', 'in consideration of her virtue and chastity and other qualities that accompany her' – obliging the husband's house to show the household of the future wife its capacity to protect their daughter.

Regarding the ownership of the dowry, the husband had control, but the possession corresponded to the wife, so that the husband ensured the dowry with his own possessions 'which he guarantees with a sufficient part of the property that he owns as a gift from his father'. On the other hand, the husband resorted to his wife for part of the material gains of the conjugal fund constructed by the marriage: 'in the custom and practice of this island he accepts from her a quarter of all the improvements . . . with the intention that the gains acquired during this period be divided between them, of which three-quarters will be obtained by the husband and the remaining quarter by the wife' (Archive of Notarial Protocols in Ibiza).

The dowry assured the wife a private domestic space in the patrimonial line of her husband. It belonged to her and protected her from the other kinship solidarities of her husband. In opposition to the lines of descent and solidarity amongst siblings, the dowry affirmed the importance of marriage as a central kinship element. The continuity of patrimonial lines could only be achieved through the creation of a conjugal fund in which relations of affinity could not be denied in the name of consanguinity.[13]

The last part of marriage settlements concerned the regulation of the family cycle created with a new conjugal fund. The clauses on future inheritance indicated the conditions governing the reproduction of the conjugal fund newly created on the basis

13. Cf. Pitt-Rivers (1977: 116–17): 'We could describe the Mediterranean by saying that it is a region in which marriage is not decided by considerations of kinship, but the other way around. Kinship, such as it is in this region, derives from matrimonial ties that are established for reasons of love, sex, friendship and land. . . , but not in accordance with any kinship structure.'

of principles regulating the formation and continuity of what we have called patrimonial lines: the hierarchical difference between the male and female sex and the difference in the order of birth between oldest and youngest.

V.3. The Matrimonial Domain

In societies with complex systems of kinship, according to the classic definition of Lévi-Strauss (1965), the choice of marriage partner is made only from negative rules. In our society matrimonial prohibitions define a domain of kinship beyond which marriage is possible. In contrast to elementary systems in which the choice of marriage partner depends on kinship categories, alliances in complex systems are formed according to considerations external to kinship such as profession, status, social class, patrimony or 'elective affinities'. Instead of belonging to a category of kinship and, in this way, seeing the attributes of a given matrimonial domain in a positive way, the preference in societies with complex structures is for attributes that situate each individual culturally and mark the limits of the different groups composing the society.

Beyond the negative definition of marriage rules that prohibit marriage between close kin and the consequent 'turbulence' (Lévi-Strauss, 1965) of matrimonial alliances, it is possible to find certain regularities in a global perspective of the marriages of a society. Although it is not defined positively by kinship categories, the matrimonial domain is determined by categories that define the membership of an individual to a given social group. *Status*, class, political affiliation and patrimony are the attributes that define each possible marriage partner within the social category of matrimonial compatibility between individuals (Zonabend 1981: 313). All these attributes are elements marking the boundary within which matrimonial alliances, that make possible the social reproduction of certain social groups, are culturally compatible. The circulation of marriage possessions and cultural and symbolic relations carried out through marriage are enclosed within the limits of different social groups. Being a landowner, labourer, farmer or sailor defines the type of matrimonial choice that each individual can make. Each choice is determined by a specific form of matrimonial compatibility imposed by the category to which the marriage partner belongs in terms of the past and present of the family, the collective norms adhered to by the individual and his family group, and the objectives of economic and symbolic maximisation that the individual is able to pursue.

Each house where there is a possible marriage partner is defined by a series of characteristics that are economic and social (value and nature of the patrimony, professional position), cultural (family background, characteristics of the members) and demographic (age of the parents, number of siblings, arrangement of the sibling group), and these characteristics make it compatible with other houses so that a possible matrimonial alliance can be considered. Although marriages in societies with complex kinship structures follow individual and family strategies, each choice takes into consideration economic and cultural elements that lead to regularities in statistical terms. In the case of Formentera, one of the most significant characteristics is the high level of local endogamy that can not be exclusively attributed to the isolation of the island.[14] The sea, on the other hand, can be considered as a means of communication. The men of Formentera emigrated temporarily to America in their youth and, yet, returned in order to marry women of the island. Few men who returned married women from outside the island, and if they did, they lived outside the island as well. A set of social and cultural factors delimited this local endogamy. From the point of view of the informants, 'marriages with women of Formentera are always better', 'marriages with women from outside always ended badly [in separations, rows, etc.]', 'the men of Formentera have a character that only the women of Formentera can understand'. This impenetrability of the male identity for certain types of marriage, which did not necessarily apply to the female identity, clearly expresses the conditions under which the emigration of men from Formentera were carried out.

14. On the high levels of local endogamy in Formentera, cf. Bertranpetit (1981: 244–70). Amongst marriages in which at least one of the spouses is from Formentera, in 88.8 per cent of cases both spouses are from Formentera, and in the remaining 11.2 per cent the majority of the marriages have one spouse from Ibiza (7.8 per cent), the rest having one of the spouses either from another of the Balearic Islands (1.6 per cent) or from outside the Balearic Islands (1.8 per cent). It should be taken into account that the high levels of local endogamy do not necessarily reflect isolation in economic and social terms. As Löfgren (1974: 34) points out: 'A restricted area of marriage in a community should not necessarily be taken as evidence of isolation. Studies of regions with a high percentage of seasonal emigration to distant places show us areas of marriage that are as restricted as regions with a less mobile population.'

Emigrant work was the condition necessary for the survival and social reproduction of the island's families. Rather than a break away from the previous social structures of the island, it was the basis of its continuity. Emigration made possible the maintenance of the houses, the creation of new patrimonies and generated the conditions necessary for an agricultural economy of small landowners mainly orientated to family consumption. Matrimonial compatibility followed the logic of matrimonial alliances between the houses of the island, although the values according to which an individual could be introduced into and considered in the matrimonial domain changed more rapidly. A sailor, son of wage labourers, who returned successfully from one of his voyages, had more options than the heir of a wealthy household, who would hardly be able to preserve the patrimony with elderly parents and a group of single sisters to maintain. The rules of the game remained the same, although the subjects could use a wider range of elements to redefine the limits of the social groups within which a matrimonial alliance was compatible.

Although the limits defining social groups within which marriage is possible vary due to changes in property distribution caused by emigration,[15] the restrictions on matrimonial exchange imposed by the different geographical zones of the island have been maintained. Local endogamy is not only defined by the limits of the island; it is also maintained by dense circuits of matrimonial exchange inside each zone of the island. From 1872 to 1959, in nearly 76 per cent of marriages both partners belonged to the same parish (Bertranpetit 1981: 265). Each zone maintained its own particular identity and defined certain close circuits of matrimonial exchange. Young men could not cross certain limits without entering the terrain of others. It was, then, in terms of marriage, a closed world that withdrew more into itself to maintain differences and preserve its own identity. Patronymics were repeated between marriage partners and were concentrated in certain zones,[16] but a distance was

15. On the continuity and change brought about by emigration to America, see above, pp. 84–6.
16. On the concentration of patronymics in Formentera, cf. Costa Ramón (1964). In this article all the family names of the rural zone of Ibiza and Formentera listed in the 1934 census are presented. In this census Formentera is divided into four zones: San Francisco, Pi des Català, El Pilar and San Fernando. On the island as a whole there were 29 different surnames (see Appendix, p. 197).

maintained between houses that permitted matrimonial alliances to function in the dense networks of relatives and neighbours. Matrimonial circuits were drawn within narrow limits, but minimal matrimonial prohibitions were maintained at the level of kinship, as well as a certain distance at the level of neighbouring houses. Neither too close as relation or neighbour nor too foreign and removed, such was the definition in Formentera of this 'neither too close nor too removed' (Zonabend 1981; Héritier 1981: 163) that defined the two limits of the alliance domain in complex kinship structures within which each family could carry out its own marriage strategies.

Possible marriage partners could be close neighbours but not socially or spatially immediate. 'Sempre hi ha hagut una distància grossa' ('There has always been a great distance') between families. 'Es guardava aqueixa distància' ('A distance was kept') that permitted the beginning of a relation with someone different, although not a stranger. On the other hand, the possible marriage partner could belong to one's kindred, if included within the wide category of 'cousins', those distant relations that were known and could be greeted but that remained outside the area of intense social interaction of the family. Although related, they were *'little family'*. Between first cousins, relations marking the close limit of the category of 'cousin', marriage was possible, although it was valued negatively and seen as the result of unusual circumstances. They were too similar, *'too much family'*, and would have created an excessively redundant alliance with consanguine kinship. The other more distant cousins were known, but their relation of kinship did not involve intense familiarity. They were distant kin related in such a way that they were known but sufficiently distant to make them possible marriage partners. 'Entre fills de cosins es poden casar, només que tenen que demanar dispensa [. . .]. Entre cosins ja es mira més. En fills de cosins ja no es mira.' ('Between second cousins it is possible to marry; it is only necessary to ask for a dispensation . . . The marriage between first cousins was considered forbidden. Between second cousins it was not.') This view expresses the limit that differentiates what is identical, 'has the same blood', from the rest, with whom it is possible to create a new alliance. It separates those who are excessively close from those who have moved away but are still known.

This structure of the matrimonial domain that organises the

sense of each alliance gives marriage a double meaning, the two parts of which seem to be contradictory but in reality complement each other.

On the one hand, marriage as a generator of a multiplicity of ties between families has a positive meaning; it encourages solidarity. 'Aquí tots ens coneixem' ('Here we all know each other'), 'tots som parents' ('we are all relatives'), 'tots som cosins' (' we are all cousins'), 'tots venim d'alla mateix' ('all of us come from the same place'), express this capacity to strengthen the solidarity between houses, making possible an identity that goes beyond the family.

On the other hand, excessively close unions, where 'ens coneixem massa' ('we know too much') and 'són molta familia' ('we are too much family') have a negative meaning, because they are an indication of the excessive closeness of neighbours' and relations' houses. Such marriages generate a closed circuit of solidarity without 'distances', in which the 'same blood' and the same interests unite. They are excessively orientated by family will and by arrangements that are overly connected to relations. The distance and difference between families is, for this reason, valued.

From this last perspective, marriage has the sense of an opening of the individual towards the outside, whereas from the other perspective marriage has the meaning of solidarity and an organised circuit of alliances between families.

The contrast between the closed world of each house and the constant game of distancing between houses gives the individual a sense of wide open choices within the restricted space of circuits of alliance and family solidarity. It makes possible the beginning of a relation between young people of both sexes without the suffocating presence of immediate family interests. When the engagement is begun 'es procurava tenir poc roce amb ses famílies fins un cert temps' ('families managed not to be in contact between them'). In this moment the elders withdraw into the background to give way to relations between young people in which individual feeling combines with family interests, in which personal mobility becomes compatible with homogamy of status and in which, finally, it is possible to speculate with private feelings and personal interests. 'L'enteniment entre ses famílies era quan ja s'havien de casar.' ('The engagement between families was arranged when young people were about to marry.') Then the importance of family relations, the matrimonial compatibility of the house and alliance as an element of family solidarity appear.

In contrast to the image of stability and internal interrelation given by the endogamic circuits of the island, there is also the opposite image of opening and mobility given to the individual by a marriage that is not too close. This double meaning of marriage (restricted circuit and open choice) explains the often contradictory descriptions to be found in the writings of travellers and folklorists of the Pitiusas as well as in the recollections of informants from Formentera. Whereas the novelist Blasco Ibáñez (1908) spoke of the great freedom of matrimonial choice enjoyed by women due to the traditional courting customs of the Pitiusas, Macabich (1967, vol. IV: 17) presented the opposite view about courting in which choice was conditioned by the will of the parents. Both images were also given by informants when they referred to marriages of the past.

On the one hand, they affirmed that marriages were contracted for economic interest, whether it was because one of the marriage partners had a good property, or because a man had just arrived back from America, or because there was an understanding between families that induced an arranged marriage between their children. Nowadays, the endogamy on the island as a whole and the internal endogamous circuits have diminished,[17] and the interplay of hierarchies that defined matrimonial compatibility between houses has also changed. A greater homogeneity has prevailed over matrimonial areas, and there has been a break away from the local idiosyncrasies that defined different spaces on the island. The close and distant limits of the matrimonial domain have been redefined, and a new system of

17. On levels of local endogamy in the period between 1960 and 1978, cf. Bertranpetit (1981: 254, Table 7.3d). Out of 401 marriages in which at least one of the spouses was from Formentera, 274 were between inhabitants of Formentera (68.3 per cent) and 127 (31.7 per cent) were with a spouse from outside the island. The decrease in the level of internal endogamy is more significant. Whereas in the period between 1872 and 1959 a quarter of marriages were between spouses of different parishes, in the period from 1960 to 1978 the proportion of this type of marriage rose to a third of all marriages. In the case of El Pilar parish (La Mola), the contrast is more noticeable: in the period 1960–78 only 36.7 per cent of marriages were between spouses of the same parish, whereas in the period 1872–1959 this proportion had been 72.8 per cent. The degree of local endogamy in La Mola has decreased by half. This difference is perceived in the statement, 'ara és una època en què hi ha molts matrimonis amb gent de La Mola' ('now is a time in which there are many marriages with people from La Mola') and its contrast with the image of a closed circuit in the past.

matrimonial compatibility organises possible alliances. The ownership of land no longer constitutes the household principle of hierarchy; neither is it the basis for the formation of a conjugal couple. The meaning of restricted matrimonial circuits that existed in the past has been lost in the present. With the homogeneity of the present, the narrow limits of family alliance are seen as too close and redundant. The distance between houses that organised the beginning of an alliance has disappeared, and only the narrowness of this space in which marriages were carried out is now seen. The networks that marriage generated and constantly renewed between families are identified with the perpetuation of the same consanguinity. 'Abans es casaven entre cosins' ('before, everyone married cousins') is the present judgement on the capacity of the alliance to generate social cohesion in restricted, although not completely closed, areas.

On the other hand, the subtle and, at the same time, passionate game played by young people in the restricted matrimonial circuits of the past – fights for sentimental reasons and 'fuites' (elopements) are constant themes for folklorists (Macabich 1967, vol. IV; Navarro 1901) and informants – can give the opposite image of freedom in matrimonial choice. This highlights the aspect of open relation that marriage implied for each house and the burden of speculation and personal risk that it involved. The greater homogeneity of matrimonial circuits as well as the loss of distance between houses – 'Sempre es mirava que hagués un poc de distància, per tenir una certa independència. Llavors la cosa era molt diferent d'ara. Ara no importa que sigui a casa des veí, sa casa més pròxima, però en aquella època, no. Sempre es mirava que no hi hagués roce amb ses famílies. Que no es coneguessin' – contrasted with the past produces the impression that things have cooled down, that today material interest and lack of freedom dominate relations between young people.[18]

This apparently contradictory double image of marriage in the past – on the one hand open, following the risk of difference, and on the other closed, assuring the reproduction of

18. Vernier (1977: 50) describes how traditional marriage on a Greek island, related to the controlled reproduction of property, is associated with love, whereas marriage today, when the restricted limits of hierarchy that existed in the past have been broken and individual inclination has acquired an important role, is associated with cold relations and purely economic values.

the identical – is drawn from the duality in which the traditional marriages of 'houses' has been situated. While these social units were facing up to the necessity of continuing, conserving, increasing and creating a patrimony, at the same time they had to circulate the elements that defined this 'symbolic capital' (inheritances and dowries, prestige and honour). Social reproduction imposed a circulation of marriages between patrimonial lines which, in spite of being socially the same (the same *status*, the same class, the same place), were not necessarily identical (identical 'blood', identical 'house', identical 'stem'). Patrimonial lines organised their marriage strategies within this duality between the definition of equality in matrimonially compatible houses, expressed in the language of social relations between individuals (to marry because of having the same interests, having the same desires and stimulating the same passions), and the definition of the identity of each house, expressed in the language of consanguine groups (being of the same 'blood', belonging to the same 'stem', having the same 'race'). By means of the mechanism of matrimonial homogamy, each social group set the boundaries of its social reproduction and each house, affirming its identity, entered the game of alliance.

Occasionally, the nostalgia for short circuits (consanguine marriages) or the principle of protection for the patrimonial line (marriage for interest) enters these household matrimonial strategies. In such circumstances, the language of consanguine groups is confused with the language of social relations, and circuits of alliance are interpreted in terms of kinship interests (closed marriages, marriages between relations, marriages between 'cousins'). In other moments the risk and individual speculation that structurally define alliance in complex structures predominates. Then the language of social relations predominates over the language of consanguinity, and kinship interests take over the language of the society (honourable marriages, marriages between good houses).

In the same way that it has been said, almost establishing a basic principle in the anthropology of kinship, that kinship relations constitute the basic language for social and economic relations in societies with simple structures, it can also be argued, although it may appear paradoxical, that social and economic relations constitute the language of kinship relations in societies with complex structures. Between these two languages the domain of matrimonial meaning is produced in societies where the house has an important role as a social and kinship unit.

V.4. Marriages Between Consanguine Kin and the Significance of Matrimonial Prohibitions

In many ways, Formentera seems to be the perfect place for a cultural analysis of consanguine marriages and, in particular, of marriages between cousins.[19] As we have already pointed out, it is an island with a high percentage of local endogamy and with some circuits of matrimonial alliance that are even more restricted in the interior of the island. A few patronymic names are scattered around the island, and their repetition in different families has created a high level of homonymy. In short, it appears to be an island that is sufficiently closed in terms of alliance for marriage to enter the domain of consanguinity.

On the other hand, there is a local discourse in the present that gives great importance to marriage between cousins in the past. References to the solidarity of families on the island in the past and the importance of self-identity often use the language of kinship; the extent to which matrimonial alliances are merely a redundant part of this image of solidarity and identity expressed in terms of consanguinity is shown by the fact that marriage within the island is identified with marriage between consanguine relations. At the same time, the matrimonial circuits of each specific place on the island that was associated in the past with a local identity, produce in the present an image of internal circularity, impenetrability and solidarity that provokes reciprocal accusations of cousin marriages between people of different localities of the island. When a peasant of Cap de Berberia states that in the Mola all the people were cousins, he expresses in terms of consanguinity the different local identities that were in the island.

The foreigners living on the island today perceive the peasant identity of the people of Formentera in relation to the idea of a matrimonial circuit between cousins and contrast it with their

---

19. This aspect was studied from the perspective of biological anthropology in the thesis of Bertranpetit (1981). On the use of information on matrimonial dispensations by biologists, cf. Valls (1982). For a sociological analysis of information on dispensations, cf. Merzario (1981).

own cultural evaluation of marriage as a process of opening towards the outside world.

Marriage between cousins seems, on the other hand, to have been a practice that grew up in the Pitiusas which provoked interventions of control on the part of the civil and church authorities. Supported by documents from the eighteenth century, Fajarnés Tur (1929: 10), a doctor and chronicler of Ibiza, presented an image of peasant farmers in which their restricted circuits of alliance inevitably led to marriages between consanguine kin:

> They move within a reduced sphere, set on an island of small dimensions, and this double isolation, favoured by difficulties of communication, by the lack of contact between individuals, in a period of blockade and frequent wars explains the absence of crossbreeding, the influence of which on species is well known by naturalists and which leads inevitably to consanguinity.

If such an image of peasant farmers could be given in Ibiza, it could certainly be applied to Formentera, an island repopulated by peasants from Ibizia, much more restricted geographically, and more isolated and marginalised.

All this information seems to support the idea, repeatedly emphasised by anthropologists, that there exists a typical 'Mediterranean endogamy'.[20] It is considered that in the Mediterranean area the daughters or sisters are retained within their own

20. Studies on Arab marriages with parallel cousins have encouraged the analysis of marriages between cousins on the northern shores of the Mediterranean. This type of marriage has generally been associated with the bilateral inheritance of land whereby lands that were separated in the grandparent's generation are united (Mira 1974: 49). For an example that contradicts this model, although one that seems to validate it, cf. Sanmartín (1982). In this study, the absence of marriages between cousins in a fishing community of the Mediterranean is explained with reference to the intensification of community links that takes place due to marriages outside the close consanguine domain, but inside the same locality, and the presence of a system of inheritance which transmits fishing rights to the oldest grandson (1982: 675–6). It should be taken into account that 'Mediterranean endogamy' refers to complex kinship structures that have no kinship category to determine marriage. As Pitt-Rivers (1977: 243) has stated: 'Mediterranean endogamy', rather than being a rule that prohibits marriage outside certain social limits, is a preference for maintaining daughters as close to the nuclear family as incest prohibitions permit.' Marriages beyond the category of cousin may exist without contradicting the kinship system. Given that there is no category to limit marriages, we believe that it is the capacity to combine close marriages with more distant marriages, rather than endogamy, that characterises the matrimonial strategy of Mediterranean families.

Table V.1   Consanguine marriages

Years	Marriages	Degrees 2 2/3 3	Consanguine marriages up to 3 degree	Degrees 3/4 4	Consanguine marriages up to 4 degree
1872–1888	235	8 8 28	44 (18.7%)	18 53	115 (48.9%)

kinship group instead of being given to other groups since the principle of accumulation and logic of prestige, derived from a group's capacity to protect its women, prevails over the logic of reciprocity basic to elementary kinship structures. In this sense Tillion (1983: 37) could argue that 'incestuous marriage is considered to be the marriage ideal' in the Mediterranean. Marriage within a group, within one's own class and according to the logic of preserving property and prestige, inevitably leads, according to the reasoning of many anthropologists of the Mediterranean area, to the search for the most closely related woman, that is, the cousin. It would seem, therefore, that we find ourselves on a purely Mediterranean island from the point of view of marriage practices, with a cultural ideal of marriage between members of the same group which translates into a high percentage of consanguine marriages. This approach seems to be clearly supported by the information on matrimonial dispensations conceded by the church to married couples in Formentera at the end of the century. Between 1872 and 1888, the total of consanguine marriages, according to the definition given in canon law,[21] represented 48.9 per cent of all marriages on the island (see Table V.1) and the cause offered most frequently (103 out of 115 cases) for conceding dispensation was the 'smallness of the place'.

Is this, then, an island with such a restricted matrimonial domain that each family is obliged to look for allies amongst their own consanguine kin or, rather, one where kindred plays a preferential role in the organisation of the matrimonial domain?

With the data and arguments so far presented, it is difficult to answer this question or understand the rules of the game

---

21. The canon system counts degrees of consanguinity by going back to the common ancestor and following the lines of descendance only once from *ego* or *alter* without including the point of departure in the calculation. If the distance from *ego* or *alter* to the common ancestor is different, the one that is closest is

according to which the matrimonial domain of the island is organised.

We shall return to the data on matrimonial dispensation between 1872 and 1888 (Table V.1). The most noticeable feature of this period is the great difference between marriages contracted in the fourth degree of consanguinity and marriages with closer degrees of consanguinity. Out of the marriages defined as consanguine that were contracted in this period, 46 per cent were between spouses with a more distant degree of consanguinity (between sons of cousins' sons), in comparison to only 7 per cent between consanguine kin of second degree (between first cousins). If we reduce matrimonial prohibitions to the third degree, the proportion of marriages between 'cousins' with respect to the total number of marriages held on the island falls considerably (18.7 per cent). The most distant degree of consanguinity concentrates half of the marriages within prohibited degrees, which would suggest that the kinship limit defined by the church exceeded the short genealogical memory of the island's houses and harmonised these marriages. This would have involved losing a precise knowledge of the degree of consanguinity since the limit of consanguine kinship set by the church, which has varied during the course of history, was not necessarily the same as the definition given by the subjects

---

counted first (for example, first with second degree for the relation between uncle and niece). See Figure below.

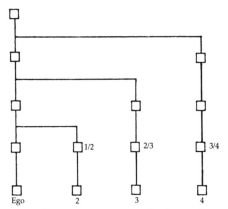

The sign □ represents masculine as well as feminine kin.

themselves who practiced the matrimonial strategies.[22]

From a formal point of view the extension of the kindred of Ego in a system of cognatic filiation can be extended *ad infinitum*. An individual, Ego, has two parents, four grandparents, eight great-grandparents, sixteen great-great-grandparents, etc. The number of ancestors increases in the proportion of 2^n, n being the number of generations that separate Ego from the ancestors in question. Assuming that each couple has a one child of each sex and that these, in turn, have another couple, and so on, and under the condition that no marriage can be carried out between consanguine kin, the number of collaterals of Ego's generation (Ego included) is the same as the number of ancestors (2^n) multiplied by the number of chains of descendants that each one of these ancestors generates (2^{n-1}), that is 2^{2n-1}. In the case of canonical prohibitions between fourth degree consanguine kin, Ego has $2^4 = 16$ ancestors, from which, continuing with the assumption made above, $2^7 = 128$ collaterals of the generation of Ego (Ego included) are descended. Between these collaterals there are $2^6 = 64$ of the male sex and $2^6 = 64$ of the female sex. If Ego then, follows the canonical rules until the fourth degree, he will have 64 collateral women of his generation included within matrimonial prohibitions. If the fifth grade of consanguinity is added, Ego will have $2^8 = 256$ collateral women, amongst whom it would be possible to marry $256 - 64 = 192$ consanguine women, even though canonical matrimonial prohibitions may be followed until the fourth grade of consanguinity. As we increase the ancestors, the collaterals of Ego multiply, and in this sense, it can be said that marriage between consanguine kin is statistically inevitable in a small population that practices a

22. In 721 the Council of Rome prohibited Christians of Roman custom (*de propia cognatione*) to marry with relatives. Kinship, as defined by Roman Law, extended to the seventh degree. Before this, in the sixth century, the area of matrimonial prohibition terminated in the fourth degree and after the Council of Toledo (653) in the sixth degree. The method of calculation was the Roman one and counted each transition in the ascendant line and the descendant line of the common ancestor separating *ego* and *alter*. Before the ninth century the church adopted the 'Germanic' method of calculation and maintained the seventh degree as the kinship limit. The adoption of this method involved, in relation to the Roman calculation, doubling the minimum number of generations that had to separate the two marriage partners if they wanted to keep to matrimonial prohibitions. This doubling of kinship degrees provoked strong tensions when the matrimonial prohibitions of the church were applied. The fourth Lateran Council (1215) reduced the number of degrees to four. Eventually, in 1915, the limit was reduced to the three.

high percentage of local endogamy. The question lies in know-
ing 'if it is consciously sought, at what level it is situated and in
what proportions it is carried out' (Héritier 1981: 147); and if
there is any category within the kindred of Ego where marriage
is favoured and in what sense kindred plays a preferential role
in the organisation of the matrimonial strategies of houses.

If we abandon the principle of progressive multiplication of
consanguinity to the point of creating an undifferentiated
population of consanguine kin, we could define the cultural
systems of kinship as mechanisms that, within this undifferentiated population, define the group of individuals who are
considered to be kin in distinction to those who are not. In this
sense, a system of kinship creates distant relatives, eliminating
consanguine kin from the kinship domain. In cognatic systems
we are faced with a problem that does not exist in unilineal
systems where a group of kin is clearly constituted through a
single line that gradually removes the ancestors from other
lines. This problem consists of defining the area of kin without
recourse to unilineality. One of the formulas for marking the
boundaries of kinship has been to measure it in terms of degrees
and to prohibit marriage within some of them. This reduces
kinship ties to a certain limit beyond which their renewal
through marriage is possible.[23]

In the kinship system of Formentera, as in other cognatic
systems, the term 'cosí' and, above all, the term 'primo', when it

---

23. This idea of consanguinity and its relation to marriage as a renewer of
dispersed ties of consanguinity is clearly expressed by St Isidor of Seville
(*Etimologías*, Book IX, 6, 29): 'Consanguinity dissolves little by little according to
the degrees of succession, until it disappears in the last degree, and kinship
ceases to exist; the law is then renewed through the marriage bond and is, in this
way, prevented from escaping.' It should be taken into account that the church
considered the positive aspect of matrimonial prohibitions: the creation of new
ties in the point of rupture of the kindred group. It portrayed matrimonial
alliance as the renewal of lost consanguine links and a form of reconstructing
kindred groups through dispersed lines. The image of cycle is present in this
conception of marriage. It is expressed in this way by St Augustine (*De Civitate
Dei*, Book XV, ch. 16) when he speaks of the 'marriage bond' as a form of
'restoring what has disappeared' in terms of consanguinity. The same image of
marriage is made by Peter Damian (*De parentelae gradibus*, in Migne, CXLV,
col. 194) when he refers to 'the bond of marriage that brings together what is
separated'. A look at the conception of 'blood' within the church can clarify the
meaning of matrimonial prohibitions, which have often been interpreted as
purely arbitrary and in opposition to the 'endogamic' tendencies of populations
under their control, without considering their positive aspects in the construction of the social fabric (cf. Du Boulay 1984).

is used in its widest sense as a classificatory term, embrace a set of collateral relations that are ordered in such a way that with them consciousness of kinship is lost. Although 'primo' can be considered as a classificatory term, we should recognise that it only unites different collateral relatives in lines parallel to Ego, in contrast to the term used in classificatory kinship systems that unite a direct line with collaterals, that is, relations. Moreover, the universe of kinship is not homogeneous as in the terminology of classificatory kinship systems. In descriptive systems there is a constant gradation in the semantic universe of kinship terms that is clearly expressed by the form in which collateral kinship is calculated in terms of degrees or by the way in which gradual distinctions are introduced into the term 'primo' through recourse to genealogy ('cosí', 'fill de cosí', 'cosí tercer', etc.). In short, in the universe of these systems there is a continual distinction between close kin at the centre of the genealogical domain and distant kin situated on the periphery. A relative who is known and recognised genealogically gradually fades to the point of becoming a relation, known but hardly recognisable through a concrete genealogy. This process continues until kinship completely disappears from the ambit in which Ego is known. In this sense, 'cousins' are situated in a very different universe of kinship, a universe in which, at a cognatic level, ties of kinship can be accurately traced. Someone who is 'cosí' or 'fill de cosí' of Ego can trace the genealogical lines that unite them. At the level of social interaction, however, the relations between brothers who have cousins are much more important than those established between cousins who, in turn, have second cousins. Social relations beyond the nuclear family begin to lose intensity until they are considered *'little family'*, although the genealogical relation is recognised. After the limit of third degree collaterals, genealogical recognition is lost, and one enters a diffuse universe of kinship, a universe in which family members are known but the genealogical relation that unites them can not be defined. They are such *'little family'* that, although they are known, they are not recognised as members of the family. They are relations who are simply 'spoken to'; they are known, but they do not have the social obligations of kinship. They are only seen at some family rituals, principally the funerals of ancestors that unite distant collateral relatives whose kinship will cease to be transmitted to future generations. Their attendance at these family rituals confirms the knowledge that they still belong to the kindred. In this way, the death of an ancestor unites those at the limit of kinship who are not going to transmit through new births. This was affirmed by one woman who considered that a man (her FFBS) she met at family funerals had to be in some way a distant relation of hers.

The disappearance of kinship with the passing of generations may be avoided by renewing it through matrimonial alliance. Beyond the delimitation of the genealogical memory of the house, the possibility exists of establishing new alliances and entering restricted circuits of reciprocity where kindreds and the linking of alliances form a dense network of relations between different houses. Matrimonial prohibitions are situated in this breaking point of kinship and not only try to deny relations of alliance, because relations of consanguinity already exist, but also to link new relations and maintain kinship relations that are dispersing, situating them through marriage at the centre of family relations. In the accounts of oral genealogy that have been collected there nearly always appears the history of some ancestors married with 'cosins', but the narrator was (or the narrators were) incapable of establishing their genealogical ties. These alliances were at the heart of a diffused kinship system where new ties that procreated were more important than ties that existed in the past. Thus kinship was reduced, lost and then renewed and maintained again through marriage.

The ambiguity of marriage between 'cousins' derives from the double universe of kinship that the term 'cousin' contains: on the one hand, a negative attitude towards marriages between close relations, relations who are genealogically recognised and socially united, as being excessively redundant because they unite what is already united; and, on the other hand, a positive attitude towards marriages within the diffuse universe of 'cousins' that are removed in kinship, but known and valued as possible marriage partners since they unite what is separated. This preference for choosing spouses in the domain of what is known and sometimes from inside the kindred explains the image of frequent 'marriages between cousins' among the peasant farmers of the past. Marriage was the principal operator of social cohesion between houses. Thus, houses thought to be separated in terms of descendance maintained social cohesion by attracting excessively distant consanguine kin towards their centre. The breaking of this matrimonial game between houses in the present has created a social void in which

Table V.2 Dispensation motives

I.	'Narrowness'	103
	'Age'	47
	'Property Preservation'	1
II.	'Poverty'	22
	'Lack of dowry'	1
	'Infamy'	15
III.	'Infamy because of elopement'	3
	'Copulation'	10
	Total dispensations	115
	(Each dispensation can allude to more than one cause.)	

the isolation of houses seems insurmountable, and an image of solidarity between families that married among themselves is projected on the past.

The church also adopted a double attitude towards marriage between consanguine kin. It was trying, on the one hand, to control an excessively familistic marriage behaviour, giving a rigid and apparently excessive general definition of kinship limits. On the other, it adopted a flexible attitude towards particular cases, conceding matrimonial dispensation.

In Table V.2 we present the reasons offered for matrimonial dispensation between consanguine kin and the number of times each one was used in the period studied. These reasons have been divided into three groups: apparently demographic motives ('restrictions of place ', *'angustia loci'*, 'advanced age of the *oratriz'*); economic reasons ('conservation of possessions', 'poverty', 'absence of dowry'); and reasons related to honour ('disgrace', 'copulation', 'disgrace due to elopement').

The motives presented in dispensation protocols and clearly codified by the church should not only be understood according to their formal and juridical appearance, but also in relation to the matrimonial compatibility of each house and the strategies to which they resorted. 'Restrictions of place' consist not so much in the quantitative absence of possible marriage partners within the island, but refers more to the preference for marrying a woman inside the kindred in response to the risk of not finding an honourable marriage outside these limits. It is not a statistical 'restriction' but rather a preference for marriage within the restricted limits of homogamy and the interplay of prestige and *status* existing between houses. The reasons for dispensation applying to women older than twenty-four represented an attempt to maintain the preference for marrying a woman within the kindred when she reached the age limit for marriage, rather than putting her honour at stake by allowing her to remain single and unprotected by the house. Reasons of an economic type ('absence of dowry', 'poverty') established the preference for circulating a woman without a dowry within the known limits of the kindred rather than outside the boundaries marking the homogamy between houses. The reasons of 'disgrace' and 'copulation' were related to the concept of honour and the preference for normalising a situation that already existed in reality.

Houses adopted a matrimonial logic that can be summed up in the following way: a marriage in the known terrain of kindred is preferable to any other type of marriage. What varied in the definition of the church was the limit of the known kinship area and the possibility for houses of combining close marriages with other more distant ones. From the third degree in canon law, families did not consider marriages between known consanguine kin as those between relations, but as marriages between 'equals', between 'distant but known houses' amongst whom knowledge of kinship was being gradually lost, and the little familiarity that had disappeared over the generations was being renewed. They were marriages inside the narrow limits of homogamy, *status* and prestige that were preferred in response to the possibility of losing the identity of the house.

V.5. Close Matrimonial Strategies

Marriages between consanguine kin form part of the global strategy of houses and should not be analysed as isolated events between families and individuals. As Bourdieu (1980: 329) points out with regard to Arab marriages:

> it is necessary to take into account, in opposition to the tradition that treats each marriage as an isolated unit, that the placement in the matrimonial market of each one of a family unit's children (that is, according to each case, sons of the same father or grandsons of the same grandfather) depends on the marriages of all the rest.

Marriages between consanguine kin are not extraordinary or exceptional occurrences in the totality of marriages or the matrimonial logic of houses. Each household introduces its children into the matrimonial market in relation to marriages in the past and others planned in the future, as well as to the possibilities that it has in each moment with respect to other houses. Both marriages within the close kinship group and those carried out at the heart of the distant kindred group form part of the game of alliances between houses in which it is possible to define the two limits of their matrimonial domain: distant marriages, beyond all knowledge of the kindred group and open to long circuits of reciprocity, and close marriages, within the recognised kindred group and with closed circuits of reciprocity. What a house cannot do, without risking the loss of its identity, is accumulate marriages that are too close in kinship terms or too removed in social terms.

With respect to the age of marriage and the internal endogamy of the island, marriages between consanguine kin follow the same norms as other marriages contracted outside the prohibited degrees of consanguinity. The average age of consanguine spouses does not vary much from the general norm in other marriages (consanguine age of women 25.34 and nonconsanguine 24.33) (Bertranpetit 1981: 442-3). Despite the fact that in 47 cases (40.8 per cent) the advanced age of the woman was presented as the reason for dispensation, the church conceded dispensations from the age of twenty-four onwards, and this was the average age of marriage in Formentera, following the late-marriage model in pre-industrial Europe (Hajnal 1965).

Neither do marriages between consanguine relations follow a different norm of internal endogamy from other marriages on the island. As Figure V.1 shows, most marriages between consanguine kin were carried out between spouses originating from the same parish (90, 78.3 per cent), with a smaller proportion between spouses of different parishes on the same island (22, 19.1 per cent) and a very low percentage of marriages in which one of the spouses was from another parish in the Balearic Islands (3, 2.6 per cent). All the parishes were interrelated through these marriages; the parishes that exchanged most spouses were Sant Francesc Xavier and Sant Ferran (14 marriages), and they established a symmetry in the direction of marriage partners. The proportion of marriages between spouses of the same parish in relation to marriages with a

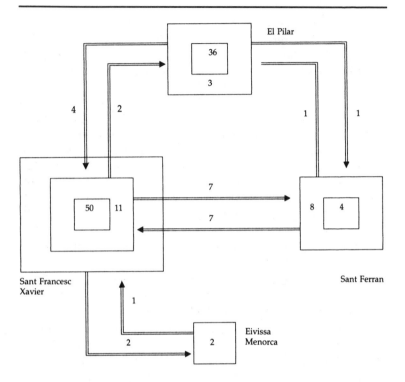

Figure V.1 Consanguine marriages up to the fourth degree in each
parish and between parishes (1872–1888)

spouse from another parish had different tendencies: while Sant
Ferran had four times more marriages (16) with one partner
from another parish than marriages with partners from the same
parish (4), El Pilar had four-and-a-half times more marriages
completely within the parish (36) than marriages with one of the
partners from another parish (8). Sant Francesc Xavier maintained an intermediate position with twice as many marriages
within the parish (50) as marriages with other parishes (20) and
three marriages outside the island.

If prohibition is reduced to the third degree in canon law
(Figure V.2), the same relation as before can be observed between marriages within the same parish (35) and marriages
between parishes (7), with only one marriage outside the island.
However, the three parishes were no longer interrelated since
marriages between El Pilar and Sant Ferran, geographically
adjacent parishes, had disappeared. Both parishes oriented

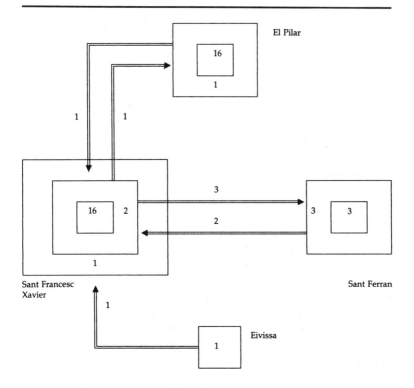

Figure V.2   Marriages up to the third degree in each parish and
between parishes (1872–1888)

their marriages towards Sant Francesc Xavier: five marriages
with Sant Ferran and two marriages with El Pilar. Sant Ferran
continued to maintain fewer marriages inside the parish (3) than
outside (5), while El Pilar concentrated its marriages, with the
exception of two, within the parish. In El Pilar a policy of
matrimonial restriction was followed, while in Sant Ferran a
matrimonial policy aimed at linking marriages already established with other parishes was developed. In Sant Fransesc
Xavier the two policies were combined.

All these aspects of consanguine marriage correspond to the
general features of marriage on the island: high levels of endogamy within the same parish; the exchange of spouses between parishes, mainly between Sant Francesc Xavier and Sant
Ferran; the relative internal isolation of El Pilar in contrast to a
higher frequency of marriages with one partner from another
parish present in Sant Ferran (Bertranpetit 1981: 265-7). Thus,

marriages between consanguine kin are not just isolated cases in the matrimonial strategies of families but form part of the matrimonial policy of concentrating the majority of marriages in the same area and establishing some alliances with the rest of the island.

Although it is possible to speak of the internal endogamy of the island, it would be inaccurate to speak of endogamy at the level of kinship units. The kindred group can even be considered as a favoured category in the search for affines of houses, yet marriage is not prohibited outside these limits. Internal endogamy, rather, represents a preference for maintaining some children with kindred boundaries, but beyond the restricted limits of the household as a patrimonial line.

Households did not accumulate marriages between excessively close kin during the development of a patrimonial line. Only seven marriages out of the 115 that requested dispensation during this period were marriages with multiple consanguinity, that is, marriages in which at least one of the partners is descended from a union within the prohibited degrees.[24] Each marriage between relations in a generation diminishes the number of collaterals of the following generation, and the closer the marriage the greater the decrease in ancestors and collaterals. If a marriage is in the second degree, the son of this marriage has two parents, four grandparents, six great-grandparents and twelve great-great-grandparents, and so on. The number of ancestors is equal to $2^n - 2^{n-g}$, n being the number of generations that separate Ego from the ancestor and g the degree of consanguinity (canonical calculation) in which the marriage of Ego's parents was consummated. If the ancestors decrease, the collaterals are also reduced. Assuming that each ancestor has a pair of children of different sexes and that these, in turn, give birth to another pair and so on, the collaterals of Ego are equal to $(2^n - 2^{n-g}) \times 2^{n-1}$. In the previous case of Ego, the son of a marriage between consanguine kin of the second degree, we obtain $(2^3 - 2) \times 2^2 = 24$ collaterals of the third degree, including Ego, instead of 32 which would have been the case if there had not been a consanguine marriage. Of the fourth degree there were $(2^4 - 2^2) \times 2^3 = 96$ collateral relations, instead of 128. The closer

24. The number of dispensations with multiple consanguinity in the period 1872–88 was: 2nd and 2nd with 3rd degree, 1; 2nd with 3rd and 3rd with 4th degree, 1; double 4th degree, 1; 3rd and double 4th, 1; 3rd and 3rd with 4th degree, 2; 3rd and 4th degree, 1. Total, 7. *Source*: Episcopal Archive of Ibiza.

the marriage of Ego's parents, the smaller the number of collaterals and, therefore, the greater the possibility of Ego marrying outside the prohibited degrees of kindred. If the same
strategy of transforming close collateral relations into affines
had been followed, the decrease in collateral relations amongst
their descendants would have been greater and patrimonial
lines would have become isolated to the point of basing their
continuity on close consanguine kin transformed into affines, a
strategy that would have prevented the creation of an extended
kindred group through affinity. Rather than relying on the
repetition of one single strategy for their social reproduction,
however, households practise the double game of open marriages and close marriages. Open marriages permit the diversification of alliances, increase collateral relations and, through
them, gain social advantages at the price of the long-term risks
involved in speculation and reciprocity. Dowries and inheritances are given to the children in exchange for attracting affines
to increase the prestige of the household. Close marriages reinforce previous relations at the price of converting close collateral relations into affines and, consequently, restricting the
kindred group with the risk of introducing affinal tensions in the
terrain of consanguinity as a result of not respecting the distance
between houses. The transformation of some uncles into
fathers-in-law or some cousins into brothers-in-law does not
necessarily mean that collaterality has neutralised the tensions
of affinity, but rather indicates the introduction of affinal de-
mands into consanguinity and the possibility of breaking the
solidarity of collateral relations.

Marriages between close relations are knots of protection
within the long circuits of the matrimonial alliance of houses
precisely because of their capacity to bring down the number of
ancestors and collateral relations. They are short circuits of
immediate reciprocity that consolidate what has already been
acquired or redefine new social units that undertake open matrimonial strategies. Closed marriages acquire special meaning
when patrimonial lines are not clearly defined or depend on
others, as is the case with marriages between non-inheritors
(marriages permitted 'due to poverty') or when a patrimonial
line is redefined or newly started. Genealogy V.3 shows a
marriage between first cousins that was carried out at the creation of a new patrimony and the redefinition of patrimonial
lines. At the level of the generation of Ego's grandparents, both

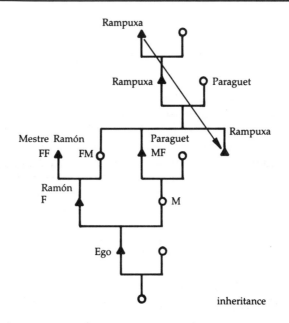

Genealogy V.3

FM and MF are siblings excluded from the inheritance. This was received by another brother (diagonal arrow in Genealogy V.3). It did not pass from father to son but from grandfather to grandson. The heir, on the other hand, lost all his patrimony, bringing to an end the patrimonial line and the house that represented it (Can Rampuxa). The two paternal grandparents (FF and FM) established a new patrimony and a new house. They worked on a property as 'majorals'; the father's father died young, and his wife bought land on which she built half a house with the money saved during this period. Their two sons worked as sailors in South America, and one of them (the father of Ego) built the other half of the house and married his matrilateral cross-cousin (the daughter of his mother's brother). A close marriage on the maternal side consolidated a patrimony started by his mother and formed a new patrimonial line after having lost the maternal line. The strategy of consolidation was directed towards maternal collateral relations that had lost the patrimony. Through a circuit of closed matrimonial exchange a new line was traced after the disappearance in the preceding generation of the other patrimonial line related by marriage to the maternal side. The two siblings (FM and MF) who became affines through the marriage of their children, although they were the same in terms of consanguinity, were clearly distinguished in the system of social denomination. Although they came from the same house, the names they received on separating from the common stem were different. The mother's father (MF) received the name of his mother (Can Paraguet), while his father's mother (FM) received the name of her father's house (Can Rampuxa) and on marrying received the name of her husband's house (Can Mestre). They received the name of the property where they worked as 'majorals' (Can Ramón), and the woman inherited this name when she built the new house and established the patrimony. From this moment her descendants were named Can Ramón as a separate patrimonial line. At first, then, we find lines that are not clearly defined, weak lines in the social game expressing the changes in name until a new name and, therefore, a new patrimonial line was established through a close marriage. These cousins, although consanguine relations, ceased to be part of the same stem, nor were they collateral relations with a common name. In terms of social classification, their parents were already separated – a distance was created that is reflected in the different name – even though none of them belonged or adhered to clearly defined lines. The marriage of their children reunited those lines that had already faded away and created, with a knot of consanguine alliance, a new clearly defined line and the possibility of entering the social interaction of long circuits of alliance.

In Genealogy V.4 we can observe a marriage between Ego and his FBDD, that is, a marriage with the daughter of his cousin, in which the married couple were related by marriage inside the second degree on the husband's side and the third degree on the wife's side according to canonical calculations. There was a generation of difference in the age of the spouses: the husband was twenty-five and the bride nineteen. Through this marriage within the close kinship group, the independent patrimonial line created by Ego's father was strengthened by attracting a collateral relation descended through the maternal route of the principal line from which the new patrimony emerged and separated. A female collateral of the principal line became an affine of the secondary line. Ego's father (Manuel) was a non-inheriting son of a clearly defined patrimonial line (Can Carlos). In 1843 his paternal grandfather gave him 'two plots of land

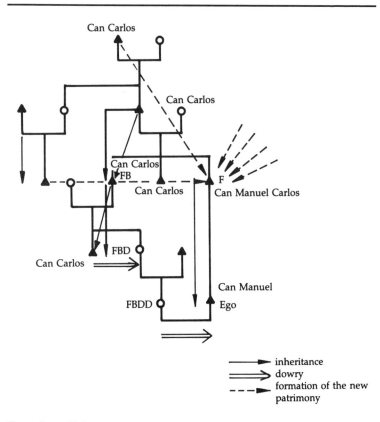

Genealogy V.4

with trees, house and cistern' situated at Cape Berberia, that he had bought a year before for 550 pesos. This gift was presented 'on the condition that he hand over to his brother Juan Tur de Carlos the sum of 550 pesos sencillos in land and that he be married or of age', and with the obligation for the rest of his life to hand over to the donee each year 'a tenth of what is produced on the land given to him'. The land and the house enabled Manuel to establish a conjugal fund. Two years afterwards he married Esperanza Juan, who brought with her a dowry of 100 pesos. Between 1849 and 1857 he built up his patrimony, always buying land from the same property of Can Gall situated next to the house and land he had received from his grandfather. With these acquisitions he carried on the strategy started by his father and continued by his older brother, Carlos, the principal heir of Can Carlos. The former bought land belonging to Can Gall in

1818, and the latter bought land belonging to the same house in 1843 from one of his cousins who had inherited it from his father who had married a woman from Can Carlos. In 1871, twenty-six years after Manuel's marriage, the heir was given all this land in payment of what was lawfully his in the inheritance of his parents. All these individual and family strategies led to the accumulation of a patrimony that was to separate from the principal line. Through the naming system two patrimonial lines began to be distinguished. When Manuel separated from the principal line he continued to maintain his dependance on it. Initially he named his house Can Manuel den Carlos in distinction from the principal house called Can Carlos and following the naming model of collateral lines. However, the consolidation of the patrimony made the line independent, and it came to be called Can Manuel, the name it had when his son Juan inherited it and which it still has today. There are, then, two collateral lines, of which one started a process of differentiation. The son of the founder of this patrimonial line married a consanguine relation that came through an intermediate affinal line rather than directly from the principal line. In this way, the secondary line was strengthened: rather than merging directly with the principal line, it received a woman of another line that had received, in turn, a woman from the principal line. Thus, the secondary line entered the matrimonial circuits of the principal line through an intermediate line, maintaining its own identity and avoiding the risk of merging with it again. The maternal grandfather of the wife was the older brother of Ego's father and the person who continued the principal line, and this line gave a woman to a line situated outside the kinship group which, in turn, gave a woman to the new secondary line. Ego, thus, received a dowry indirectly from the same place he had received hereditary possessions in the preceding generation. In this way, the principal line continued, through an intermediate line, to maintain alliances with a collateral patrimonial line that was consolidating independently. At the time of Ego's marriage (1882) his father, the initiator of the secondary line, had already died, and the son that had been named as heir had also died. The widowed mother handed over the direction of the patrimony to her son Juan. As indicated in the marriage contract, she gave 'to the aforementioned son all that corresponds to him and may correspond to him as a result of the intestate death of his brother Manuel, reserving the usufruct during her life'. The

intention here was to protect the new line through other collateral relations in the principal line who became affines. This
marriage transformed the first cousins into relatives by affinity
(the male cousin was the son-in-law and the female cousin was
the daughter-in-law) and, through them reaffirmed an alliance
with the line from which the preceding generation had separated and from which it continued to receive possessions, this
time in the form of a dowry. On the other hand, the distinction
between principal and secondary lines was maintained, as is
clearly expressed by the position of the donor of the first line
and the change in terminology of the cousins who became
affines: the male cousin from the second line was the son-in-law
of the female cousin (mother-in-law) from the principal line.
Through this terminology the distinction between older and
younger brother that produced the two asymmetrical collateral
lines continued to be affirmed. After this close marriage the new
matrimonial line entered other circuits of alliance and used other
strategies to maintain the continuity of the patrimony.

In Genealogy V.5 we can observe a marriage between Ego and
his FFBDD, that is, the daughter of a female cousin of his
parents, a marriage between 'fills de cosins', consanguine kin in
the third degree that were also in the fourth degree because of
her being daughter of a marriage between cousins of the third
degree (FFFBDSD). It was the marriage of an heir of a clearly
constituted patrimonial line (Can Talaiasa) that followed a clear
strategy of patrimonial indivision, establishing a man as single
heir in the five generations. As heir the father of Ego established
himself as the reorganiser of the patrimonial line, acquiring new
patrimonies, buying the legitims of his brothers and paying the
dowries of his sisters in cash. In 1895 his father named him heir
of the house, and between 1899 and 1922 he made a series of
purchases from strangers and relatives directed towards increasing and preserving the patrimony. In his will of 1922 he left
the patrimony to his son Juan (Ego), who two years later married a second cousin. He bought land from other owners with
the aim of giving dowries to his non-inheriting children. In 1899
he bought the property of Can Vincent den Guillem from a sailor
living in Ibiza, and this acquisition enlarged the inheritance that
his son Juan received. In 1906 he bought the property Es
Turrent Fondu from the heirs of M. Valerino, 'trader and resident in the suburb of Marina' in Ibiza, who had acquired the
property in payment of a debt contracted in 1832 by a brother of

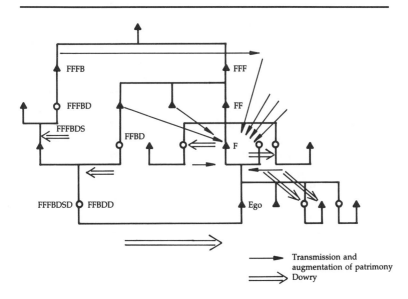

Genealogy V.5

his father's father. In this way he recovered the property that one of his distant collateral relations had lost. After this he handed it over to the non-inheriting son of the house when he wrote his will. In 1922 he bought another property in Sant Francesc Xavier and in the same year passed it on to one of his married daughters in that parish. The other daughter, who was also married, inherited 'the dowry in cash that he gave her'. He also gave dowries in cash to his two sisters and afterwards bought from each one 'the participation that corresponds to them in the undivided property of Can Talaiasa'. The two non-inheriting brothers of his father also sold to their nephew 'the legitims that correspond to them in the property of Can Talaiasa'. We are dealing, here, with a hereditary strategy of patrimonial integration and preservation that attracted to the principal line the parts that could remain dispersed in secondary collateral lines. The matrimonial alliance of his son was organised in keeping with these strategies of patrimonial concentration: to attract collateral kinship relations, that were already dispersing, towards the centre of the principal line. His marriage with a female cousin of the third degree who was, in turn, the daughter of another marriage between cousins of the third degree, managed to simplify collateral relations and attract, at the same time, a removed affinal line (the line where the mother of the wife's father married) towards the principal line. Ego received a dowry from a secondary collateral line through intermediate alliances in the same way that – through his father – he received the share of the house to which these secondary collateral lines had the right. At the beginning of the century, when the impact of emigration was being felt, important changes were occurring in the structure of property, and the social crisis was so profound that even many heirs of households had to emigrate. At this time, the matrimonial alliance of a non-emigrating heir belonging to a well-established patrimonial line was formed within the kinship group since, with the difficulty of finding an honourable alliance beyond the kindred circle, this was the only means of preserving the line. The heir lived in the house of his father, who continued to manage the patrimony and freed him from hereditary obligations with his brothers. The father had already handed over dowries to his daughters and given the legitim to his other son. This legitim was eventually to enlarge the patrimony of the principal line when the emigrant son died single.

This was a marriage in which the principal line – represented by the father of Ego – maintained the role of organiser, arranging the other collateral lines not only into relations of inheritance, but also into relations of alliance. This strategy of avoiding the dispersion of patrimony led to the simplification of collaterals and their attraction towards the centre through the consanguine marriage of the heir.

Another way of creating strong links of alliance between lines, that avoids consanguinity but follows the same logic as marriage between consanguine kin, consists of double marriages: two brothers with two sisters (parallel double marriage) and the exchange of sisters (crossed double marriage) (see Figure V.3).

Like consanguine marriages, double marriages are redundant. They are alliances enclosed within the kinship domain which restrict the lines with which Ego is united by affinity since they renew the same alliance in the same generation with the same line. If my brother married my sister-in-law (the sister of my wife) I would would no longer be able to form an alliance with another line. The children of such a marriage lose collateral relations in exchange for doubling relations of consanguinity (FBS = MZS in parallel double marriages and FZS = MBS in crossed ones) and having the same common grandparents in the

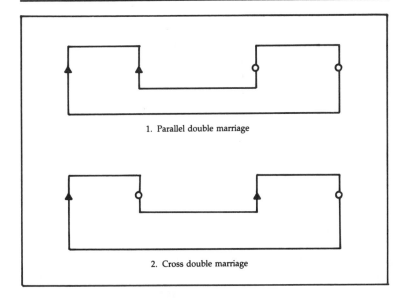

1. Parallel double marriage

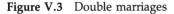

2. Cross double marriage

Figure V.3 Double marriages

two lines. This reduces the number of ancestors that create or carry on a line. In this way, relations between two houses are reinforced through the creation of double links between lines at the cost of decreasing the links with other houses. When a consanguine relation marries the affine of a consanguine relation, relations of collateral kinship are simplified, and this permits, at a given moment, the delimitation of lines that are not clearly defined in the kindred domain.

In crossed double marriages the difference of sex in the sibling group is emphasised in order to carry out an asymmetric exchange of sisters. Compensation for the asymmetry of sexes in the sibling group is immediately achieved through another asymmetric pair. In the case of the two marriages being carried out on the same day, when one dowry is given, another one is immediately received. The opening of the house necessary in each marriage is immediately closed again when another identical dowry is received from the same affines. This creates a circle of immediate reciprocity that doubles the links with the affinal line at the cost of not entering the extended circuits of reciprocity through longer chains of alliance with other lines that are more distant in kinship and affinity.

In parallel double marriages importance is given to the identity

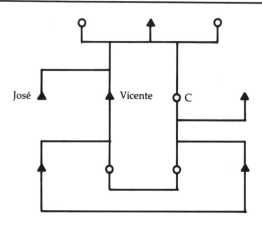

Genealogy V.6

of siblings of the same sex. If the lines make the distinction between 'adult' and 'young' in the sibling group, there is a group of 'young' siblings who are identical, in the same way that sisters are identical to each other in relation to siblings of the opposite sex. Thus lines are stabilised, and the area of kinship is reduced so that a line is united with another through two affinal ties of the same kind.

These double marriages strengthen ties of affinity between lines, above all if the two lines were already united by a previous marriage. In this way, they recover ties that are becoming distanced in the collateral domain or had been terminated by death. In Genealogy V.6, two sisters married into a line in which their grandfather had already established an alliance. A parallel marriage strengthened the ties of the two lines in the previous generation of two brothers and a half-sister who had the same father and different mothers. The first marriage of the grandfather of the two sibling pairs had one daughter (C), and in his will signed in 1883, he made this daughter 'heiress to half of his possessions', and named 'his sons José and Vicente as heirs to the rest', both of whom were from his later marriage. One of these heirs was the father of the two sisters that married two sons of the heiress of the first marriage. Through this double marriage an affinal tie that had broken with the death of the grandfather's first wife was renewed, and a tie that had truncated was recovered and directed towards another line. The inheritance handed over to the daughter (C) of the first marriage continued to attract two sisters from the other line as if a double

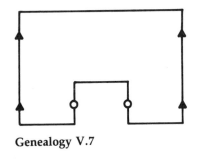

Genealogy V.7

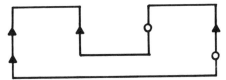

Genealogy V.8

alliance was required to renew the tie that had been lost with the other house.

These double marriages are the closest and most simplified of matrimonial models that, like marriages between consanguine kin of the second degree, develop other matrimonial forms more removed than immediate circuits of alliance. They are found in the privileged terrain of the matrimonial domain, for example when two cousins (Genealogy V.7) marry two sisters. These distanced collateral relations were reunited through an identical pair of sisters. The parallel lines that had separated closed a matrimonial circle by renewing an alliance through the consanguine relations of affines, and the sons of these cousins had the respective wives of more distant collaterals as immediate collaterals.

These circuits in wider matrimonial strategies become longer, and through various marriages, alliances that return to their point of origin are formed. Like marriages between consanguine relations, they reduce the kindred area and define its lines, as when Ego marries the daughter of the brother of the wife of the brother of his father (Genealogy V.8) bringing together two relations by affinity who are going to become the grandparents of the children of this marriage.

Another close matrimonial strategy carried out between affines involved the marriage of a widow or widower with a

Table V.3   Marriages in the degrees of affinity

Marriages	Degrees of affinity							
	1	1/2	2	2/3	3	3/4	4	Total
	3	–	3	2	2	2	2	14

	Degrees of affinity with consanguinity			
widowers/	1 aff. &	1 aff. &	2 aff. &	3/4 aff. &
bachelors	2/3 cons.	3/4 cons.	3/4 cons.	4 cons.
27	1	1	1	1

	Dispensation motives		
'narrowness'	'copulation'	'age'	'poverty'
10	8	6	3

consanguine relation of the former spouse (Table V.3). In the period 1872–88 half of the marriages (14 out of 27) between a widow/widower and a single man/woman needed dispensation due to affinity. Despite the number of marriages of this type being much lower than the number of marriages with dispensation due to consanguinity, one can observe a reverse tendency in marriages between affines. While marriages between consanguine relations increased considerably from the third degree, in marriages between affines there were more marriages in close degrees (ten up to the third degree), and they decreased in the last degrees (four marriages of third with fourth degree and between fourth degree). On the other hand, there were four marriages that, besides dispensation due to affinity, needed dispensation due to consanguinity. They were marriages of Ego with consanguine relations of a husband/wife that was at the same time a consanguine relation, in other words, marriages inside the kindred domain.

Marriages within close degrees of affinity followed the logic of the continuity of alliance between households, so that if an alliance was broken because of the death of one of the marriage partners it was renewed in the same generation usually through a close consanguine relation of Ego's affines. These marriages followed the norms of others on the island. Alliances were established preferably inside the parish, although a few marriages served to relate parishes with each other (see Figure V.4). Affinity was recovered within the narrow kindred limits of affines (in 10 dispensations out of 14 'smallness of place' was given as the reason), and often these marriages had already

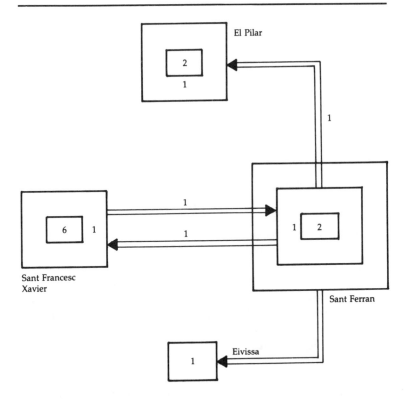

Figure V.4 Marriages in the degrees of affinity in each parish and between parishes (1872–1888)

been carried out before asking for dispensation (in eight cases 'copulation' was indicated as the reason).

A comparison between consanguine marriages needing dispensation in the period 1872–88 and those contracted between 1941 and 1976 shows a significant decrease in close marriages. During latter period the church only demanded dispensation up to the third degree, so we cannot know the number of marriages in the more removed degrees that considerably increased the number of marriages between consanguine relations in the earlier period. If we restrict the comparison to the third degree in the two periods, we can observe a decrease in this type of marriage of more than half in the latter period. Between 1872 and 1888, 18.7 per cent of all marriages in Formentera were between consanguine spouses up to the third degree, whereas between 1941 and 1976 the proportion fell to 7.6 per cent (see

Table V.4   Consanguine marriages up to the third degree

Years	Marriages	Degrees			Consanguine Marriages
		2	2/3	3	
1872–1888	235	8	8	28	44 (18.7%)
1941–1976	706	5	5	44	54 (7.6%)
1941–1950		3	1	13	17
1951–1960		2	2	12	16
1961–1976		–	2	19	21

Table V.4). In the latter period the number of marriages between consanguine relations of the third degree (44 marriages) was 4.4 times more than the number of those in the other two closer degrees (10 marriages), while in the period 1872–88 there were only 1.75 times as many marriages of the third degree (28 marriages) as those of the other two degrees (16 marriages). In the last fifteen years of the second period (1961–76) there were no marriages between second degree relations, two marriages between second and third degree relations and nineteen between third degree consanguine relations. The proportion of close marriages decreased, while marriages within the recognised limits of kinship maintained their importance. Families became socially isolated, and kinship ties tended to be forgotten. The diffuse universe of collateral kinship contracted, starting from first cousins, so that an alliance in which the spouses were removed in kinship was considered possible, although not preferred.

During this period (1940–76), the average age of marriage between consanguine relations remained high (30.6 for men and 25.8 for women) like the other marriages of the island among which the average age only started to fall from the 1960s onwards.[25] In marriages between consanguine relations spouses

25. Cf. Bertranpetit (1981: 211, Table 6.7):

The average age for men: and for women:

1940–9 = 28.55   1940–9 = 24.42

1950–9 = 29.32   1950–9 = 24.42

1960–9 = 30.24   1960–2 = 25.70

1970–8 = 26.93   1970–8 = 22.97

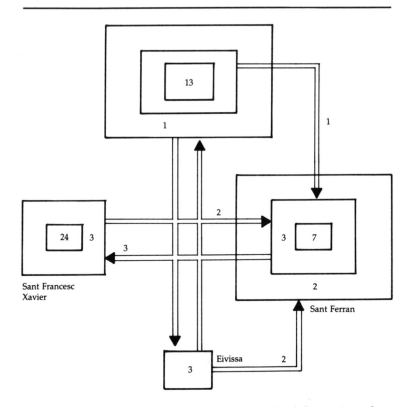

Figure V.5 Consanguine marriages up to the third degree in each parish and between parishes (1941–1976)

from the same parish (44 marriages) were preferred, but there was some matrimonial exchange between the three parishes, mostly between Sant Francesc Xavier and Sant Ferran (one marriage between El Pilar and Sant Ferran and five marriages between Sant Francesc Xavier and Sant Ferran), and also with the neighbouring island of Ibiza (four marriages) (see Figure V.5). The break away from the trend of internal endogamy that marriage on the island had followed since the 1960s (see above pp. 164–5) did not occur in consanguine marriages between 1961 and 1976: there were 18 marriages in which the spouses were from the same parish, three with one of the spouses from Ibiza and no marriage between spouses of different parishes. It would seem, therefore, that the opening up of internal endogamy caused an increased closure of consanguine marriages that impelled them to resort to neighbours or recover relations living on the other island. The proportion of consanguine marriages decreased, although they continued to maintain the norms of internal endogamy of past marriages.

The decrease in consanguine marriages between 1940 and 1976 can be related to the widening of the limits restricting matrimonial alliance at the end of the last century. The return of temporary emigrants made the distribution of property more homogeneous and, as a result, produced a decline in the hierarchy between households defining the matrimonial domain in each sibling group. The new social homogeneity brought with it a widening of the matrimonial compatibility of houses, and the entrance of each individual into the matrimonial market no longer depended on his position in the sibling group or the position of the house in the social hierarchy. Marriages between consanguine relations ceased to be an important element in the strategy of protecting patrimonial lines. The game of distances between houses gradually disappeared, and the particular identities of each zone started to dissolve. Between 1961 and 1976 the intensification of social and cultural homogeneity widened the matrimonial domain of the island in keeping with the disappearance of excessively close marriages (second degree). The social and cultural 'narrowness' of the matrimonial domain of the island is disappearing and, among the reasons for giving matrimonial dispensation, 'narrowness of place' has lost the importance it had at the end of the last century. From 1941 to 1976, in 25 out of the 54 marriages between consanguine relations the reason presented for giving dispensation was 'the advanced age of the *oratriz*', in 18 cases '*angustia loci*', in 10 cases 'the lack of a dowry' and in only one case 'copulation'. The restricted circuits that linked alliances within the kindred have disappeared as the homogeneity of the island has increased. From this new organisation of the matrimonial domain, the circuits of marriages in the past are perceived as excessively restricted and close, a time in which houses as kinship units maintained their identity by means of the double game of seeking close alliances within the kindred group and forming others in order to open new relations outside kinship and, in this way, to enlarge the kindred group.

Appendix

Census of Surnames on Formentera in 1934

	1	2	3	4	Total
Mayans	41	46	131	44	262
Ferrer	59	71	31	62	223
Juan	21	51	41	38	151
Castelló	73	26	12	36	147
Escandell	29	38	46	13	126
Serra	65	37	–	18	120
Tur	37	32	29	21	119
Marí	31	35	7	39	112
Torres	10	35	29	12	86
Riera	30	20	15	2	67
Costa	11	13	21	20	65
Colomar	45	16	1	–	62
Verdera	14	40	–	4	58
Roig	4	4	30	1	39
Guasch	11	15	1	12	39
Cardona	12	9	7	9	37
Ribas	19	1	–	10	30
Yern	18	2	–	2	22
Ramón	2	7	1	1	11
Portas	–	1	4	5	10
Suñer	8	1	–	–	9
Planells	2	2	–	3	7
Roselló	3	4	–	–	7
Ros	6	–	–	–	6
Noguera	2	–	2	1	5
Benet	1	–	–	3	4
Vidal	–	–	–	4	4
Sala	1	–	–	–	1
Soler	–	1	–	–	1
Total	*555*	*507*	*406*	*360*	*1,830*

Bibliography

Abad y la Sierra, M. (1907), 'Breve noticia del Estado natural, civil, militar y político que tienen hoy las islas de Iviza y Formentera, con sus adyacentes en 1786', *Boletín de la Real Academia de Historia*, LI (VI): 417–46

Alarco von Perfall, C. (1981), *Cultura y personalidad en Ibiza*, Madrid: Editora Nacional

Anderson, M. (1971a), *Family Structure in Nineteenth Century Lancashire*, Cambridge: Cambridge University Press

Anderson, M. (ed.) (1971b), *Sociology of the Family*, London: Penguin

Anderson, M. (1980), *Approaches to the History of the Western Family, 1500–1914*, London: Macmillan

Antoun, R.T. (1968), 'On the Significance of Names in an Arab Village', *Ethnology*, 7: 158–70

Arensberg, C.H. and Kimball, S.J. (1968), *Family and Community in Ireland* (2nd edn), Cambridge, Mass.: Harvard University Press

Ariès, P. (1973), *L'enfant et la vie familiale sous l'Ancien Régime*, Paris: Seuil

Assier-Andrieu, L. (1981), *Coutume et rapports sociaux*, Paris: Editions du C.N.R.S.

Augustins, G. (1977), 'Reproduction sociale et changement social, l'exemple des Baronnies', *Revue Française de Sociologie*, XVIII: 465–84

—— (1979), 'Division égalitaire des patrimoines et institution de l'héritier', *Archives européennes de sociologie*, XX: 127–41

—— (1982), 'Esquisse d'une comparaison des systèmes de perpetuation des groupes domestiques dans les sociétés paysannes européennes', *Archives européennes de sociologie*, XXIII: 39–69

Barnes, J.A. (1961), 'Physical and Social Kinship', *Philosophy of Science*, 28: 296–9

—— (1964), 'Physical and Social Facts in Anthropology', *Philosophy of Science*, 31: 294–7

—— (1980) 'Kinship Studies: Some Impressions of the Current State of Play', *Man* (N.S.), 15: 293–303

Beattie, J.H.M. (1964), 'Kinship and Social Anthropology', *Man*, 130

—— (1965), 'The Content of Kinship', *Man*, 38

Bell, R.M. (1979), *Fate and Honour. Family and Village. Demographic and Cultural Change in Rural Italy since 1830*, Chicago and London: University of Chicago Press

Bender, D.R. (1967), 'A Refinement of the Concept of Household: Families, Co-residence and Domestic Functions', *American Anthropologist*, 69 (5): 441–59

Berkner, L. K. (1972a), 'Rural Family Organization in Europe: a Problem in Comparative History', *Peasant Studies Newsletter*, 1: 145–56

—— (1972b), 'The Stem Family and the Development Cycle in the Peasant Household: an Eighteenth-Century Austrian Example', *American Historical Review*, 77: 398–418

—— (1973), 'Recent Research on the History of the Family in Western Europe', *Journal of Marriage and the Family*, 35 (3): 395–405

—— (1975), 'The Use and Misuse of Census Data for Historical Analysis of Family Structure', *Journal of Interdisciplinary History*, V (4): 721–38

—— (1976), 'Inheritance, Land Tenure and Peasant Family Structure: a German Regional Comparison' in J. Goody et al. (eds), *Family and Inheritance*, Cambridge: Cambridge University Press, pp. 71–111

—— and Mendels, F.F. (1978), 'Inheritance Systems, Family Structure and Demographic Patterns in Western Europe, 1700–1900', in C. Tilly (ed.), *Historical Studies in Changing Fertility*, Princeton: Princeton University Press, pp. 209–33

Bertranpetit, J. (1981), *Estructura demogràfica i genètica de la població de Formentera*, Ph.D. dissertation, Department of Biological Anthropology, University of Barcelona

Bisson, J. (1977), *La terre et les hommes aux îles Baléares*, Aix-en-Provence: Edisud

Blasco Ibáñez, V. (1908), 'Las islas Baleares', in *La Nación* (reproduced in I. Macabich, *Historia de Ibiza*, IV: 12–20)

Bloch, M. and Guggenheim, S. (1981), 'Compadrazgo, Baptism and the Symbolism of the Second Birth', *Man* (N.S.) 16: 376–86

Bourdieu, P. (1962), 'Célibat et Condition Paysanne', *Etudes rurales*, 5–6: 32–135

—— (1972a), 'Les stratégies matrimoniales dans le système de reproduction', *Annales*, 27 (4–5): 1105–25

—— (1972b), 'La maison ou le monde renversé', in *Esquisse d'une théorie de la pratique*, Geneva: Droz, pp. 45–9

—— (1980), *Le sens pratique*, Paris: Minuit

Brandes, S.H. (1975), *Migration, Kinship and Community*, New York: Academic Press

Breen, R. (1980), 'Naming Practices in Western Ireland', *Man* (N.S.), 17 (4): 701–13

Brooke, M.Z. (1970), *Le Play: Engineer and Social Scientist*, London: Longman

Buchler, I.R. and Selby, H.A. (1968), *Kinship and Social Organization. An*

Introduction to Theory and Method, New York, Macmillan

Campbell, J.K. (1964), *Honour, Family and Patronage*, Oxford: Oxford University Press

Cerdá, J., (n.d.), 'Reflexiones sobre los capítulos matrimoniales de Ibiza y Formentera', unpublished manuscript

Chamberlin, F. (1927), *The Balearics and their People*, London and New York: John Lane

Charles, L.H. (1951), 'Drama in First-Naming Ceremonies', *Journal of American Folklore*, 64 (251): 11–35

Chayanov, A.V. (1966), *The Theory of Peasant Economy*, Homewood, Ill.: Richard D. Irwin

Cole, J.W. and Wolf, E. (1974), *The Hidden Frontier: Ecology and Ethnicity in an Alpine Valley*, New York: Academic Press

Collomp, A. (1972), 'Famille nucléaire et famille élargie', *Annales E.S.C.*, 27 (4–5): 969–75

—— (1978), 'Maison, manières d'habiter et famille en Haute Provence aux XVII et XVIII siècles', *Ethnologie française*, 8 (4): 301–20

—— (1983), *La maison du Père*, Paris: P.U.F.

Compagnon, A. (1980), *Nous, Michel de Montaigne*, Paris: Seuil

Corblet, J. (1881), *Histoire dogmatique, liturgique et archéologique du sacrament du Baptême* (2 vols), Paris: Société Générale de la Librairie Catholique

Costa Ramón, A. (1964), 'Apuntes sobre los apellidos de las Islas Pitiusas. Zona Rural de Ibiza y Formentera', *Boletín de la Cámara Oficial de Comercio y Navegación de Palma de Mallorca*, 664–5: 175–86

Costa Ramón, J. (1958), 'Derecho Foral Ibicenco', *Ibiza*, 5: 19–58 (first published in 1946)

Davis, J. (1977), *People of the Mediterranean. An Essay in Comparative Anthropology*, London: Routledge & Kegan Paul

Davis, N.Z. (1977), 'Ghost, Kin and Progeny: Some Features of Family Life in Early Modern France', *Daedalus*, 106 (2): 87–113

Donzelot, J. (1977), *La Police des familles*, Paris: Minuit

Dorian, N.C. (1970), 'Substitute Name System in the Scottish Highlands', *American Anthropologist*, 72: 303–19

Douglass, W.A. (1969), *Death in Murelaga. Funerary Ritual in a Spanish Basque Village*, Seattle and London: University of Washington Press

Du Boulay, J. (1974), *Portrait of a Greek Mountain Village*, Oxford: Clarendon Press

—— (1984), 'The Blood: Symbolic Relationships between Descent, Marriage, Incest Prohibitions and Spiritual Kinship in Greece', *Man* (N.S.), 19: 533–56

Durkheim, E. (1888), 'Introduction à la sociologie de la famille', in *Textes* III (1975): 9–34, Paris: Minuit

—— (1892), 'La famille conyugale', in *Textes* III (1975): 35–49, Paris: Minuit

—— (1897), 'Zur Urgeschichte der Ehe. Prof. J. Kohler', *Année Sociologique*, 1: 306–19

—— (1915), 'La sociologie', in *Textes* I: 109–18, Paris: Minuit

Elias, N. (1978), *The Civilizing Process*, Oxford: Basil Blackwell

—— (1982), *La sociedad Cortesana*, Mexico: Fondo de Cultura Económica (Eng. edn: *The Court Society*, Oxford: Basil Blackwell, 1983)

Esmein, A. (1881), *Le mariage en droit canonique* (2nd edn, 2 vols), Paris

Fajarnés Tur, E. (1929), *Los matrimonios consanguíneos en la antigua población ebusitana*, Palma de Mallorca: Imprenta de la Hija de J. Colomar

Faus i Condomines, J. (1902), 'Els Capítols Matrimonials a la Comarca de Guissona', *Revista Jurídica de Catalunya*

Fine-Souriac, A. (1977), 'La famille-souche pyrénéenne au XIXe siècle: quelques refléxions de méthode', *Annales*, 32 (3): 478–87

Flandrin, J.L. (1976), *Familles, Parenté, Maison, Sexualité dans l'Ancienne Société*, Paris: Hachette

Fleury, M. and Henry, L. (1976), *Nouveau Manuel de dépouillement et d'exploitation de l'Etat Civil Ancien* (2nd edn), Paris: Institut Nationale d'Etudes Démographiques

Fontanella, J.P. (1916), *Tractat dels Pactes Nupcials, o Capítols Matrimonials, que escrigué*, ed. F. Maspons i Anglasell, Barcelona: Ibérica

Fortes, M. (1958), 'Introduction', in J. Goody (ed.), *The Developmental Cycle in Domestic Groups*, Cambridge: Cambridge University Press

—— (1970a), *Time and Social Structure and Other Essays*, London: The Athlone Press

—— (1970b), *Kinship and the Social Order*, London: Routledge & Kegan Paul

—— (1978), 'An Anthropologist's Apprenticeship', *Annual Review of Anthropology*, 7: 1–30

Foster, J. (1974), *Class Struggle and Industrial Revolution*, London: Methuen

Fox, R. (1963), 'Structure of Personal Names in Tory Island', *Man*, 63: 153–5

—— (1967), *Kinship and Marriage, an Anthropological Perspective*, London: Penguin

—— (1975), *Encounter with Anthropology*, Harmondsworth: Penguin

—— (1978), *The Tory Islanders*, Cambridge: Cambridge University Press

Freeman, J.D. (1961), 'On the Concept of Kindred', *Journal of the Royal Anthropological Institute*, 91: 192–220

Galeski, B. (1972), *Basic Concepts of Rural Sociology*, Manchester: Manchester University Press

Geertz, H. and Geertz, C. (1964), 'Teknonymy in Bali: Parenthood, Age Grading and Genealogical Amnesia', *Journal of the Royal Anthropological Institute*, 94: 94–108

—— (1975), *Kinship in Bali*, Chicago and London: University of Chicago Press

Gellner, E. (1973), *Cause and Meaning in the Social Sciences*, London: Routledge & Kegan Paul

Gibbon, P. and Curtin, C. (1978), 'The Stem Family in Ireland', *Comparative Studies in Society and History*, 20: 429–53

Gibert, J.M. (1845), 'Relación de la visita practicada en las islas de Ibiza y Formentera al tenor de la Real Orden de 25 de Agosto de 1845, por el jefe político de la provincia', in I. Macabich, *História de Ibiza*, II, 1966: 250–71

Gil Muñoz, C. (1971), *Formentera. Una comunidad en evolución*, Barcelona: Dopesa

Gilmore, D.D. (1982), 'Some Notes on Community Nicknaming in Spain', *Man* (N.S.), 17 (4): 687–99

Goldschmit, W. and Kunkel, E.J. (1971), 'The Structure of the Peasant Family', *American Anthropologist*, 73: 1058–76

Goode, W.J. (1963), *World Revolution and Family Patterns*, Glencoe, Ill.: Free Press

Goodenough, W.H. (1956), 'Residence Rules', *Southwestern Journal of Anthropology*, 12: 22–37

Goody, J. (ed.) (1958), *The Developmental Cycle in Domestic Groups*, Cambridge: Cambridge University Press

Goody, J. (1972), 'The Evolution of the Family', in P. Laslett (ed.), *Household and Family in Past Time*, Cambridge: Cambridge University Press, pp. 103–24

—— (1973a), 'Bridewealth and Dowry in Africa and Eurasia', in J. Goody and S.J. Tambiah (eds), *Bridewealth and Dowry*, Cambridge: Cambridge University Press

—— (1973b), *The Character of Kinship*, Cambridge: Cambridge University Press

—— (1976), *Production and Reproduction*, Cambridge: Cambridge University Press

—— (1983), *The Development of the Family and Marriage in Europe*, Cambridge: Cambridge University Press

——, Thirsk, J. and Thompson, E.P. (eds) (1976), *Family and Inheritance*, Cambridge: Cambridge University Press

Gordon Darroch, A. (1981), 'Migrants in the Nineteenth Century: Fugitives or Families in Motion?', *Journal of Family History*, 6 (3): 257–77

Goubert, P. (1977), 'Family and Province: a Contribution to Knowledge of Family Structure in Early Modern France', *Journal of Family History*, 2: 179–95

Gudeman, S. (1972), 'The Compadrazgo as a Reflection of the Spiritual and Natural Person', *Proceedings of the Royal Anthropological Institute for 1971*: 45–71

—— (1975), 'Spiritual Relationships and Selecting a Godparent', *Man* (N.S.), 10 (2): 221–37

Habakkuk, H.J. (1955), 'Family Structure and Economic Change in XIXth Century Europe', *The Journal of Economic History*, XV (1): 1–12

Habsburgo Lorena, Luis Salvador (1886–90), *Las Baleares. Las Antiguas Pityusas*, (2 vols), translated from the German by F. Manuel de los Herreros, Palma de Mallorca

Hajnal, J. (1965), 'European Marriage Patterns in Perspective', in D.V. Glass and D.E.C. Eversley (eds), *Population in History*, London: Arnold Press, pp. 101–43

Halbwachs, M. (1973), *Les cadres sociaux de la mémoire*, Paris and The Hague: Mouton (first published in 1925)

Hammel, E.A. (1972), 'The Zadruga as Process', in P. Laslett (ed.), *Household and Family in Past Time*, Cambridge: Cambridge University Press, pp. 335–73

Hammel, E.A. and Laslett, P. (1974), 'Comparing Household Structures over Time and between Cultures', *Comparative Studies in Society and History*, 16: 73–109

Hammel, E.A. and Yarbrough, C. (1973), 'Social Mobility and the Durability of Family Ties', *Journal of Anthropological Research*, 29: 145–63

Hareven, T.K. (1977a), 'Family Time and Historical Time', *Daedalus*, 106: 57–70

—— (1977b), 'The Family Cycle in Historical Perspective: a Proposal for a Developmental Approach', in J. Cuisinier (ed.), *The Family Life in European Societies*. Paris and The Hague: Mouton

—— (1982), *Family Time and Industrial Time*, Cambridge: Cambridge University Press

Hausmann, R. (1938), 'Recherches ethnoanthropologiques sur les Pityuses', *Revue anthropologique*, XLVIII (4–6): 122–45

Héritier, F. (1981), *L'exercise de la parenté*, Paris: Gallimard-Seuil

Homans, G.C. and Schneider, D. (1955), *Marriage, Authority and Final Causes*, Glencoe, Ill.: Free Press

Ibiza   Archive of Notarial Protocols

Ibiza   Episcopal Archives

Iszaevich, A. (1979), *Social Organization and Social Mobility in a Catalan Village*, Ph.D. dissertation, University of Michigan

—— (1980), 'Household Renown: The Traditional Naming System in Catalonia', *Ethnology*, XIX: 315–25

—— (1981), 'Corporate Household and Ecocentric Kinship Group in Catalonia', *Ethnology*, XX: 277–90

Jolas, T., Verdier, Y. and Zonabend, F. (1970), 'Parler Famille', *L'Homme*, X: 5–26

Jolas, T. and Zonabend, F. (1970), 'Cousinage et voisinage', in J. Pouillon and P. Maranda (eds), *Echanges et Communications. Melanges offerts à Cl. Lévi-Strauss*, Paris and The Hague: Mouton, Vol. I: 169–80

Kakane, Chie (1964) *Kinship and Economic Organization in Rural Japan*, London: The Athlone Press

Karnoouh, C. (1971), 'L'oncle et le cousin', *Etudes Rurales*, 42: 2–53

—— (1979), 'Penser maison, penser famille. Résidence et Parenté. Deux modèles opposées', *Etudes Rurales*, 75: 35–76

Kertzer, D.I. (1977), 'European Peasant Household Structure: Some Implications from a Nineteenth-Century Italian Community', *Journal of Family History*, 2: 333–49

Kessing, R.M. (1975), *Kin Groups and Social Structure*, New York: Holt, Rinehart and Winston

Klapisch-Zuber, (1980), 'Le nom "refait". La transmission des prénoms à Florence (XIV–XVI siècles)', *L'Homme*, XX (4): 77–104

Kroeber, A.L. (1909), 'Classificatory Systems of Relationship', *Journal of the Royal Anthropological Institute*, 39: 77–84

Lalinde Abadía, J. (1965), *Capitulacione y donaciones matrimoniales en el Derecho Catalán*, Barcelona

Lamaison, P. (1979), 'Les stratégies matrimoniales dans un système complexe de parenté: Ribennes en Gevaudan (1650–1830)', *Annales*, 34 (4): 721–43

Langham, Ian (1981), *The Building of British Social Anthropology*, Dordrecht: D. Riedel

Laslett, P. (1972), 'Introduction: The History of the Family', in P. Laslett and R. Wall (eds), *Household and Family in Past Times*, Cambridge: Cambridge University Press, pp. 3–89

—— (1977), 'Characteristics of the Western Family Considered over Time', in P. Laslett, *Family Life and Illicit Love in Earlier Generations*, Cambridge: Cambridge University Press, pp. 12–49

—— (1978), 'The Stem Family Hypothesis and its Privileged Position', in K.W. Wachter, E.A. Hammel and P. Laslett (eds), *Statistical Studies of Historical Social Structure*, New York: Academic Press, pp. 89–112

Laslett, P. and Wall, R. (eds) (1972), *Household and Families in Past Times*, Cambridge: Cambridge University Press

Leach, E. (1951), 'The Structural Implications of Matrilateral Cross-Cousin Marriage', *Journal of the Royal Anthropological Institute*, 81: 23–55

—— (1961), *Pul Eliya, a Village in Ceylon: a Study of Land Tenure and Kinship*, Cambridge: Cambridge University Press

Le Play, F. (1862), *Sur la Méthode d'observation dite des monographies de famille propre à l'ouvrage intitulé les Ouvriers Européens*, Paris: Société d'Economie Sociale

—— (1871), *L'Organisation de la famille selon le vrai modèle signalé par l'Histoire de toutes les races et de tous les temps*, Paris: Tequi

—— (1874), *La Reforme sociale en France* (3 vols), Tours: Alfred Mame et fils

Levine, D. (1977), *Family Formation in the Age of Nascent Capitalism*, New York: Academic Press

Lévi-Strauss, C. (1965), *The Future of Kinship Studies*, Huxley Memorial Lecture
—— (1966), *The Savage Mind*, London: Weidenfeld and Nicolson
—— (1968), *Les Structures eléméntaires de la parenté* (2nd edn), Paris and The Hague: Mouton
—— (ed.) (1977), *L'Identité*. Paris: Grasset
—— (1983), 'Histoire et Ethnologie', *Annales* 38 (6): 1217–31
—— (1984), *Paroles donées*, Paris: Plon
Leyton, E. (1975), *The One Blood: Kinship and Class in an Irish Village*, Toronto: Memorial University of Newfoundland
Löfgren, O. (1974), 'Family and Households among Scandinavian Peasants', *Ethnologia Escandinavica*, 1974: 17–52
—— (1982), 'The Swedish Family: a Study of Privatisation and Social Change', in P. Thompson (ed.), *Our Common History. The Transformation of Europe*, London: Pluto Press, pp. 233–50
—— (1984), 'The Sweetness of Home. Class, Culture and Family Life in Sweden', *Ethnologia Europaea*, XIV: 44–64
Lounsbury, F.G. (1964), 'The Formal Analysis of Crow- and Omaha-type of Kinship Terminologies', in W.H. Goodenough (ed.), *Explorations in Cultural Anthropology*, New York: McGraw Hill, pp. 351–94
Macabich, I. (1966–70), *Historia de Ibiza* (5 vols), Palma de Mallorca: Daedalus
Macfarlane, A. (1978), *The Origin of English Individualism*, Oxford: Basil Blackwell
—— (1979) , 'Review of L. Stone (1977)', *History and Theory*, XVIII (1)
McLennan, J.F. (1886), *Studies in Ancient History*, London and New York: Macmillan
Maranda, P. (1974), *French Kinship*, Paris and The Hague: Mouton
Malinowski, B. (1930), 'Kinship', *Man*, 30 (2): 19–29
Maspons i Anglasell, F. (1907), *Nostre dret familiar*, Barcelona
Medick, H. (1976), 'The Proto-industrial Family Economy: the Structural Function of Household and Family during the Transition from Peasant Society to Industrial Capitalism', *Social History*, 3: 291–315
—— (1981), 'The Proto-industrial Family Economy', in P. Kriedte, H. Medick and J. Schlumbohm (eds), *Industrialization before Industrialization*, Paris and Cambridge: Maison des Sciences de l'Homme and Cambridge University Press
Medick, H. and Sabean, D.W. (1979), 'Family and Kinship. Material Interest and Emotion', *Peasant Studies*, 8 (2): 139–60
—— (1984), 'Interest and Emotion in Family and Kinship Studies: a Critique of Social History and Anthropology', in H. Medick and D.W. Sabean (eds), *Interest and Emotion*, Paris and Cambridge: Maison des Sciences de l'Homme and Cambridge University Press, pp. 9–27
Merzario, R. (1981), *Il paese streto. Strategie matrimoniali nella diocesi di Como. Secoli XVI–XVIII*, Turin: Einaudi

Milden, J.W. (1977), *The Family in Past Time. A Guide to Literature*, New York and London: Garland

Mintz, S.W. and Wolf, E.R. (1950), 'An Analysis of Ritual Co-Parenthood (Compadrazgo)', *Southwestern Journal of Anthropology*, 6: 341–68

Mira, J.F. (1974), *Un estudi d'antropologia social al País Valencià*, Barcelona: Edicions 62

Mitterauer, M. and Seider, R. (1982), *The European Family*, Oxford: Basil Blackwell

Moll, F. de B. (1959), *Els Llinatges Catalans*, Palma de Mallorca: Editorial Moll

Morgan, Lewis H. (1871), *Systems of Consanguinity and Affinity of the Human Family*, Washington, Smithsonian Contribution to Knowledge

Navarro, V. (1901), *Costumbres de las Pithiusas. Memoria sobre derecho consuetudinario y economía popular*, Madrid: Real Academia de Ciencias Morales y Políticas

Needham, R. (1954), 'The System of Teknonyms and Death-Names of the Penam', *Southwestern Journal of Anthropology*, 10: 416–31

—— (1960), 'Descent Systems and Ideal Language', *Philosophy of Science*, 27: 96–101

—— (1962), *Structure and Sentiment*, Chicago: University of Chicago Press

—— (1974), *Remarks and Inventions. Sceptical Essays about Kinship*, London: Tavistock

Netting, R. McC. (1979), 'Household Dynamics in a Nineteenth-Century Swiss Village', *Journal of Family History*, 4: 39–58

—— (1981), *Balancing on an Alp. Ecological Change and Continuity in a Swiss Mountain Community*, Cambridge: Cambridge University Press

—— and Wilk, R.R. (1984), 'Notes on the History of the Household Concept', in *Households. Comparative and Historical Studies of the Domestic Group*, Berkeley, University of California Press

Nieto, J.A. (1976), *Tourism: Its Penetration and Development on a Spanish Island*, Ph.D. dissertation, New York: New School for Social Research

Parsons, T. (1943), 'The Kinship System of the Contemporary United States', *American Anthropologist*, 45: 22–38. Reprinted in *Essays in Sociological Theory* (revised edn 1954), New York: Free Press, pp. 177–96

Perier, P. (1956), *Los tipos familiares franceses y catalanes según las encuestas sociales de F. Le Play y sus discípulos*, Barcelona: Publicaciones del Patronato de la Escuela Social

Peristany, J.G. (ed.) (1976), *Mediterranean Family Structures*, Cambridge: Cambridge University Press

Pitt-Rivers, J. (1971), *The People of the Sierra* (2nd edn), Chicago and London: University of Chicago Press

—— (1973), 'The Kith and the Kin', in J. Goody (ed.), *The Character of*

Kinship, Cambridge: Cambridge University Press, pp. 89–105
—— (1976), 'Ritual Kinship in the Mediterranean: Spain and the Balkans', in J.G. Peristany (ed.), *Mediterranean Family Structures*, Cambridge: Cambridge University Press, pp. 317–34
—— (1977), *The Fate of Shechem or the Politics of Sex*, London, New York, Melbourne: Cambridge University Press
Puig Ferriol, L. and Roca Trias, E. (1979), *Fundamentos del Derecho Civil de Cataluña. Vol. II: Derecho Familiar Catalán*, Barcelona: Bosch
Radcliffe-Brown, A.R. and Forde, D. (eds) (1950), *African Systems of Kinship and Marriage*, London: Oxford University Press
Rebel, H. (1982), *Peasant Classes. The Bureaucratization of Property and Family Relations under Early Habsburg Absolutism*, Princeton: Princeton University Press
Rivers, W.H.R. (1907), 'On the Origin of the Classificatory System of Relationship', in *Anthropological Essays presented to E.B. Tylor*, Oxford: Clarendon Press
—— (1914), 'Kin, Kinship', in J. Hasting (ed.), *Encyclopaedia of Religion and Ethics*, Vol. VII, Edinburgh: T. and T. Clark.
Robin, J. (1980), *Elmdon: Continuity and Change in a Northwest Essex Village, 1861–1964*, Cambridge: Cambridge University Press
Rullán, J. (1882), 'La fiesta de las comadres. Costumbres Ibicencas', *Almanaque Balear para el año 1883*, Palma de Mallorca: Pedro José Gelabert
Sabean, D.W. (1976), 'Aspects of Kinship Behaviour and Property in Rural Western Europe before 1800', in J. Goody et al. (eds), *Family and Inheritance*, Cambridge: Cambridge University Press, pp. 96–111
Sanmartín, R. (1982), 'Marriage and Inheritance in a Mediterranean Fishing Community', *Man* (N.S.), 17: 664–85
Schneider, D.M. (1964), 'The Nature of Kinship', *Man*, 217
—— (1965), 'The Content of Kinship', *Man*, 108
—— (1968), 'Rivers and Kroeber in the Study of Kinship', in W.H.R. Rivers, *Kinship and Social Organization*, London: The Athlone Press, pp. 7–15
—— (1972), 'What is Kinship All About?', in P. Reining (ed.), *Kinship Studies in the Morgan Centennial Year*, Washington, D.C.: Anthropological Society, pp. 32–63
—— (1976), 'Notes Toward a Theory of Culture', in *Meaning in Anthropology*, Albuquerque: University of New Mexico Press
—— (1979), 'Kinship, Community and Locality in American Culture', in A.J. Lichtman and J.R. Chalinor (eds), *Kin and Communities. Families in America*, Washington D.C.: Smithsonian Institution Press
—— (1980), *American Kinship. A Cultural Account* (2nd edn), Chicago: University of Chicago Press
—— (1984), *A Critique of the Study of Kinship*, Ann Arbor: University of Michigan Press
Segalen, M. (1977), 'The Family Cycle and Household Structure: Five

Generations in a French Village', *Journal of Family History*, 2–3: 223–36
——(1978), 'Cycle de la vie et transmission du patrimoine en Bretagne. Analyse d'un cas', *Ethnologie française*, 8 (4): 271–7
——(1980), *Mari et femme dans la société paysanne*, Paris: Flammarion
——(1985), *Quinze Générations de Bas-Bretons. Parenté et société dans le pays Bigouden Sud*, Paris: Presses Universitaires de France
——(1986), *Historical Anthropology of the Family*, Cambridge: Cambridge University Press
Severi, C. (1980), 'Le nom de lignée', *L'Homme*, XX (4): 105–18
Shanin, T. (1972), *The Awkward Class*, Oxford: Oxford University Press
Shorter, E. (1975), *The Making of the Modern Family*, New York: Basic Books
Seider, R. and Mitterauer, M. (1983), 'The Reconstruction of the Family Life Course: Theoretical Problems and Empirical Results', in R. Wall, (ed.), in collaboration with P. Laslett and G. Robin, *Family Forms in Historic Europe*, Cambridge: Cambridge University Press, pp. 309–46
Simmel, G. (1977), *Sociología: Estudios sobre las formas de socialización* (2 vols, 2nd edn), Madrid: Revista de Occidente
Spelbrink, W. (1936–7), 'Die Mittelmeerinseln Eivissa und Formentera. Eine Kulturgeschichte und lexikographische Darstellung', *Butlletí de Dialectologia Catalana*, XXIV: 184–281 and XXV: 1–147
Stone, L. (1977), *The Family, Sex and Marriage in England 1550–1800*, London: Weidenfeld and Nicolson
—— (1981), 'Family History in the 1980s. Past Achievements and Future Trends', *Journal of Interdisciplinary History*, XII (1): 51–87
Strathern, M. (1981), *Kinship at the Core*, Cambridge: Cambridge University Press
—— (1982), 'The Place of Kinship: Kin, Class and Village Status in Elmdon, Essex', in A.P. Cohen (ed.), *Belonging*, Manchester: Manchester University Press, pp. 72–100
Tax, S. (1937), 'From Lafitau to Radcliffe-Brown. A Short History of the Study of Social Organization', in F. Eggan (ed.), *Social Anthropology of North American Tribes*, Chicago: Chicago University Press, pp. 443–81
Thomas, W.I. and Znaniecki, F. (1927), *The Polish Peasant in Europe and America* (2 vols, 2nd edn), New York: Alfred A. Knopf
Tillion, G. (1983), *The Republic of Cousins*, London: Al Saqui Books
Vallés, R. (1973), 'El poblamiento de las islas de Ibiza y Formentera', *Revista de la Facultad de Filosofía y Letras de la Universidad de Valencia*, XXIII: 177–89
Valls, A. (1982), *Antropología de la consanguinidad*, Madrid: Universidad Complutense
Van Gennep, A. (1909), *Les rites de passage*, Paris
—— (1943), *Manuel de folklore français contemporain*, Paris: Auguste Picard
Verdon, M. (1973), *Anthropologie de la colonisation au Québec*, Montreal: Les Presses de l'Université de Montreal

—— (1979), 'The Stem Family: Toward a General Theory', *Journal of Interdisciplinary History*, X (1): 87–105

—— (1980), 'Shaking off the Domestic Yoke, or the Sociological Significance of Residence', *Comparative Studies in Society and History*, 22: 109–32

Vernier, B. (1977), 'Emigration et déréglement du marché matrimonial', *Actes de la recherche en sciences sociales*, vol. 15

—— (1980), 'La circulation des biens, de la main d'oeuvre et des prenoms à Karpathos: du bon usage des parents et de la parenté', *Actes de la recherche en sciences sociales*, 31: 63–87

—— (1984), 'Putting Kin and Kinship to Good Use: the Circulation of Goods, Labour and Names of Karpathos (Greece)', in H. Medick and D.W. Sabean (eds), *Interest and Emotion*, Paris and Cambridge: Maison des Sciences de l'Homme and Cambridge University Press, pp. 28–76

Vilá Valentí, J. (1950), 'Formentera: Estudio de Geografía Humana', *Estudios Geográficos*, 40: 384–442

Wall, R. (ed.), in collaboration with P. Laslett and G. Robin (1983), *Family Forms in Historic Europe*, Cambridge: Cambridge University Press

Wallerstein, I., Martin, W.G. and Dickinson, T. (1982), 'Household Structure and Production Process: Preliminary Theses and Findings', *Review*, V (3): 437–58

Wheaton, R. (1975), 'Family and Kinship in Western Europe: The Problem of the Joint Family Household', *Journal of Interdisciplinary History*, 5 (4): 601–28

Wittgenstein, L. (1976), *Los Cuadernos Azul y Marrón*, Madrid: Tecnos (Eng. edn: *Preliminary Studies for the 'Philosophical Investigations', generally known as the Blue and Brown Books*, Oxford: Basil Blackwell, 1958).

Wolf, E.R. (1970), 'The Inheritance of Land among Bavarian and Tyrolese Peasants', *Anthropologica*, XII: 99–114

Wrigley, E.A. (1977), 'Reflections on the History of Family', *Daedalus*, 106 (2): 71–85

Yanagisako, S.J. (1979), 'Family and Household: The Analysis of Domestic Groups', *Annual Review of Anthropology*, 8: 161–205

—— (1985), *Transforming the Past. Tradition and Kinship among Japanese Americans*, Stanford: Stanford University Press

Yver, J. (1969), *Egalité entre héritiers et exclusion des enfants dotés. Essai de géographie coutumière*, Paris: Sirey

Zabeeh, F. (1968), *What's in a Name? An Inquiry into the Semantics and Pragmatics of Proper Names*, The Hague: Martinus Nijhoff

Zonabend, F. (1977), 'Pourqoi nomer?', in C. Lévi-Strauss (ed.), *L'Identité*, Paris: Grasset, pp. 257–86

—— (1978), 'La parenté baptismale à Minot (Côte d'Or)', *Annales*, 33 (4): 656–76

—— (1979), 'Jeux de noms. Les noms de personne à Minot', *Etudes*

Rurales, 76: 51–85

—— (1980a), *La Mémoire Longue*, Paris: P.U.F.

—— (1980b), 'Le nom de personne', *L'Homme* XX (4): 7–23

—— (1981), 'Le très proche et le pas trop loin. Réflexions sur l'organisation du champ matrimonial des sociétés à structures de parenté complexe', *Ethnologie française*, 11 (4): 311–18

Index